C000138434

The Pioneering Life of
PETER KIRK

From Derbyshire to the Pacific Northwest

Saundra Middleton

Copyright 2021 Saundra Middleton

ISBN 978-1-09837-091-6 (paperback)
ISBN 978-1-09837-092-3 (eBook)

All rights reserved. No part of this work may be reproduced in any form or by any means, including electronic and Internet reproduction, without permission of the author, except for brief passages for critical review and certain other noncommercial uses permitted by copyright law.

Published by Genetically Inclined, Anchorage, Alaska
Direct inquiries to the author at saundramiddleton.com

Printed in the United States of America

First Edition

Front cover and internal design by BookBaby.com
Front cover photo of Peter Kirk courtesy of Kirkland Heritage Society, Kirkland, Washington.

I have strived to interpret and relate the researched material accurately. Any mistakes are my own.

"If I chase my dreams,
Will they let me catch them?"

SLM

Contents

List of Illustrations

Preface

I grew up in Alaska, far away from relatives outside our nuclear base of six. Many of my friends belonged to multi-generational families. I envied their gatherings with aunties and uncles, cousins, cousins of cousins, and grandparents. At about ten years old, I asked my Dad about our family, and he said, "One of your relatives started a town." Dad said the man's name was Peter Kirk, and he had started the town of Kirkland, near Seattle, Washington. I was skeptical. That name did not match up with the ones I knew from my grandparents. I suspected Dad might be pulling my leg, but it did not stop me from bragging to my friends about it just the same.

Events in my early adulthood solidified my interest in Peter Kirk's story and genealogy in general. First, my uncle Morris Middleton shared a family lineage chart listing Peter Kirk as my second great-grandfather. It also documented Peter's ancestry to 1750 in the town of Chapel-en-le-Frith, England. I found I had cousins of cousins and grandparents galore.

I discovered other sources, too, like Arline Ely's book, *Our Foundering Fathers*, about Kirkland history. Ely's book revealed that Peter Kirk emigrated from England to start a steel mill. Integral to her research were three detailed essays by Geoffrey Peter Kirk covering the Kirk iron business and family history. Based on his extensive research, Kirk's writings remain a solid base from which to expand the Kirk story.

Kids, college, and careers came and went before I again delved into Peter Kirk research and my general genealogy interest. In 2004, armed with a new-fangled computer, internet service, and the recently launched

Ancestry.com, my hunt began in earnest. Excitement overtook me when I saw actual census and other documents from a hundred years ago, even though it took ten minutes to download one page at dial-up speeds. I also sent away to government offices for vital records. With these first fundamental documents, my family story took shape.

I wanted more. I wanted to *know them*. Who were they? How did they live? How did they handle the struggles I had read about in history books?

Computer speeds improved, as did access to documents. The Library of Congress launched a digital newspaper archive, enabling me to explore from home. I rose every morning with a plan: "I'll just search for a bit while I have a cup of coffee. Then I'll have breakfast." Slipping into bathrobe and slippers, I headed straight to the computer. The coffee went cold before the cup emptied and breakfast was long forgotten as tidbits of information rolled in.

I found Peter Kirk's obituary, which included many details of his life and iron business. It also offered a snapshot of his character:

> Mr. Kirk was a man of generous impulses, and never forgot the
> hospitable ways that to the stranger wins his esteem and friendship.
> He was modest and of a rather retiring disposition, bore adversity
> bravely and enjoyed propriety quietly. By these virtues of true
> manhood, he attracted to him many friends by whom he will be
> greatly missed…[1]

Peter's matter-of-fact nature muddled his own history. The only journals he kept were pocket notebooks with cryptic undated notes, iron ore sample analyses, shopping lists, and math tallies.[2] He rarely granted interviews, giving credence to one reporter's remark: "Mr. Kirke does not like much publicity."[3]

Photos also were scarce. His daughter, Florrie, who returned to England, wrote to him, "I am delighted with the photo of you with Clara's little baby. Do you know I have not had a photo of you since I was married."[4]

I transcribed the articles into a master document arranged chronologically. To this, I added all the birth, marriage, and death records. Notes and letters from archives followed. Newspaper fragments like "Peter Kirk was at the Hotel Northern" on May 26, 1894 made a lot more sense when another article surfaced mentioning protest hearings for the Kirkland companies spearheading Kirk's steel mill.[5] He had a stake at attending the hearings. I wondered how these events affected him and longed to find HIS words. One day I did:

> We invested $300,000 in building the iron works in Kirkland, in
> Seattle suburbs, years ago but the outcome for any profit is buried
> in the womb of the future. They are going to build a smelter there
> and my friends have invited me to go over and see it, but with my
> experience before me I tell them I'll wait and see what the result
> will be, as my enthusiasm is pretty well gone.[6]

My research led me to local libraries, archives, and museums in places where Peter Kirk had lived. Recognizing how Peter and his family had made their mark upon the world, previous family historians had donated family papers and their own research to institutions in England and Washington. Without these records, we would not have the genealogical chart tracing Peter Kirk's ancestors to 1750 or know of references to a family curse. We would not know Peter Kirk's favorite composer was Mendelssohn, nor would we be privy to his concerns about a relative "dribbling away" an inheritance.[7]

In 2014, I traveled to England to study Peter Kirk's life and family there, starting in his hometown of Chapel-en-le-Frith, a quaint little hamlet nestled in the mountains of the Peak District. It astonished me to imagine all the Kirk generations who had lived in that valley. The notion differed greatly from my more recent ancestry, including several great-grandparents who immigrated to the United States, then lived in multiple states during their lifetimes. Conversely, the Kirk family launched their iron enterprise dynasty before our thirteen colonies had formed a nation. Even more astounding, Kirks had lived in that little pocket of England since before Columbus sailed the oceans blue. It made me wonder why Peter's father moved his children away from an area steeped in history and security.

I spent weeks at the Derbyshire Record Office examining documents saved over generations and then donated by modern, but distant, Kirk relatives. A typical day of research at the archives started with a brisk twenty-minute walk to the old stone building. The automatic door beckoned me in, while the metal detector remained the true portal to the check-in clerk. I signed in each day with a special library card used to access the records. My coat and backpack went into a locker, the rules allowing me only a pencil, notebook, and laptop computer in the archive room. Staff unlocked the door each time anyone moved in or out of the glass-walled room. Whispers and head nods replaced conversation.

Archivists retrieved the records I requested from their fireproof stronghold. The collections came in office boxes full of packets of varied sizes. Slate-blue file folders and specially constructed boxes protected each record, secured with a beige cotton ribbon. The archivists allowed me only one packet at a time, weighing each item before handing it to me. I never knew the secret contents until I opened it. Was it the marriage record that might unveil the mysterious bride of an ancestor? Maybe it was a will listing all the children of a forefather. As I pondered the contents, each walk back to my table reminded me of Christmas mornings.

One packet revealed a stiff yellowed parchment with red wax seals dangling from it on red satin ribbons. Unfolding the parchment, I found the date…1657! Graceful and precise, the writing proved difficult for my 21st century eyes to read. I remembered 's' looked like 'f' and 'e' mimicked 'o'. Deciphering the documents, I combined phonetics with a lot of guesswork. For instance, one record recounted the exploits of a group of 16th century Kyrkes who *"dyd riotouslye assembled and gathered grete store of money to meynteyn their unlawfull doings."*[8]

With some packets, I needed only a minute or two to figure out they were unrelated to my research. Documents written in Latin were an automatic return. Other records I kept a full day deciphering letters or transcribing a parish list of subscriptions. When finished with an item, I repackaged and retied it into its packet, then reverently returned it to the archivist, who weighed it once again.

Some facts did not come wrapped in quaint little packages, however. I searched parish registries only to find inadequate details and missing records. The names Peter, Henry, Thomas, Ann, and Elizabeth populated generations of Kirk family lines. I often met brick walls simply because I could not determine to which branch a particular person belonged. At times, only the perseverance of our shared DNA kept me digging for the crumbs of Peter Kirk's history.

On one occasion, a cloudy but dry December day greeted me at the Chapel-en-le-Frith church cemetery, where I had gone to find Kirk graves. Groundskeepers kept only some sections maintained and manicured. A huge rhododendron tree the size of a small house occupied much of one sector of the graveyard. Tenacious moss covered most everything else.

I searched for the grave of Peter's father, hoping he occupied one of the three tombs included in a site belonging to Peter's grandfather, Henry Kirk. The memorial inscription book said wrought iron fencing sur-rounded Henry's grave, appropriate for an iron founder.[9] I finally located a candidate in an untended part of the cemetery. Thorny blackberry creepers and a carpet of clumped grass had overgrown the raised tomb. I waded through ivy, thistle, brambles, cow parsnip stalks, and other weeds to read the inscription. A thick layer of moss covered all three stones, hiding the occupants' identity.

Compelled to find out whose names the slabs contained, I entered through a broken section of the iron fence. I tried to pull away some of the moss to read the writing beneath, only to find it securely rooted through decades of fallen leaves decayed into a layer of mud. Thorny brambles snaked across the entire grave site and wove through the iron railings.

I kicked and scraped at the thick mat with my boots. I used the moss as protection for my hands to pull away the barbed vines. Clumps of weeds gave way with my two-handed grunt work. I scraped one corner of the first stone slab with the side of my boot. "IN MEMORY" appeared at the top. I scoured more moss and mud aside. "HENRY KIRK, of TOWN END." I went into a frenzy of scratching and digging with both hands. On my knees, I took the moss clumps and turned them face down to wipe the mud from the stone. "Iron Manufacturer." I had found Peter's grandfather! A couple more hours of work cleared all three stones. Several family members were there, but not the one I hoped for. I left disappointed but satisfied. Such is the journey in research.

During my explorations, I found some information from certain sources differed from official records. I found articles about Peter Kirk often mirrored the same tired narrative: Peter Kirk, the wealthy Englishman, came to America to build a steel mill in Washington and failed. But the Kirkland mill venture occupied only a few years of this man's life. Surely, idleness and twiddling of his thumbs did not engage the other 70-odd years of his existence.

Indeed, they had not. Peter registered many patents for new rail products and devices to maximize profits in his England steel mill. A gifted musician, he housed a pipe organ in his mansion—a pipe organ! He cared for his family members by helping them establish businesses and land investments.

Scrutiny of the records also revealed less complimentary information about Peter Kirk. He was a shrewd businessperson, yet he got wrapped up in a scheme in Arizona in which the president of the smelter business faced charges for investor fraud. I struggled with that. I wondered if Peter was part of the scheme. I wanted to ignore it, minimize it, but had to remember he was human and had faults. Readers can decide for themselves in the pages ahead if he was complicit in the Arizona fraud. They may also discover other insensitivities and missteps.

The purpose of this book is to expand Peter Kirk's story and experience in America and compile it in one place, knowing the journey of discovery might not be possible for everyone. I followed pieces of his story sprinkled like breadcrumbs from his birthplace in the quaint rural village of Chapel-en-le-Frith to Workington, where his family's iron experience and his education culminated in a successful business life. The trail led to America, where Peter carved a town out of the virgin forests of the Pacific Northwest, eventually ending up on San Juan Island among sheep paddocks and rolling hills, where he lived out his later years surrounded by family.

A warning: Despite my extensive research, Peter Kirk's story remains incomplete, some of it lost, some forgotten. Some details will not fit within the confines of this work. What readers will discover, however, is his extensive family history in the iron business as well as how tales of his ancestors informed his journey. I also offer an alternative to the tired story of failure. Peter Kirk gave up everything to follow his dreams, no matter the cost. His pioneering efforts enriched the iron industry and drew international attention to the Seattle area.

Acknowledgements

Great appreciation goes to Geoffrey Peter Kirk, who laid out the path for more research with his writings. His charming letters from England eloquently bridged the thousands of miles, and generations of our common Kirk family, offering an Alaskan girl a new view of the world and her place in it. Thanks as well to Geoffrey's son Robert, who patiently answered my questions, hunting through his father's notes to find information.

I extend thanks to many cousins near and far who offered information, particularly Barbara Dickinson, Penny Craven, and Dan Morrill. My appreciation extends to the Capron family for donating many items to the University of Washington Special Collections and Kirkland Heritage Society. Without these items, it would have been difficult to tell Peter's story and get to know him beyond what the newspapers depicted.

My family deserves much thanks for their extreme patience and encouragement. To my grandson, Adrian, who even though he stalled at bedtime asking for family stories inspired me to learn more. And to Jeff Sherman, my personal tech support.

Thanks to the many helpful archivists and historians including Kevin Loftus, Loita Hawkinson, Helen Cunningham, Elly Todhunter, and Russell Barnes. Thanks to Elizabeth from St. Beckett's Parish, who selflessly walked me around Chapel-en-le-Frith one snowy day to show me the ancient Kirk estates.

I greatly appreciated the patience of the Derbyshire Record Office with this Yank who wanted to see EVERYTHING, occupying one of their tables in the archival vault for over a month. Acknowledgement must be extended to the many families who have contributed centuries-worth of documents to tell the region's history.

I am eternally grateful to Deb Vanasse, whose editorial expertise and encouragement helped me bring the thousands of bits of information into a cohesive story.

Author's Note

The extended Kirk family had a propensity for naming sons after fathers and uncles, causing a cascade of generations and familial branches bearing the same names: Peter, Henry, and Thomas. The subject of this book is but one of several Peters named in this history. For ease of reading, I have assigned them a nickname. For example, the subject of this book will be "Victorian Peter" in contrast to "Peter the Widower," "Peter the Elder," and "Peter the Younger" who will enter the pages ahead. Likewise, each generation of iron-producing brothers will have a descriptor to distinguish their era.

The book's subject, Victorian Peter, is mainly referenced simply by first or last name (or both), depending on the context. Here is a list of all of them with their time periods:

- Peter the Elder—1770 Blacksmith Brothers.
- Peter the Younger—1812 Iron Forge Brothers.
- Peter the Widower—Peter Kirk & Brothers (circa 1848).
- Victorian Peter—Kirk Brothers & Company (circa 1860) and others.

Introduction

"Mr. Kirk had long heard of America and its wonderful opportunities. He longed to see the states, and finally induced the chief engineer of his company, John G. Kellett, of his Moss Bay works, to accompany him on a trip through the states."[1]

Seattle Post-Intelligencer, 1916

In 1886, Peter Kirk stood on a Seattle wharf, gateway to the Pacific Northwest frontier. The luggage at his feet contained top hat, tailcoat, and gold coin. More significant than his neatly stacked shirts and trousers were the vast expertise and ingenuity he carried with him, along with his quiet audacity and steadfast perseverance. Most important of all, in his pocket, Peter Kirk carried a dream, one he had followed from his ancient British roots in Chapel-en-le-Frith to his successful steel mill in Workington and now to a New World.

Rails manufactured at Peter Kirk's Moss Bay Hematite Iron & Steel Company arrived in North America years before he did. The iron mogul had benefited from Great Britain's tenacious iron industry that turned out rails that linked towns and cities throughout Queen Victoria's reign. In turn, the railways made the industry lucrative and vibrant. Other nations, including the United States, followed Britain's lead. In North America, railways connected the far-flung coasts of Canada and the United States. Ranked the world's top iron and steel manufacturer for decades, Britain began losing production to America.

In response, Kirk engineered more efficient processes within his steel mill. He invented new machines and rail products. His company expanded to include mining operations so they could control their products—and

1

profit—from the ground up. It was not enough. The American iron and steel industry took more and more of the market. However, there was another way for his ironworks to compete.

Kirk closely tracked the world markets and their fluctuations, knowing their effects on his own Moss Bay ironworks, which sold rails around the world. Prudently, he kept abreast of international laws affecting sales. Well aware of US regulations, which favored her citizens and tariffed others, he traveled to America on a fact-finding mission, possibly with an eye for expansion.

Peter Kirk, Esquire, arrived in New York on August 23, 1886, after crossing the Atlantic in a first-class cabin of the *RMS Umbria*.[2] The Cunard line had lavishly decorated the *Umbria* with contemporary Victorian trappings of ornately carved furniture and heavy velvet curtains. Passengers enjoyed fine dining rooms and a music room. In the smoking room, gentlemen discussed world events and great enterprises. Kirk's life-long experience with machinery probably gave him an appreciation for the *Umbria*, which was equipped with the latest technological innovations of the day. This included three large masts for auxiliary sails in addition to her single-screw propulsion. The Cunard Line prided itself on her speed. Capable of attaining 19 knots, the luxury liner was among the fastest amid the fleet of ships crossing the Atlantic. Kirk's voyage took less than six and a half days from Liverpool to New York.

He traveled with John George Kellett, the ironwork's young mechanical engineer. Possessing an inventive mind, Kellett was keenly interested in the possibilities of the future. His family later claimed he invented "a device that made it possible to lay rails in the desert which to steel makers was a matter of greatly increased business."[3]

Once on the American continent, Kirk and Kellett checked in with his company's US representative.[4] The office had recently received a rail purchase inquiry from the Seattle, Lake Shore & Eastern Railroad (SLS&E), a fledgling railway in Seattle, Washington Territory. Daniel H. Gilman, owner of the SLS&E, included with his railroad's prospectus an analysis of the iron ores in Seattle's nearby Snoqualmie Mountains. Gilman later stated, "Mr. Kirk and associates were immediately struck by the ore analysis and he decided to examine it for himself."[5] Having spent decades decoding ore analysis to produce the best quality iron, Kirk was intrigued. He contacted Gilman, requesting a meeting on the opposite coast.

Kirk and Kellett continued with their original plans to investigate various American steel mills. Kellett kept a small journal of their trip. In it, he mentioned their "American agents were the Messrs. Wallbrun & Co. in Pittsburgh who placed one of their offices at Mr. Kirk's disposal, so we spent some time there."[6] He also noted the methods and equipment used in the large steel mills they visited. He specifically mentioned they visited the Pittsburg Steel Foundry Company and were impressed with the company's "specialty of steel castings, both crucible and Bessemer." Kellett further noted, "Mr. Hainsworth's Bessemer casting is a splendid job, as sound as if they were forged, not the slightest indication of Honeycomb."[7]

Later reports said, "Kirk and his associates visited and inspected all the mines and iron and steel works of Pennsylvania and were offered inducements to locate in Pittsburgh. However, they wanted to go farther west."[8]

In what Kellett described as a "weary journey" crossing America, travel to Seattle included a long trek on roads, rails, and ships. And yet there were rewards. "The scenery coming over the Rockies and down the Columbia River and all the way to this place is worth coming a long way to see," he wrote. "There are some splendid waterfalls, one 800 feet high. We had a run through Portland on a bus; from Portland to Tacoma by rail; and then by steamer from there to this place up Puget Sound."[9]

Traversing the United States by rail in late summer surely gave the men a sense of America's expanse and diversity. The train whisked them passed fields of tall corn stalks and Great Prairie grasslands gone to seed. The higher elevations of the Rockies brought the coolness of impending autumn and aspen forests ablaze with color. Reaching the Pacific coast surely struck them as familiar, as the salty tang of the sea invigorated the breeze as it did at their home near the Scottish border.

Arriving on Puget Sound, the Englishmen may have marveled at the landscape. Comparable in size, England and Washington Territory both benefited from warm and wet ocean currents that kept the regions temperate. But that was the extent of familiarity. Kirk's residence in Workington, in the county of Cumberland (present day Cumbria), counted about 23,000 citizens, though the area comprised many more thousands in the interconnected communities supporting the local iron and mining industries.[10] In contrast, Seattle's citizens numbered about 15,000, inhabiting a young town rough-cut out of a thickly forested frontier.[11]

The volcanic Cascade Mountains stretching from Canada to California cordoned the western side of Washington Territory, including Seattle, from the rest of the continent. The jagged spine of the range sent up miles-high glacier-covered cinder cones that stood like sentinels surveying the expansive Pacific Ocean. Not so with Kirk's homeland, where glaciers had retreated to the Arctic thousands of years earlier, leaving only low-lying hills. Likewise, old forests had long ago relinquished their roots to farms and sheep paddocks partitioned by living hedgerows or stones piled three to four feet high. In turn, those agricultural pursuits had given way to the iron industry and resource extraction. Cobbled streets lined with stone buildings formed towns and cities interconnected by a spider web of railroads.

Seattle and the Pacific Northwest had few, if any, of these features. America's intercontinental railroad had only recently entered Washington Territory, with the line to Puget Sound barely in operation for three years prior to Kirk's arrival.[12] In fact, nearly everything manmade was new, with a prevalence of buildings made from lumber cut from old growth timber by rowdy young men who swaggered over muddy roads.

By the time he reached this frontier, Peter had experienced a good number of rainy winters. Born three years into Queen Victoria's reign, he had joined the line-up of Peter and Hannah (nee Oliver) Kirk's five children in 1840.[13] He was the youngest born to the couple during their ten years of marriage.[14] Owner of a large iron forge, Peter's father supported his family as an "iron founder." The family lived in Townend, a small collection of houses and businesses at the edge of Chapel-en-le-Frith, in the county of Derbyshire, where generations of Kirk brothers had collaborated in a profitable iron manufacturing business for over a hundred years. Their success coincided with England's expansion from the Industrial Revolution to the prosperous and enlightening Victorian Era.

Standing on the Seattle wharf, Peter Kirk also carried the family baggage of that history, namely, the propensity for those named "Peter" to leave the family business.

Part I: Peter Kirk's Origins

Figure 1 Chapel-en-le-Frith countryside
Photo by author, 2014.

One—The Kirk Blacksmiths of Chapel-en-le-Frith

"The Chapel-en-le-Frith Ironworks is one of the oldest iron works in the Midlands being founded by the Kirk family probably round about the year 1770. The Forge and Rolling Mills…were formerly famous for their brand of Kirk best hammered scrap merchants bar iron and forgings, which found ready markets in all parts of the world."[1]

Mr. Chaloner, 1943

Peter Kirk's birthplace, Chapel-en-le-Frith, in the heart of Derbyshire county in England, was a small, unobtrusive village lodged in the middle of the Peak Forest. Derbyshire is a landlocked county more than 150 miles northwest of London. Craggy and bare hilltops enclosed the hamlet's rolling hills, once described by a local scholar as "clothed with stunted oaks and underwood, and their bases surrounded by treacherous bogs and reedy pools."[2]

In ancient times, the Peak Forest was set aside to protect game for the hunting pleasure of the King and his nobles.

The red deer browsed in great numbers through the sunny glades. The wild boar sharpened his tusks against the rugged bark of the forest trees: whilst from their mountain fastnesses the hungry wolves came howling in search of prey. The wild cat prowled with stealthy tread through the heather, waiting for the chattering grouse or timid hare, and the shriek of the golden eagle was heard from the dark heights of Kinder [mountain]. In the stagnant pools the otter sank with a sullen plunge, frightening the wild ducks from their home amongst the reedy banks.[3]

The King was more apt to pay his foresters, verderers, and sheriffs in land than money, coin being scarce in the 11th and 12th centuries. Eventually, the foresters and keepers became so numerous that in 1220, they bought land on a small knoll to build a chapel. They called the place Chapel-en-le-Frith (chapel in the forest) and named their church St. Thomas Beckett.

Cobblestone streets descended from the churchyard and meandered through the village and into the valley, a reminder that many local and ancient bloodlines did the same. In those early times, when the population was small, townsfolk did not use last names. As the population grew, common first names often needed a descriptor to help distinguish one Henry, Thomas, or William from another. Place names and occupations were widely used. Local historians believe the name Kirk (and its variants) came from the Norse for church, *kirkja*, meaning "dweller by the church."[4] Certainly in the case of Peter Kirk's known ancestors, this proved true, as they lived, farmed, and later worked the iron forge near St. Thomas Beckett Church.

1770 Blacksmith Brothers

Over the centuries, the king relinquished more land and rights to his subjects. The legends of Robin Hood gave way to farming concerns. Mineral resources of iron ore, coal, lead, and limestone enriched the economy of the area. Residents had long developed transportation systems that moved these valuable raw materials to markets. Chapel-en-le-Frith stood at a crossroads, as did the Kirk iron works. The earliest known forebears of the Kirk ironworks included Victorian Peter's great-grandfather, Thomas Kirk Jr., and his older brother Peter, here nicknamed, "Peter the Elder." These brothers were born about 1750 and 1748, respectively.[5] Both lived in Townend, on the edge of Chapel-en-le-Frith. These two men are the "1770 Blacksmith Brothers."

Lack of records prevents discovery of how the Blacksmith Brothers came into the iron business. In fact, much of 18th century Kirk history remains shrouded due to an absence of suitable sources. The accepted start of the business in 1770 was derived from modern sources passed down from earlier common knowledge.[6] As young men, ages eighteen and twenty, Thomas and Peter likely had help from their father in establishing the foundry.

Parish records of marriages and baptisms often listed the brothers' occupations as blacksmiths.[7] This indicated they had a smithy where they worked with iron, but there remains the question of whether they produced iron or metal items from pre-casted or pre-forged pig iron. Nor is it clear how large an operation they had.

The ability to work with metal was a boon as the Industrial Revolution took hold. By 1770, the young Blacksmith Brothers had already witnessed improvements to industry mechanizations. When they were teenagers, the spinning jenny revolutionized the textile industry by automating the weaving of cloth. A year before they established their ironworks, James Watts of Scotland added a condenser to the existing steam engine and produced a machine with improved power and greater efficiency than the original. Industries rapidly embraced these new technologies, making them key components in the Industrial Revolution.

This era coincided with replacing wood with iron for machines and tools. For decades to come, Britain's pig iron production doubled every ten years.[8] The Kirk enterprise benefited from this factory-launching, machine-building, tool-making boom. Any business capable of turning iron ore into metal to cast or shape into the plethora of metal parts needed for new factories found a ready market.

The Blacksmith Brothers also benefited from their strategic location. Chapel-en-le-Frith was less than 20 miles southeast of Manchester on a major road connecting it with other cities, including London. Manchester's population during the Blacksmith Brothers' era quadrupled as it became the first industrialized city in the world. The early Kirk ironworks also profited from the 15-mile Peak Forest Canal linking Manchester to Chapel-en-le-Frith. The canal project, coupled with the Peak Forest tramway, connected the coal and limestone quarries to manufacturing towns. The

Kirk foundry had easy access to these new Industrial Revolution systems and the raw materials needed for iron manufacturing.

Producing iron was a hot, labor-intensive job. To make one ton of pig iron, a foundry needed approximately two tons of iron ore, one ton of coke, and half a ton of limestone. The 1770 Blacksmith Brothers hauled in wagonloads of iron ores such as hematite and magnetite, then heated them to high temperatures in their furnaces, reducing the ore to molten rock. Iron producers used limestone as a flux to remove impurities in the ore. Chemical reactions decomposed the limestone to calcium oxide, also known as quicklime. This combined with any siliceous minerals in the ore to form slag, which separated from the molten iron and floated to the top. Workers channeled the liquid ore to a sand bed designed with multiple outlets (resembling a pig). These outlets collected the molten iron to mold into pig iron ingots.

The ingots still contained impurities, which caused brittleness, but not enough to prevent shaping them into cast iron products. The Kirk forge produced wrought iron by reheating and hammering out these additional impurities. This process produced a stronger, more malleable material than cast iron. Manufacturers shaped the wrought iron into any form they chose, including the large rolled-out sheets used for shipbuilding and the small rivets used to attach them.

Methods for iron production also improved during the Industrial Revolution. Invented in 1784, a new process called *puddling* facilitated the smelting of pig iron in a blast furnace. Men stirred the liquefied iron with long metal rods that further oxidized the carbon as the rods melted into molten ore, increasing the purity of the iron. Family historian Geoffrey Peter Kirk described purification as, "White hot, pasty lumps of iron [which] emerged, like a dumpling in a gravy of molten impurities."[9] The puddler and his assistant extracted these lumps, or "puddles," with large tongs. An experienced team could produce puddles at a rate of almost 300 pounds per hour. The puddles underwent further development in hammering and rolling mills. Puddling streamlined the entire process, enabling the mass production of wrought iron for the first time. However, it required strenuous labor and a high degree of skill in knowing when to pluck the puddles from the molten pool.

In April 1794, the older Blacksmith Brother, Peter the Elder, signed a 42-year lease for a piece of land in Townend, near the tramway and canal system, with plans of erecting a forge and waterwheel.[10] It is possible the Kirk enterprise intended to expand their original business and take advantage of the boom in the iron trades and the new puddling technology. Perhaps they intended to install a drop hammer in use at the time. Waterwheels powered drop hammers by pumping water through pipes, operating a ram connected to the hammer. This action raised and lowered the hammer repeatedly, striking a piece of hot metal to pound out the impurities, resulting in wrought iron. This automated process allowed for greater production by greatly reducing the manual labor of pounding the metal.

For decades, the 1770 Blacksmith Brothers thrived in their business, but mortality caught up with them. In April 1811, approaching life's end and without a child of his own, Peter the Elder passed his estate to his wife, his brother, and his brother's children. The inheritance included several houses and parcels of land already owned by his nephews, Peter the Younger and Henry, sons of his brother Thomas. He bequeathed the ironworks, listed as "all that edifice and building together with the watercourse, water wheel and the implements therein occupied and employed by me as an iron forge" to his nephews and his wife. The document ended with one other stipulation. "It is my particular desire and recommendation that the business that I do now have lately carried on shall be continued in like manner by my said brother Thomas, my nephews Peter Kirk the Younger and Henry Kirk and my said wife jointly for their equal benefit and advantage in life during their joint lives."[11]

Whereas Peter the Elder's words and directions remained strong and determined, his hand was not. He signed his will in a small, crooked script before passing away in 1812, a few months after his brother Thomas.[12] Peter the Elder intended the forge to care for his household, stipulating equal benefit to his heirs. But intent and interpretation often conflict in such matters. His like-named nephew's wife later embarked on a rant, invoking a curse upon her brother-in-law, Henry, with eviction from Chapel-en-le-Frith.

1812 Iron Forge Brothers

Kirk iron passed to a new generation as the younger brother, Henry, supplanted his older brother, Peter, as heir to the ironworks. Although Henry's story stood out, it certainly intertwined with Peter's and, to a lesser degree, of their half-brother, Thomas's stories. For simplicity and to facilitate the timeline, these men are dubbed the "1812 Iron Forge Brothers," reflecting the year they took over the ironworks and how they expanded the business.

As the Industrial Revolution took hold, job titles changed with the burgeoning demand for iron production. With advancing technology, it became possible for the simple village blacksmith to evolve to iron master, as did the 1812 Iron Forge Brothers within their lifetime.

Church of England parish records identify Henry and Peter's father and uncle as blacksmiths throughout their lives. At least four other smithies existed in the Chapel-en-le-Frith area, and no other term other than "blacksmith," "smith" or "smithy" identified this occupation in the parish records.[13] The Iron Forge Brothers began their careers as blacksmiths, but by the 1820s, they were classified as "forgeman" and "iron forger," indicating they super-heated the metal with the aid of a bellows system.[14] A waterwheel powered some of their machinery.

In the city directory for 1829, the 1812 Iron Forge Brothers both claimed to be farmers and iron founders for Bowden Edge, a district surrounding part of Chapel-en-le-Frith.[15] This is the first indication of the size of the Kirk ironworks. The term "iron founder" identified the supervisor of a blast furnace producing iron, indicating the brothers oversaw other blacksmiths and forgemen in their facility, some of them relatives.

However, local trade journals listed the younger brother, Henry, as the "iron manufacturer" for Chapel-en-le-Frith.[16] This title referred to the owner of a large-scale enterprise with multiple blast furnaces and many employees. By 1837, Henry's signature extended the agreement between their uncle Peter the Elder and Robert Needham for leasing the mill and the stream running through the property for another forty-two years.[17] It identified Henry as an ironmaster, a new term coined during the Industrial Revolution for entrepreneurs who ran large iron-producing operations. The contract gave Henry permission to "erect a weir, reservoir and goit" (a water channel). This expansion of the waterworks supplied more water, enabling Henry to increase the foundry automation. During this era, many ironworks employed tilt hammers driven by waterwheels for hammering out the metal. The Kirk ironworks employed a noisy, belching Naesmith steam hammer that "bumped away night and day and [was] heard all over the place."[18]

The Needham lease conspicuously omitted the other Iron Forge Brother, Peter the Younger. England's first census in 1841 further hinted at a change within the Kirk iron dynasty.[19] It enumerated Henry as an iron founder while Peter the Younger listed himself as a farmer. Their sons followed their fathers' example. They all lived close to each other in their respective residences of Reddish Green and Hawthorne House. Their half-brother Thomas, a forgeman, lived nearby as well. But apparently Peter no longer worked in the iron business with his brother.

An explanation was scratched out in a brown leather-bound note-pad, scarcely the dimensions of a business card. Peter the Younger's son penned, "December 11th 1841—Received a letter from Mr. Adam Fox stating that Henry Kirk has agreed to give £1800 for my Fathers annuity and enclosing £10 as a deposit and is part payment of the purchase money."[20] With this arrangement, Peter Kirk (the Younger) relinquished his share in the family business and moved from the compound, the first to distinguish himself of the many Peter Kirks who would follow suit. He sold the house where he and his children were born and the Townend properties passed to him by his uncle, Peter the Elder. He bought a respectable farm at Dove Holes Meadow, a few miles outside Chapel-en-le-Frith. The notebook mentions no animosity between the 1812 Iron Forge Brothers, nor does it say what prompted the annuity. But Peter the Younger's wife, Rachel, had a problem with it.

According to some of Peter the Younger's descendants,

> Henry Kirk by means of some trick or other got [his brother] Peter to sign a paper handing the ironworks over to him and was cleared out with an annuity. The tale goes that this so enraged [Peter's wife] that she went to Henry Kirk's house at Reddish Green and gave him her mind in rather forcible language saying that she would live to see the day when there was not a Kirk of their branch in Chapel [Chapel-en-le-Frith].[21]

Living to the ripe old age of ninety years, Peter's wife, Rachel (Thornhill) Kirk, did witness the day when her brother-in-law and all his children had gone to their graves. However, she did not witness the full extinction of Henry's line as plenty of grandchildren remained in Chapel-en-le-Frith. The Kirk ironworks remained strong, with Henry's heirs operating the levers.

Henry may have had no choice but to buy out his brother in the ironworks. The business may not have been able to support both families. The heavy build-up of iron production and mechanization during the previous decades had saturated the markets. By the time Henry divested Peter the Younger from the business, an economic recession that would continue through the early 1840s had gripped many industries. Economic conditions worsened with the Mines Act of 1842, which outlawed child labor in the coalmines. In the mines, children had received a lower wage than their adult counterparts, keeping labor costs down for the collieries. In this era, coal was king, powering the steam engines that ran all the machinery.

Their wages decreased, people from Chapel-en-le-Frith and the surrounding area rose up and went on strike in August 1842. Mobbing local factories, they forced a work stoppage, reminiscent of the Luddite Riots of 1811 when textile workers aggressively protested the mechanization that had stolen their jobs. Several thousand local men and women dissenters strove to "have the same rate of wages as they received in 1840, and that they would have it before they went to work again."[22]

The mob started at New Mills, north of Chapel-en-le-Frith, and forced all the workers out of the mills. Strikers marched to the print works at Furnis and did the same. The mob even put out boiler fires and let off the steam to prevent completion of the work. The rioters forced all employees to leave work at the Bugsworth cotton mills and the paper factory near Chapel-en-le-Frith. They blocked carts on the road. Learning that the Furnis print factory had resumed work, the rioters marched back and let off the reservoir to make sure the facility had no water for operating the steam-powered machines. The rabble forced work to stop at limestone quarries, coalmines, and kilns. They progressed to the Kirk ironworks and compelled the workforce to leave.[23]

Forced closures were hard on an ironworks. It took a lot of coal to build up enough heat to melt the ore. To damper the fires required an expensive and time-consuming re-firing to return to proper smelting temperatures once work resumed. Two generations of Kirks manned the forge by this time, namely Henry and his sons Peter, Henry Jr., and Thomas, along with Henry's half-brother Thomas and his son, Samuel.[24] Perhaps the six men could have kept the essentials going if the mob had let them.

Having weathered the storms of recessions and riots, the Kirk ironworks grew to a full-scale iron manufacturing operation. Activity during England's industrial age again escalated to a feverish pitch. Railroad building began in earnest, and it is likely the Kirk ironworks manufacture of "small rounds, squares, and flats hammered out with their water-powered helve hammer" found a lucrative market.[25]

Likewise, Chapel-en-le-Frith developed from an ancient village to a bustling, thriving community of three thousand people. Situated in an extensive fertile valley girdled by lofty hills, the region's uplands contained good pasture dotted with sheep. Bold and picturesque scenes rewarded the town's residents when they looked up to the rocky mountaintops. Despite the industrial growth of the area, good stands of forest populated with game bordered the moors. A fine reservoir supplied the canal system with water for the town's mining and cotton manufacturing ventures.

Standing at the crossroads to larger towns like Manchester, Nottingham, and Sheffield ensured Chapel-en-le-Frith had a steady traffic of goods in addition to daily mail service and a cadre of coaches arriving at inns with names like the *Bull's Head*, *Pack Horse*, and the *Three Tuns*.

Town shops included coopers, corn millers and cotton spinners, butchers, blacksmiths, and boot makers. Wheelwrights worked alongside carpenters, stonemasons, tanners and nail makers. The town boasted curriers, tailors, milliners, and dressmakers. A paper manufacturer set up business along with druggists, surgeons, and even an attorney. And of course, an iron manufacturer owned by the Kirk clan, filled the ranks of a bustling business community.[26]

By the time Henry Kirk died in 1848, three generations of Kirks were laboring in the iron works. Ironically, the 1812 Iron Forge Brothers (Peter the Younger and Henry) died within two months of each other, mimicking the close deaths of their father (Thomas) and uncle (Peter the Elder) earlier in the century.

The Kirk iron foundry passed to Henry's three adult sons.

Peter Kirk & Brothers

In 1851, Henry's sons, Peter, Henry Jr., and Thomas all lived at Townend in separate yet nearby houses. All listed their occupation in England's census as "Iron Founder partner in the firm Peter Kirk & Bros. empl[oying] 24 men."[27] This was a significant operation, especially since other forges existed in the area. Importantly, this is the first reference to an actual name for the Kirk iron foundry, though whether the "Peter" referred to Peter the Elder, Peter the Younger, or Henry Kirk's oldest son, born in 1805, is unclear.

This latter Peter Kirk married his mother's cousin, Hannah Oliver in 1830. During the next ten years, Hannah bore him five children: Henry, 1831; Joseph, 1833; Thomas, 1835; Anne, 1837; and Peter, 1840, known here as Victorian Peter.[28]

Doubling down with baptisms in both the Church of England and the nonconformist church did not spare Hannah (Oliver) Kirk from the ravages of consumption (tuberculosis).[29] Considered the 19th century's biggest killer, this highly infectious lung disease spared neither the rich nor the poor. Hannah died a year after Victorian Peter's birth.[30] It was miraculous the infant survived—or any of his siblings, for that matter. His mother likely had harbored the infection for years. His father did not remarry and so will be designated "Peter the Widower" to help keep separate the many Peter Kirks.

Perhaps losing his wife motivated him to champion the cause of widows and orphans through the Odd Fellowship, where Peter the Widower held the office of secretary.[31] He raised his children in the Wesleyan Church and was superintendent of the Sunday school.[32] He supported the efforts of Chapel-en-le-Frith's Wesleyans to form a Band of Hope for young people to encourage lifelong abstention from alcohol.[33] Generosity towards the unfortunate was evident in a short address at a workers' supper years later, in which he spoke to the "advantages arising from a state of mutual friendship between employers and employed."[34]

This leadership policy for the ironworks was passed down through the generations. It built loyalty amongst the workers. Peter the Widower's sons worked in the family enterprise as forgeman. His oldest son, Henry, later described the Kirk Brothers' work environment, stating he saw only one man quit in the first decade after his father and uncles took over. He said, "Never any of the hands were brought to the workhouse, or received parish relief, or needed a stone yard, or soup kitchen. Everybody was properly provided for without such miserable and pauperizing methods."[35]

He went on to describe what life was probably like for all the Kirks raised in the ironworks:

There were 30 of us, but everyone did his share of actual productive work. There was no timekeeper, and nobody whatever, except the workers themselves, to see that everyone did his duty. Every man worked just as if the place belonged to him, and was only paid out of the actual profits. Boys soon caught the spirit and worked as hard and as faithfully as the men. The wages were not raised in brisk times nor were they dropped in slack times. The only immediate benefit to the workers was a little extra time worked, but that was not generally very much because the master kept the place going more or less in bad times as well as in good. His orders were mainly confined to a few standard sorts and sizes, generally used by his best customers. And as he was not impoverished by high wages, irregular and bad work, and restricted production in high times, he generally had money left to lay in a large stock of finished iron ready for the better times to come. I will remember the master's cheery words during the dark days, which followed the boom of 1845-6, 'work away, lads, work away, it'll come in.'[36]

1851 Great Exhibition

Victorian Peter and his siblings grew up in the early years of Queen Victoria's reign when innovation and prosperity propelled many British subjects into another age of advancement. Railroads linked every corner of Britain during his youth, and telegraph lines bridged communication barriers in a similar way. Peter had more access to written works with the advent of the steam-driven rotary printing press. He and his siblings were the first generation of Kirks who used fountain pens and mass-produced pencils for their studies. Also, standardized tool designs greatly improved the mechanization of the Industrial Age factories. Many of these advances were highlighted by the first world's fair.

It is likely their father, Peter the Widower, took his young family to the Great Exhibition of the Works of Industry of All Nations. They may have traveled by the special train reserved for bringing visitors directly to

London's Hyde Park during the summer of 1851. The Crystal Palace, housing the Great Exhibition, was stunning. The massive iron-framed structure was built over the trees in the park and was completely constructed of large plate glass panels, a novelty of the time.

Walking around the Crystal Palace took the Kirks on a virtual trek around the world as they visited booths sponsored by Great Britain, her colonies, and dozens of other countries. Visitors followed "the course of the sun," pondering the thousands of exhibits in the natural light pouring into the giant greenhouse. The industrious Kirks surely found something of interest in the four categories of raw materials, machinery, manufacturers, and fine arts. Hundreds of metallurgy items graced the exhibit halls, including a specimen of iron casting from New Zealand, the first of its kind from iron-sand instead of ore. Finished products made of iron were on hand, too, including Samuel Colt's new revolver. Electrical telegraphs, microscopes, ingenious medical devices, daguerreotype photographs, and a variety of Austrian clocks tantalized visitors.[37]

Curiosities like artificial human eyes, an ice cream freezer, a barometer that used leeches to predict the weather, and Queen Victoria's own Koh-I-Noor diamond, the largest in the world, likewise beguiled onlookers.[38] The Kirk family may even have spent a penny to use the first flushing lavatory, introduced at the exhibition. Surely, they would have toured the Machinery in Motion Gallery. Viewing so many innovations may have served as a catalyst in launching eleven-year-old Victorian Peter on his future path of inventions in the iron industry, marking a place for him in the 19th century.

The Great Exhibition ushered in changes to the archaic and cumbersome British patent registry system. The government streamlined the application process and began printing a weekly pamphlet of the registered patents. The cost to register an invention dropped considerably, from £100 to £25.[39] These changes allowed for an explosion of patents around the country during Peter's teen years. Any new idea or change to an existing part of any machine could generate a new patent in this transformative time.

These changes fostered a Second Industrial Revolution marked by technological innovations such as the telephone, electricity, vulcanized rubber, new processes for steel production and refining petroleum for fuel. Later came the introduction of the internal combustion engine. The increased use of steel caused a great increase in railroads and shipbuilding. Via these forms of mass transit, huge migrations of people traveled from farm to factory and across the seas.

The onslaught of new ideas at the Great Exhibition may have also triggered Peter's father, Peter the Widower, to move his family out of Chapel-en-le-Frith. While the family's deep and ancient roots in the village may have offered them a sense of place and history in their world, the move helped to propel them out of the secluded and perhaps limiting valley.

1853 Leaves Chapel-en-le-Frith

During the second year following the world's fair, partnerships dissolved between Peter the Widower and his brothers, Henry and Thomas, iron and brass manufacturers of Peter Kirk & Brothers.[40] Peter the Widower handed over the business to his younger brothers, marking the second Peter Kirk to leave the family business and move away. Perhaps continued grief over his wife's death spurred his departure, or perhaps he viewed Chapel-en-le-Frith as too limiting for his young sons in the fast-changing times of Victoria's reign. His youngest son and namesake had reached his teens, and it is possible his father sought better schooling in a larger metropolis for his son.

He might also have hoped to escape the ravages of tuberculosis. He and his children had miraculously escaped the disease that cut short the lives of so many, including his wife. His brothers had contracted it, though, and probably some of his sisters. Henry would not survive the decade, and Thomas would succumb in the next. In the prime of their lives, aged 52 and 47 respectively, both left widows with young children.[41] Their hardy oldest brother, Peter, would live a full life of 70 years, outlasting all his eight siblings.[42]

For now, Peter Kirk & Brothers became H&T Kirk, Iron Foundry, represented by Henry and Thomas. Having left the partnership, Peter the Widower moved north to Stockport, part of the greater Manchester area. There, he continued producing wrought iron at the Star Ironworks.[43]

Stockport shared the explosive growth of Manchester, both cities influenced by a preponderance of textile factories. Hat manufacturing was Stockport's specialty. The city's extensive industrialization garnered its fitting description as "one of the duskiest, smokiest holes"[44] in the district. Kirk's ironworks surely added to the pollution belching from the smokestacks.

The Kirk household took up residence in the suburb of Romiley, a couple miles east of Stockport. Even though it sat on the outskirts of a metropolis, Romiley retained its rural character, like Chapel-en-le-Frith. Both towns' agricultural landscape gave way to a residential area of a few thousand people. Nearby canals and rivers separated Romiley from the greater industrial expanse of Stockport and the even larger metropolitan area of Manchester. The Kirks probably benefited from proximity to the advantages a city offered, such as shopping, culture, arts, and higher education.

Less than 15 miles from Chapel-en-le-Frith, Stockport became the first leg of a sojourn for young Victorian Peter that would eventually extend halfway around the world to America. As he reached adulthood, another move catapulted the family forward. In 1858, their father dissolved his partnership in the Stockport ironworks.[45] In response, Peter and his brothers relocated north to Workington and established Kirk Brothers Iron Manufacturers. Each bore the name of one of their illustrious iron producing ancestors—Henry, Thomas, and Peter Kirk.

Two—New Life in Workington

"Another enterprising firm has established itself here and is nearly ready to commence operations with the smelting of iron. They will combine the rolling process, which will employ a large number of skill and workmen. The firm is the Messrs. Kirk Brothers, of the New Yard Iron Works. There is every prospect of success. Their long experience in the manufacture of iron, having been in existence for about a century, and those now connected being thoroughly practical men, can prepare iron for any particular purpose."[1]

Carlisle Patriot, 1861

Workington was a hotbed of iron manufacturing when Victorian Peter and his brothers arrived in 1860.[2] Located northwest of Stockport near the Scottish border, Workington lay on a treeless coastal plain. It possessed good harbors and an area rich in iron ore, limestone, and coal.

Peter and his brothers immediately bought an idle plant called New Yard Iron Works, situated near the Workington harbor, to house Kirk Brothers & Company.[3] They produced wrought iron by the puddling process. Kirk Brothers established itself as the sole producer of wrought iron in the area.[4] The brothers maintained the family business practice of a "close union between masters and men, all working honestly and heartily together for the common good" to build a loyal workforce.[5] Their combined expertise fueled their prosperity, especially that of Peter's oldest brother, Henry, who possessed "first-hand knowledge of being an expert roller, furnaceman, and shingler."[6]

Kirk Brothers advertised their manufactured, rolled wrought scrap bar iron as "well tried, tested and proved with a uniform quality. It was applicable for all purposes where strength, tenacity, and solidity were required, particularly for mining, ship building, engineering, and railway purposes, but also for general smith's purposes. No iron can excel it."[7]

The claim was hard-won, however. Their forge was little more than a blacksmith shop used as a drawing-out forge to make the metal longer and thinner while hot. They renovated the works to produce bar and rod iron to sell to intermediaries who worked it into finished products. As historians noted, "Unexpected difficulties hurt them from the outset, of both manual and mental application."[8] The area's iron proved "splendid," but only in the cold state. It possessed "hotshortness," a condition of the metal rendering it brittle and unfit for smithing purposes when reheated, often due to high phosphorus content. They learned of the defect after sales of their first manufactured product proved defective forcing customers to return it to the Kirk ironworks.

"Bitter experience taught our firm in the early days of iron making at Workington," wrote Peter's brother, Henry to the Iron and Steel Institute. "Though hematite iron, might be worked very successfully, and might be made entirely free from hotshortness experimentally (with coal and fettling of a different nature from those of Cumberland, and with puddling cinder from iron of an entirely different character); we did not find it possible to accomplish the same end under the altered conditions of another class of fettling, with a surous coal, and with the cinder produced by the puddling of the hematite pigs themselves."[9]

Kirk Brothers kept testing, often with poor results, eventually resorting to scrap and Scotch pig iron to make their merchant bars. They continued to experiment, and in time, their persistence paid off, solving the hotshortness problem. They soon manufactured a high-quality bar iron that obtained good prices. They intended to produce enough specially smelted iron to supply all the local mills.

Kirk Brothers expanded their enterprise when their brother-in-law, Charles J. Valentine joined them. They collaborated in purchasing the Derwent Iron Works, an idle plant they "fitted up with new machinery of a superior class."[10] The partners acquired Marsh Side Works and Ellen

Rolling Mills near Maryport. They also installed more puddling furnaces and rolling mills along with an enlarged blast furnace at New Yard.

Yet despite all this success, something was amiss. Ten years after their father left the family ironworks in Chapel-en-le-Frith, Victorian Peter left Kirk Brothers in Workington, the third Peter Kirk to leave the family business in as many generations, and the youngest to do so.[11] At 23 years old, Peter set up his own iron business though, unlike his father, he did not leave town—yet.

The reasons for Peter's break from his older brothers remain speculative. Did he feel overshadowed by them? Was he compelled to make something of himself on his own? Possibly, he craved a more modern approach than the old family tradition of wrought iron, like the newly developed process for making steel. There was room in the market, and in the family, to diversify. Whatever the reason, Peter's departure from Kirk Brothers Iron was oddly bracketed by two marriages in three years. His upward career mobility from a mere puddler to iron merchant and partner in his own enterprise was the singular change; his bride remained the same.

Mary Ann Quirk

Figure 2 Mary Ann (Quirk) Kirk
Photo courtesy of Kirkland Heritage Society.

Mary Ann Quirk's surname hinted that her ancestors sailed from the Isle of Man. Her family's prosperity charted a course from mariners to merchants in the bustling port of Whitehaven, fueled by England's extensive textile industry.[12] One of her forefathers gained success with investments in valuable iron ore deposits.[13] Failing to take up the life of his mariner father, her father, James Quirk, owned leather shops in Whitehaven and Workington. In his work as a currier, he applied the final processes to the tanned leather, rendering it flexible and waterproof and adding color. Quirk's shops boasted an "extensive stock of ladies', gentlemen's, and children's boots and shoes made of his own manufacture numbering over 3000 pairs."[14] His death from tuberculosis at the age of 43 left his widow with eight children.[15]

Her father's death left Mary Ann, fresh into her 18th year, with two strong and independent women to guide her. Her mother, Hannah (nee Gibson) Quirk, carried on her husband's robust business for a number of years.[16] Investing in companies in the Whitehaven/Workington area, particularly those that would benefit her nieces and nephews, her aunt, Mary Gibson, also contributed to Mary Ann's welfare and future.[17] Both women were the daughters of Peter and Mary Ann (Campbell) Gibson. Peter Gibson was a successful sailcloth manufacturer. Beginning in the early 1830's, his shop and residence were located on the main street in front of the Whitehaven harbor.[18] His daughters became entrepreneurial financiers, unusual for women of the times. Mary Ann Quirk later mirrored these women's successes. For now, her destiny lay in meeting the industrious, dashing, grey-eyed young Peter Kirk.

A leisurely half-hour train ride along the beautiful and rugged Cumberland coast connected Whitehaven and Workington. The Kirk Brothers frequented the area, conducting business with their agent on Roper Street, who had exclusive right to sell Kirk wrought iron.[19] Strand Street, a main thoroughfare connecting Whitehaven's harbor to the train depot, intersected with Roper Street near the Peter Gibson home and sailcloth factory. Peter Kirk and Mary Ann could have met any number of ways. Perhaps a chance meeting occurred on the train as Peter headed to Mr. Whittle's office and Mary Ann went to visit her grandfather. Perhaps they met at the Quirk shoe shop. Perhaps they attended the same church or social gathering. Perhaps it was no chance meeting at all but an arrangement by their elders, a common practice in those days to secure business alliances or status in the community.

Whatever the circumstances, Mary Ann set her sails with Peter soon after he arrived in Workington. Once properly introduced, they found common ties. Besides the obvious similarity of their last names, Kirk and Quirk, both were born in 1840. Both their families had links to the iron industry and enjoyed the same social status. Each had lost a parent in their young lives to tuberculosis. Each had a mother named Hannah.

Yet in some respects, Peter and Mary Ann were opposites. Mr. Kirk's upbringing grounded him with an ancient family name in a pastoral land-locked valley, while Miss Quirk had grown to womanhood in a bustling international port. Peter was the youngest amid a small band of men; Mary Ann was second oldest in a large crew comprised mostly of women. Her formal education probably included studying foreign languages, art, literature, and music. As a young Victorian maiden, she would have learned to navigate parlour decorum, perfecting social graces, embroidery, and conversation. Peter's training and skills were industrial: ore analysis, market reports, and finessing more heat out of a slag pile.

Their courtship was not lengthy. Peter arrived in Workington about 1860. In August 1862, the newspaper announced in the "Marriages" section:

At the Wesleyan Chapel, Workington, on the 20th inst., by the Rev. J. Mortimer, Mr. Peter Kirk; puddler, to Miss Mary Ann, second daughter of the late Mr. James Quirk, Washington Street.[20]

These few lines are telling of the couple. The Wesleyans believed in "love your neighbor as you do yourself." They favored abolitionism and women's rights. They were early proponents of women's suffrage. Equality may have been a fundamental aspect of Peter and Mary Ann's relationship.

No official governmental certificate associated with this publicly announced ceremony exists. The parties involved submitted and paid for the newspaper notices for births, marriages, and deaths, which makes a second, almost identical, marriage notice for Peter and Mary Ann even more curious. Published three years later in September 1865, it read:

> *At the Parish Church, Workington, on the 7th inst., Mr. Peter Kirk, of the firm of Messrs. Kirk and Dixon, iron merchants, to Mary Ann, second daughter of the late Mr. James Quirk, Washington Street, Workington.*[21]

Unlike the first, this second announcement aligns with an official government certificate, which notes Peter's occupation as an iron founder.[22] With the marriage, Mary Ann gained a father, Peter a mother. Their families complemented each other. Peter gained more sisters, and each gained two more brothers.

Why the multiple announcements, each citing a different church as the venue? Marriage protocol for that era included a short civil ceremony at the government's register office, immediately followed by a chapel ceremony. At the time, the Wesleyan church for Workington was not licensed for marriages, and so the ceremony would not have been legally recognized. An archivist has suggested the mix-up might have been caused by an innocent misunderstanding on Peter and Mary Ann's part as to the necessity of the registry office ceremony, coupled with lack of oversight by the Wesleyan minister, who may have assumed the couple already had the legal ceremony.[23] But registration of births, marriages, and deaths with Britain's government had commenced decades earlier. Peter's three siblings had married since then, and it is doubtful he would be ignorant of the requirements.[24]

Another explanation: Peter and Mary Ann's first marriage comprised a virtual promise of sorts. They bound themselves in the Wesleyan ceremony, knowing the legality fell short until a certified marriage occurred.

Why the delay? The other telling remarks included in the marriage notices reference Peter's occupation. Perhaps his profession was the problem.

Separates from family business

The Kirk Brothers ironworks was small when the men first arrived. They brought a lot of talent and experience with them to Workington, amassed by generations over the previous 100 years. They soon received repeated orders from Scotch and Irish shipbuilders needing rivets and other iron products.[25] The skilled brothers worked in the ironworks themselves, adding hired laborers as they built their enterprise. Peter worked as a puddler at the time of the first marriage announcement. The puddler had to possess a keen sense when the puddles became ready. The job involved strenuous, long hours dealing with heat and fumes while stirring the melted iron with rods before extracting large, spongy balls of heavy iron. Undoubtedly, it was an important job in the process of converting pig iron to wrought iron, but the title of puddler failed to impress against his brothers' titles of iron manufacturers.[26]

Coupled with the fact that Peter was the youngest Kirk (his brothers were nine and five years older) and therefore less experienced in the business, a puddler's lack of prestige may have caused concern with Mary Ann's prominent family. This may also explain why, a year after the first marriage notice, Peter separated himself from his brothers' business.[27] When Peter and Mary Ann officially married in 1865, he was an iron merchant in his own company, Kirk & Dixon.

The year after the legal wedding, Peter and Mary Ann's first child arrived, in the fall of 1866 at Marshside in Workington. They rebelled against the ancestral naming pattern and called him Frank.[28] Like clockwork, Mary Ann gave birth every two years thereafter, blessing the couple with nine children. The couple named some after family members: Hannah Oliver (Peter's mother, and later called "Olive"), Mary Gibson (Mary Ann's aunt, and later called "Marie"), and Peter Junior. Fanny Valentine's name honored Peter's aunt Fanny (Seville) Kirk and his brother-in-law, Charles

Valentine. (The former may have been instrumental in Peter's early life after his mother died.) The last child's name, Arnold, resurrected the memory of the ancient Kyrke bloodline. The names of their other daughters, Florence, Clara, and Jessie, had no family connection.

The regularity of birth certificates for their offspring provides a snapshot of the family's movements. Peter and Mary Ann lived at Marshside for several years, near his father and brothers and their families. Perhaps due to their growing household, they moved to Senhouse Terrace between Olive and Marie's births. Another move between Fanny and Peter Jr.'s births took the family to Bankfield Mansion, their final home in Workington.[29]

The homes got bigger, and so did Peter's ironworks. As his business flourished, Peter expanded the operation, employing more people. His occupation title changed from iron manufacturer to, ultimately, iron master, indicating he owned a large-scale foundry employing hundreds of workers. Driving his success was Britain's heady iron market and his quality product. The entrepreneur also had a knack for cutting costs by re-engineering the iron manufacturing process.

Three—Masterminding Success

At age 26, Peter Kirk registered his first British patent in 1866.[1] Over the next twenty years, he would register at least fifteen more. His inventions considered all aspects of iron and steel production, from heat for the furnaces that melted the ore to special ovens that cooled the ingots to rolling mill machines as well as tram rails and railroad ties of his own design. Some patents combined with others into one idea, such as a patent for a rail tie and one for the machinery for its manufacture. Kirk also generated new patents by improving his older ones. For example, his rolling mill patent progressed from a three-roll configuration to seven rolls. Most of his ideas reduced fuel use and labor costs. Some were unsuccessful or became obsolete with subsequent changes in the industry, while others proved more efficacious. He registered the most successful patents abroad, in France, Belgium, Germany, Spain, the United States, and Australia.

Kirk's first improvement to rolling metals incorporated three rollers stacked upon each other and joined with bolts.[2] The novel concept allowed adjustment of the middle roller, up or down, in conjunction with the top and bottom rollers, to vary the thickness of the iron. To transport the heavy metal bar to the respective rollers, he created an elevator system for a hydraulic platform.[3] The iron passed through one roller, raised to the next level, and advanced through another roller, or vice versa. In subsequent inventions, he expanded on the idea:

> I employed five rolls—that is to say, I combined a set of 'three-high rolls' with an ordinary two-roll mill, the intention being to obtain two reductions [rolling of the steel bar] by passing the ingot or bloom between the lower rolls, and then to obtain a further

31

reduction with the same heat by lifting the ingot or bloom to the upper rolls in the three-high set.[4]

This strategy also eliminated one of the engines, instead relying on the inherent power within the various sets of rollers "to communicate motion from the more powerful set of rolls to the weaker set by friction." Peter further developed this model, resulting in a rolling mill with seven rollers working in tandem with each other.[5] This allowed for four rolls of the metal without having to reheat between each, thus achieving a great economy of energy and labor in conveying the bar to and from the reheating ovens and the rolling mills.

In his final patent concerning rolling mills, Kirk eliminated the hydraulic platform that lifted the metal to the higher cylinders. Instead, he placed the sets of rolls so the ingot (or the smaller equivalent, the bloom) passed through one set and then, shifted over by a bar, proceeded through another set, exiting the machinery where it entered. "By means of my Invention," he said, "I am enabled at one heat to roll a very heavy bloom, say about fifteen inches square, into a rail long enough to cut up into six or more rails."[6]

Peter Kirk's experience as a puddler gave him insight into that process. Another early patent, registered in 1869, improved puddling furnaces by forcing more hot air in and around the furnace chamber.[7] Building on an existing idea in the industry, he used grates that circulated more heat as air flowed freely over and through them. His design incorporated unique hexagon-shaped fire grates with slats and spaces that allowed clinkers (embers) to fall through to an ash pit. Workers collected the embers and used them as a residual heat source. The innovation also involved blowing forced air over the ash pit and surrounding parts to increase the heat of the puddling furnace and supply the hearth fire with additional oxygen. In its travels, hot air contacted the furnace bottom and other surfaces, keeping them hot and further shrinking fuel usage.

Another mechanism further improved the operation of puddling furnaces. Kirk's goals for the device were "to promote economy in the consumption of fuel, to obtain regularity in the working of the furnace, and to provide for the regular discharge of the incombustible constituents of the fuel." He noted this improvement was not restricted to puddling and heating furnaces for manufacturing iron, but also "applicable to reverberatory, steam, generator, and other furnaces in which fuel [was] consumed upon grates."[8]

"The most important feature," he wrote, "[was] the employment of a grate bottom revolving on a horizontal or nearly horizontal axis carrying forwards the fuel and delivering the clinkers into the ash-pit."[9] In fact, he had recorded a separate patent two years earlier for an appliance for residential fireplaces based on a similar concept.[10]

These early patents constitute only a fraction of Peter Kirk's catalogued innovations. The products of his drawing board would determine the course of his ironworks.

Workington Iron Company

A new venture between Peter Kirk and his brothers-in-law, Charles J. Valentine and Peter Gibson Quirk, coincided with a wrought iron boom between 1869 and 1872. The men took a lease out for land at Moss Bay and erected blast furnaces to manufacture pig iron.[11] The site of the works (between Workington and Harrington) formed a triangle, wedged between the Solway Firth—the fjord separating England and Scotland—and the Derwent River with its expansive wharves. Winding through the mill yard, railways connected both ends of the property. The partners named the enterprise Workington Iron Company. The company experienced subsequent name changes; to reduce confusion, references here will be by its location at Moss Bay.[12]

Kirk and Valentine's personalities complemented each other, with Peter described as quiet and more concerned with the day-to-day management of the works. Charles, on the other hand, appeared more extroverted (in later life he entered politics) and, some say, possessed of significant vision and drive.[13] The amicable partnership would last for decades.

Historians hailed Peter Kirk and his colleagues as "very much alive to the trends and changes of their times."[14] The operation expanded in 1877 when the partners added a Bessemer steelmaking plant to their integrated ironworks. This facilitated a restructuring and name change to the Workington Hematite Iron & Steel Company.[15] Wrought iron was king during most of the 19th century, yet the industry blazed with talk about a new, revolutionary process of producing stronger and less expensive steel. The new method also required less labor to manufacture, an aim central to Kirk's enterprise.

Patented by Henry Bessemer in 1858, the new method used a special tilted blast furnace that pushed large amounts of compressed air through molten pig iron to burn away impurities and make steel. Bessemer did not invent steel; he improved the process. The expensive nature of steel production before his innovation only allowed small quantities for manufactured items such as cutlery. Bessemer's invention rocked the iron world as it reduced steel production costs from the £40 per ton price of smelting wrought iron to about £4 a ton. But the new method required the iron ore and other raw materials to possess specific chemical properties. England's northwest county of Cumberland claimed the iron ore, limestone, and coke with the perfect attributes. In particular, the area surrounding Workington held the low-phosphorus iron required for making Bessemer steel.

The Moss Bay managers produced little pig iron for resale, instead using it to construct rails. In this way, they controlled the quality of the iron and the finished product while avoiding the middleman's markup. The company housed a large laboratory, staffed with chemists, who analyzed the resources received and the product at different stages of manufacture as well as the finished merchandise.[16] Other production tactics conserved time and labor while maintaining excellence. As Kirk explained, "Keep a good supply of all material—ore, charcoal, limestone, coke, and cinder, so that no change [in production] is necessary for want of stock. If these items are attended to and the furnace manager keeps a constant look-out for changes and regulates or anticipates the same in advance, the cost of smelting will be reduced considerably, and the plant will become a good paying investment."[17]

Like a conveyor system, seven locomotive engines snaked raw materials and finished product on almost six miles of track inside Moss Bay's yard. The company's annual consumption amounted to 100,000 tons of coke, 40,000 tons of limestone, and 160,000 tons of iron ore, totaling over 300,000 tons of various rocks. Reducing the mountains of minerals into rails also required large-scale buildings and engines plus a lot of heat. A portion of the workforce labored in two twelve-hour shifts, continuously filling wheelbarrows with the 800 tons of resources needed per day for the operation. Cages lifted the minerals, weighed, and measured in precise proportions, to the top of the six-story furnaces where the smelting process began.[18]

An engine-house containing four blowing engines supplied four furnaces with the necessary blast. The furnaces reached sixty feet high, eighteen feet in diameter. Between the engine-house and furnaces stood thirty boilers supplying steam to the blowing engines and other smaller engines around the plant. The efficiency-minded managers powered twenty-five of those boilers by the waste gas from the blast furnaces, with coal fueling the rest.

Once the ore had been heated to a molten state, ladles dipped out the liquefied iron and moved over a series of molds. Above each, a tap opened in the bottom of the ladle, allowing it to pour into the cast until full. Each mold formed a 15-inch diameter iron pillar weighing over a ton.[19] Even though the metal began to set within five to ten minutes, producing a hard shell, the inside remained in a semi-fluid state for some time, making it too soft to pass through the rollers. While solidifying to the right temperature, the ingots lost great amounts of heat, so they needed reheating to become pliable enough for rolling. To avoid reheating the ingots, many methods had been tried, none fully successful.

Peter Kirk eventually devised a "cellular furnace" to house the ingots while they solidified.[20] The furnace also kept the blooms at the right temperature before they went to the rolling mill. Standard industry practice had involved transporting ingots to warming furnaces in bogies (carts or heavy wheelbarrows). This caused excessive cooling at uneven rates, which affected the quality of the metal. It also forced the warming furnace to undergo additional firing. The cellular ranges Kirk developed used the latent heat of ingots for uniform curing to the proper temperature before rolling. He built the cellular furnace within reach of the ingot crane to avoid uneven cooling during transport to other locations.

With Kirk's method, the ingots went from the mold to an individual cell as soon as the outer crust formed. A series of flues blew hot air along the range of cells to move the heat and refresh it. Peter reasoned the ingots could be "kept for a considerable time with a comparatively small consumption of gas and the heat better regulated than in the ordinary heating furnace...to conserve the heat of the ingot and make it more uniform throughout the length of the ingot."[21]

When the ingots were ready, workers removed them from the heating furnaces and sent them to the rolls of the blooming mills. Machinery passed the iron through several grooves until it was diminished in thickness and increased its length to between 80 and 130 feet. Afterward, laborers transferred the metal to roughing mills, repeating the process until it became a rough-shaped rail. Finally, it ended up in the finishing rolls, where it received the form and finish of a desired shape and weight. Other automated machinery moved the metal through a small circular saw, cutting it into the proper lengths, then shifted it to benches where workers smoothed off the rough edges. The rails underwent a final straightening before going to the steam drills that bored holes for the fastening bolts. In passing through the last groove of these mills, the rail received the stamp of the firm as well as the date and name of the purchaser, along with a final inspection (both physical and chemical) before being loaded for shipment to its destination.

Four—Bankfield

Figure 3 Bankfield 1882
Photo courtesy of Kirkland Heritage Society.

Peter Kirk, Esq., did not chain himself to the inkwell of an engineer's desk, however. With his brothers and Charles Valentine, he joined the Iron and Steel Institute, a professional organization to further the ideas of metallurgy.[1] He performed his civic duty by serving on the local court's grand jury.[2] He was also elected for terms as the parishioners' warden at St. Michael's Parish Church.[3] (He and his siblings had given up on Workington's Wesleyan church because that particular congregation was "suspicious and narrow," often making the Kirks feel like "interlopers.")[4]

Peter and Mary Ann also attended civic events, such as joining many special guests invited aboard the *Alme Holme* when Workington christened the town's new dock.[5] They attended concerts in the area, often sitting in the front row to enjoy the orchestrations of their good friend, Walter W. Williams.[6] At times, Peter joined him on stage. Both men belonged to the Workington Glee Society. They sang bass while Peter's sister Ann sang treble and her husband, Charles Valentine, sang tenor for the same group, which gave a benefit concert to raise money for a coal charity. Both Charles and Walter conducted also.[7]

In 1875, Peter moved his loved ones into the newly constructed Bankfield Mansion. He and Charles Valentine shared the twin residences attached side by side. (The British call this type of housing a "semi-detached.") For a time, they also used the mansion for their business offices. Situated on a prominent hill above the city, Bankfield stood like a castle, and a mighty fortress it was. Peter and Charles used steel rails for the supporting beams in the roof and ceilings. Wooden tramways connected their steel mill to their extensive property at Banklands, transporting bogies (railway trucks) filled with iron mill slag up the hill to the construction site. The partners added these tailings to the cement to make it stronger, a practice ultimately detrimental to Bankfield, as the iron eventually rusted and deteriorated the cement.[8]

A great expanse of lawn rolled out like green carpet in front of Bankfield, making the estate appear all the grander by highlighting its three-storied façade. The mansion exemplified Queen Victoria and her times, with a scepter tower standing on one end and a widow's walk at the crown.

Light flooded the entire house from the numerous door-sized windows set every few feet around its exterior on all floors. Heavy velveteen curtains draped the panes in the thirteen main rooms that graced Peter and Mary Ann's residence; these included a drawing room AND a library, a dining room, offices, several bedrooms, and a nursery.[9] A large kitchen was equipped with the necessary sculleries, storerooms, and larders. Not tallied in the thirteen-room count were any bathrooms, shops, warehouses, and closets (resembling small anterooms for storage as opposed to present-day hall closets), but of course, the residence would have included these as well. Bankfield dwarfed other houses in the neighborhood, most half its size.[10]

The Kirks' eclectic taste mixed Victorian luxury, old world charm, and a penchant for modern technology. Two suits of foreign armor greeted entrants to Bankfield's front hall. On a long marble table sat a Fitzroy barometer that monitored the fickle Cumbrian coastal weather.

Three of the many large windows wrapping Bankfield illuminated the grand drawing room. Gilt cornices and fringe dressed each window and, coupled with a chandelier hanging from the tall ceiling, gave evidence to the claim the room was "furnished with a refined taste."[11] A beautiful seven-foot Amboyna wood wall cabinet graced the room, featuring glass doors and gilded mounts. Another exquisite cabinet included three doors crafted with plaques of inlaid precious stones in the manner of Pietra dura. The room's main feature, however, was the walnut grand piano. A matching Canterbury sat nearby; its upright slots filled with sheet music. Peter Kirk's favorite composer, Felix Mendelssohn, was surely among the selections.[12]

"Mr. Kirk was an ardent lover of music and an accomplished musician, devoting considerable time to its study," a family member later recalled. "For years he officiated as organist at the Episcopal church."[13] His passion for music also prompted him to furnish Bankfield with a pipe organ, perhaps housed in the open-raftered, high-ceilinged, upper floor ballroom, large enough to mimic the expanse of a church. On this organ, he often composed his own songs. Later in life, some of his daughters likewise composed and published their own music.

The Kirks furnished Bankfield with pieces ornately carved from Spanish mahogany, American ash, Italian walnut, rosewood, and ebony. Horsehair, leather, and satin upholstered the many couches and chairs throughout the home. Walls displayed oleographs and water-colored drawings. Figures under glass shades, bronzes, vases, and other ornaments graced claw-footed Loo tables. The dining room contained a telescoping mahogany table with matching chairs and sideboards.

In the library, a Devonport desk, its drawers opening to the side, stood among over-sized wall cabinets replete with books and adornments. One carved walnut bookcase had previously belonged to the Marquis of Hastings. It stood 8½ feet tall and extended 15½ feet along one wall, undoubtedly filled with a great assortment of literature. A gilded clock on a marble base ticked away the time on the embellished hearth mantle. A large gilt-framed mirror reflected the light and warmth of the room's fireplace.[14]

In fact, every room in Bankfield had a fireplace, each fitted with a protective but decorative fender and fire irons; in the drawing room, these were silver-plated. Ever mindful of efficiency, Peter likely had the hearths of Bankfield equipped with his special fire-grates, patented in 1873.[15] The design included a hopper that, with a turn of a lever, dropped coal to the back of the fire onto a revolving grate. He constructed the hopper and flues of heat-conducting metal such as cast iron to radiate more warmth back into the room. He also had two bedrooms equipped with modern gas heaters.[16]

Several Bankfield bedrooms featured large wardrobes made of expensive mahogany, oak, or American ash. Other furniture matched each wardrobe's wood. Washstands with marble slabs held the chamber ware of pitchers, basins, and other toiletry items. Bankfield's nursery probably boarded a few of the youngest members of the brood, with the children graduating to other rooms as age allowed. A child's rocking chair sat in one corner, a treadle sewing machine in another.[17]

The kitchen was the heart of any home, and Bankfield's was no different. The dominant features were the gas plate and stoves, which heated the water pumped to other rooms in the house. The kitchen area included separate chambers for the scullery, where servants cleaned food and dishes; the pantry, where the china, glass, and silver were stored; and separate larders for fresh and dried food storage. For some of their meat and dairy needs, the Kirks kept a cow and rabbits.[18] Other groceries entered Bankfield's kitchen at the rear of the house, where a short, pebbled driveway connected Newlands Lane with the main residence, the servants' house, and the carriage house. The Kirk and Valentine residences shared these buildings. The separate quarters for domestic help were a departure from the norm.[19]

Huge double doors opened into the carriage house. Glinting in the light, three sets of silver-mounted harnesses and other tack hung on one wall. Two horses pulled the four-wheeled buggy, large enough to convey several Kirks at once.[20] One eventful ride occurred on a summer day when the Kirk children and their nurses were en route to the Quirk house on Nook Street. Rounding a corner, the carriage overturned, violently throwing its passengers to the ground. One passenger's head suffered a severe cut, while another lost several teeth. Others were bruised and shaken.[21]

Bankfield's grounds were large enough to have both a kitchen and an ornamental garden, said at one time to contain 500 plants.[22] Primroses were a hardy perennial and may have been included in the gardens, along with violets, calendula, and various roses. A good many edible plants probably graced the grounds also, including lavender, thyme, chamomile, and mint. These were lovely, fragrant, useful, and tolerant of the weather in Northwest England.

On nice days, Peter Jr. might have brought his pet crow out to the garden to play while the family sat overlooking the grand view of Workington and its harbor.[23] The whistle and puff of the steam locomotives may have interrupted their conversation as they chugged past the expansive Kirk iron industries on their way along the rugged Cumbrian coast.

The large room referred to as the ballroom on the top floor of Bankfield probably served as office space for Peter and Charles' ironworks. Each residence had a staircase accessing this area. "Behind the two identical great staircases were ornamental-coloured windows. In one of these the initials PK and, opposite, the date 1875 can be seen, subtly incorporated in the decorative design of two glass panes," noted Geoffrey Kirk, grand-nephew to Peter.[24]

Peter's office at Bankfield most certainly combined comfort with function, furnished as it was with overstuffed leather armchairs and handy side tables. The hearth warmed the room with a fire that crackled over the rhythmic ticking of the eight-days clock. A metal safe occupied one corner. On a large, elegant worktable, Peter might have spread his daily work or whatever invention he wished to ponder. A twenty-pound brass prototype of a railroad tie, of Peter's invention, might have sat conspicuously there, weighing down the rolled corners of draftsman designs as Peter contemplated adding a rolling mill or blast furnace.[25]

Five—Life Tests Peter Kirk's Mettle

It seemed Peter had the world by the tail. By his mid-thirties, he was a freethinking innovator with the talent to increase profits with his cost-cutting ideas. His burgeoning ironworks grew in scale as he added more blasts furnaces and other equipment. He enjoyed a growing family in a mansion that bore evidence of his success. All that was missing in his grand estate was his son Frank.

Prior to the family's move to Bankfield, the household had grown to four children, and Mary Ann was pregnant again. Though the Kirks lived at Senhouse Terrace, this child arrived at 10 Nook Street, the Quirk family home. This was not the first time Mary Ann had returned home since her marriage. She and infant daughter Olive were enumerated there in February 1871 while Peter, Frank and Florence remained at Seaton.[1] Mary Ann's mother died a few months later, and it is possible she stayed at Nook Street to care for her ailing parent.

Quite suddenly, in the summer of 1874, Peter and Mary Ann's oldest child, Frank, became ill with a sore throat and fever. Ulcerated lesions soon appeared in his mouth and throat as his condition erupted into strep throat. Seven-year-old Frank's face and body flushed red with a rash as rough as sandpaper. The doctor could not help the suffering little boy, who had contracted the dreaded scarlet fever.

The scarlatina epidemic raged for decades throughout England during the years 1840-1880.[2] Mary Ann and Peter knew how fast the disease might spread to their other children. Certainly, they knew of families who lost all their children within weeks to the fast-incubating disease. To protect their daughters from the toxic germs spewed with Frank's every cough, sneeze, and labored breath, the young family, including pregnant

MaryAnn, likely quarantined at her brother's house. A nursemaid cared for the fragile boy and verified Frank's death at the Kirk home in July.[3]

Still grieving this sudden dreadful loss of her firstborn son, Mary Ann delivered another daughter to the family, Fanny Valentine Kirk, a month later.[4] Bittersweet this was for the Kirk clan, who found themselves at church for a burial and a baptism within weeks of each other, the cadence of their lives forever changed.

Boiler explosion

Accidents, injuries, and machinery breakdowns plagued the iron industry. Peter's Moss Bay works were no different. A year after Frank's death and two weeks after his father's death, amid a heavy September rain, many townspeople awoke at daybreak to what sounded like a distant clap of thunder. Presumably, Peter heard it too. Approaching one of the many large Bankfield windows that faced the harbor and the ironworks district, he would have seen a barrage of shrapnel raining down upon his ironworks. Installed a year earlier to one of the blast engines, a boiler had suddenly exploded without warning.[5]

The explosion was so massive that a large section of the boiler, launched thirty feet in the air, fell upon the rail sidings outside. Another section rocketed even higher, clearing the 45-foot blast engine house before coming to rest on the railway-weighing machine. As the blast propelled bricks and other debris in all directions, steam and water hissed and gushed from broken pipes. Projectiles crashed through the roofs of offices and workshops, bombarded the engine house tank, and fell into the sea.

Kirk probably wasted no time in investigating the cause of the explosion, but it is not known what he discovered. The news article had noted the malfunctioning boiler was single-flued. This incident may have prompted him to adopt a new business practice of adding a backup flue. In later years, he recommended "an additional pipe stove so that one can be laid off and the stoves can be kept clean and in good repair without stopping the furnace. Frequent stoppages have often occurred through repairing and cleaning the stove. This is very serious, as regularity of working is most important and when the furnace is regulated, the stoves will have more air to heat. This can only be done by keeping the stoves clean."[6]

Thankfully, the only injury was to Moss Bay's pocketbook. The mill sustained £1,000 in damages (over $100,000 in current US dollars), but insurance only covered the £100 in damage to the boiler. And while repairs were underway, orders were delayed. This was a hard hit since the industry was in the midst of a five-year depression that "brought about the complete and final stoppage of more than one half of the finished ironworks in the north of England."[7] Peter's plant survived only to meet with another major setback.

Pattern shop fire

It started out a quiet evening in late April for the Moss Bay facility. The depression had ended, and business had returned. Some departments had finished for the day, others kept working. A guard made his rounds, and at half-past ten, walked by the pattern shop, finding nothing unusual except that a machine he heard earlier in the evening had gone silent. The new shop, built of considerable dimensions, sat next to the foundry. The expert staff in the pattern shop translated two-dimensional blueprint images of metal parts into three-dimensional molds. The shop basement housed the steam engines that operated the variety of saws, lathes, drills, planers, trimmers, and other machines located on the ground floor. Large quantities of dry wood piled in the workshop belied the museum-like quality of the pattern storeroom built over the work area. Renowned as one of the largest and best collections, Kirk's well-organized patterns were valued at some thousands of pounds.[8]

After the guard passed, a huge blaze began, rapidly engulfing Moss Bay's pattern shop. The roof collapsed with a tremendous crash, awakening many townspeople. Many blast furnace workers raised the alarm, but the inferno had already consumed the end of the building adjoining the foundry. The pattern shop burned so fast and hot the lead flashings on the skylights of the foundry melted and streamed down the roof. Knowing the pattern shop was lost, the men directed their efforts to saving the foundry.

Lack of fire engines and hoses forced the men to hoist ladders to the roof and douse the flames with a bucket brigade. One of the wooden ventilators caught fire, and workers feared the blaze would spread. Braving flames and intense heat, a young man threw a ladder against the wall, ran up, and busted apart the ventilator framework with a hammer.

It took an hour for the inferno to gut the pattern shop and burn itself out while the men worked to save the foundry. Damage was extensive. This time, insurance covered most of the loss, but the devastation of the pattern shop crippled the enterprise until the partners rebuilt and restocked.

The pattern shop was the heart of the steel works. Within, the Moss Bay ironworks had made their own repairs to their machinery, fashioning any new tool or part needed. They had designed new machinery required for implementing Kirk's ideas. They had cast the company's rollers to save money and ensure a quality product. Those machines rolled 70,000 tons of steel rails a year, with capacity fast approaching 100,000 tons. For the company's production increase, many people credited the laborsaving machinery devised and erected by Peter Kirk, machinery fabricated in a building now reduced to a pile of ash and charred debris.[9]

Though likely devastated by this catastrophe, Peter Kirk registered three new patents, including two new products, by year's end.[10]

The company goes public

For years, Kirk and Valentine's steel plant boasted annual profits averaging over 25 percent. Yet lack of funds in 1881 forced the company into liquidation. They restructured into a public holding called Moss Bay Hematite Iron & Steel Company, Limited. Reports noted Peter Kirk, Charles Valentine, Peter G. Quirk, and Joseph Ellis, partners in the old company—and bound together through marriages—held over 6600 shares of the new corporation, amounting to about a third interest in the syndicate.[11] Undoubtedly, other family members also held shares. The company prospectus cited as reason for the restructuring its ongoing obligations to pay out deceased partners' interests over the previous eight years of operation.[12] Couple this with the expansions, renovations to accommodate processes based on new patents, and conversion to steel production a few years earlier, all of which had undoubtedly strained the private company.

Making matters worse, coal prices had doubled in the region.[13] Iron producers in eastern England manufactured products at a much-reduced price. Competition cut into sales. Even so, the Moss Bay associates built an international reputation resulting from "valuable connections with various railway companies and other large buyers in the United Kingdom, the Colonies, India, and other countries."[14]

All considered, the Kirk ironworks needed a public corporation to entice new investors. The Joint Managing Directors of the new company included Peter Kirk and Charles James Valentine, each receiving £1,000 per annum salary.[15] To further the public offering of the steel mill, Kirk mortgaged Bankfield for £9,000 to the Yorkshire Penny Bank.[16] This liability brought hardship in future years when Kirk attempted to expand the business even further. Going public also meant shareholders and a board of directors had a say in what the company would do. In later years, this, too, would cause Kirk to stumble.

Over the years, the company had diversified and expanded into an integrated iron works which included blast furnaces, a large Bessemer steel rail mill, a steel sleeper mill, a brass foundry, and a forge at the quayside. Though prices for rails declined somewhat, newspapers reported high output and other optimistic news, and Moss Bay shares were in demand.[17]

Moss Bay, Ltd. modernized by installing an electric lighting system.[18] Other steel works in the area had already invested in similar upgrades in addition to adding telephones that connected plants to company offices. It is possible Kirk followed suit and replaced its telegraph system.[19] But these improvements did little to buffer the plant from breakdowns that in one instance caused the mill to stand idle for two months to accommodate extensive repairs.[20] Even so, the company finished its first year of incorporation with a tidy profit and a 10 percent dividend—this despite a depression that year in the iron and steel trades.[21]

The following year, Moss Bay, Ltd. employed 1,000 men who produced 93,800 tons of pig iron, 88,000 steel ingots, and 7,300 tons of steel tracks.[22] The company acquired leases for some iron ore royalties and limestone quarries. This enabled the organization to control their manufacturing from the ground up, literally from rocks to rails.

At Kirk Brothers & Co., Peter's brothers had also done well over the years, but they had to adjust to changing times as well. A decade after Peter left the partnership, so did Thomas, moving east to Hartlepool, in the county of Durham. Family historian Geoffrey Peter Kirk summed up his departure: "With the financial backing of Workington friends, two failed ironworks producing blast furnace pig iron were taken over—The Carlton Iron Co. Ltd. and the Seaton Carew Iron Co. Ltd. He was Managing Director of both, modernizing but not changing their essential character, operating them successfully and prudently until his death."[23] When scientists found a way to use slag for agricultural fertilizer, he also served as Managing Director of Basic Phosphate Co. Ltd. at the Carlton works.

Coincidentally, Henry Kirk at Kirk Brothers had to restructure from heavy debt the same year Peter's mill went public.[24] Kirk Brothers claimed forty-three puddling furnaces, four rolling mills, and a brass foundry within their different enterprises at New Yard, Marsh Side, and Derwent Rolling Mills. Both companies manufactured pig iron for their own use though Henry employed half as many workers as Peter. Kirk Brothers' annual production included 25,000 tons of pig iron, 25,000 tons of bar and rivet iron of various sizes and qualities, and 650-1,000 tons of iron and brass castings.[25]

Peter and his brothers had each found their own niches in a highly competitive market. The Kirk companies were not the top producers in the Workington area, but neither were they at the bottom of the heap among the many entities producing pig iron, Bessemer steel, castings, and other iron products.

But as Britain's market slackened due to over-saturation, problems intensified. As in most enterprises, directors often targeted labor costs to offset a depression in trade. In 1883, most producers in the area, including Peter's Moss Bay, Ltd., sought an all-round wage reduction of ten percent.[26] Workers disagreed, triggering a strike, and forcing the ironworks to dampen down the furnaces until they resolved the issues.

At the time, iron mills had the semblance of union work without the representation and protections labor practices would eventually entail. Within each department of the iron works—the Bessemer plant, the puddlers, the blast furnace men, and so on—a departmental manager contracted with the company to operate that department for a fixed sum. The manager then struck bargains with the men for carrying out the work. If a department manager miscalculated the expense or got too greedy and drove too hard a bargain with the workers, workers in only that department might strike. This caused volatility in the industry as one disgruntled department could shut down the entire plant.[27]

More products steeled Peter's resolve

As the iron trade slump continued, Moss Bay directors assured shareholders they were "using every effort to seek fresh outlets for their productions and were especially endeavoring to develop a trade in other branches of the steel industry besides rails."[28]

The company's upgrades paid off with a considerable reduction in the manufacturing cost and the added benefit of increased production. Even after a long stoppage, they could produce rails in a shorter time with less cost. Dampening the furnaces due to lack of orders was expensive for the company and harmful to the thousand workers depending on paychecks. Early in 1885, newspapers reported a depressed market at all Workington mills and predicted more work stoppages.[29] This affected the whole area since mining, shipping, railways, etc. all depended on a steady iron market. Kirk's rail mill and Bessemer departments had already been idle for weeks due to repairs and alterations.[30]

However, Peter continued to diversify. His brothers' ironworks had leased the Quay Forge from Peter's enterprise, but it had gone idle and the contract had expired. Peter planned to use Quay Forge for smaller kinds of steel manufacture, such as bars, plates, tinplate works, tramrails, and rail ties specifically connected to his recent patents.[31] Notwithstanding explosions, fires, labor and other shutdowns, market fluctuations, and other vulnerabilities that stretched finances, Kirk's ironworks continued delivering a decent profit and dividend to shareholders.[32]

Peter Kirk played with a design for manufacturing tram rails, usually an expensive process requiring specially built rolling machines, by turning the metal on an incline in a regular rolling machine.[33] This idea ushered in a series of innovations to railroad ties, also called sleepers. His patent for combined chair and sleepers was a huge success.[34] An economy of metal, labor, processes, and parts streamlined production of the invention, benefiting railroad builders with the same. The local newspaper reported at the time, "As the sleeper and chairs are in one place, and as there are neither rivets, bolts, nor loose pieces of any kind, the work of laying down [of track] can easily be done at the rate of a mile a day."[35]

Most railroad ties were made of wood, which rotted quickly in wet climates, so iron ties increasingly replaced them. Metal brackets, called chairs, fastened the rails to the ties, usually with rivets, holding the track in place. Kirk fabricated his sleeper with a thicker band either on one side or at specific places; later, this was punched with slots or holes. The chair piece received molded tongues or jaws fitted into the slot. A weld secured the cooled chair piece to the hot sleeper "so that the contraction of the sleeper caused it to tighten its grip upon the chair," reasoned Kirk.[36] He later formed clips or jaws directly out of the thickened section of the sleeper, replacing the chair piece altogether. For him, the two-fold benefit "obtained sufficient strength in the clips, jaws or chairs without rendering the sleeper excessively heavy."[37]

But he also had to overcome another disadvantage of metal sleepers. The flexibility of wood allowed the whole line to bend and flex under the weight of the train. Kirk needed a pliable steel tie. He believed constructing the chairs (or connecting jaws) from rolled steel would achieve this "as a more elastic grip upon the rail is obtained than when wrought iron or cast malleable iron [was] used."[38] He also fastened the jaws more securely to the sleeper with a "key" wedged between the jaws, which added a certain amount of lateral give to the rail.[39]

Kirk laid 200 yards of rail in the iron works yard to test the new product in an area of heavy use. Locomotives weighing 47 tons drove over the test line at high rates of speed, with and without brakes, "without the slightest variation in gauge."[40] Locomotive engineers agreed the line had sufficient elasticity and strength to hold the parts together. Peter Kirk found ready markets in India, Africa and Australia and other places where wood was not practical.[41] The following year, Moss Bay Ltd. delivered 160,000 to Bombay alone.[42]

Market succumbs to US production

Even though 1886 began with news that Moss Bay Ltd. had received another large order for the new rail ties, the year overall proved grim as the market downturn continued. For the first time since the company's formation, it reported a loss of over £15,000, making it a canary in the coalmine for the industry. "Moss Bay Iron Works was a striking illustration of the dullness of the iron and steel trade in West Cumberland during the year 1886," reported the *Carlisle Journal*.[43]

Financial troubles descended upon many Workington plants. A disruption of the Railmakers' Association in the spring of the year sent the price of rails plummeting by 25 percent, while the cost of raw materials dropped only slightly. For months, rail orders could not be obtained at any price. For three months, Moss Bay, Ltd. went idle. Peter Kirk, however, remained active.[44]

Kirk and his company read the landscape of the industry. Great Britain had lost ground as an iron producer to the United States. When Peter Kirk went into partnership with Charles Valentine, Britain was producing over fifty percent of the world's iron, while the United States supplied fourteen percent.[45] A decade later, when Moss Bay Co. went public, America had taken another seven percent of the market from Britain. Now, in 1886, the two countries closely matched each other in their iron production, but experts predicted America would soon overtake Britain. Knowing times would not change on their own, Kirk sought to change the times. He looked for a solution beyond the western horizon.

Having already connected a vast country coast to coast with rail, the United States was now racing to expand the network. America's northern neighbor was following suit, the Canadian Pacific Railroad having launched its coast-to-coast service in the spring of 1886. Peter's steel mill supplied some of the tracks within these two great transportation systems.[46] China and South America also stood poised for rail expansion. Altogether, the situation presented Peter Kirk with an opportunity to expand his firm into a fresh, burgeoning market beyond Britain's confining shores.

Part II: Exiting England

Six—Arrive in Seattle

"After arriving in Seattle [the Englishmen] decided that here was God's own country."[1]

Seattle Post-Intelligencer, 1916

Having travelled across America's great expanse in September 1886, Peter Kirk and his young engineer, John Kellett, finally reached her western shores. Encouraged by the Denny iron mines ore analysis they had seen in Seattle Lake Shore & Eastern Railroad's prospectus, the pair extended their tour within America's Far West. Standing on a wharf with their trunks and suitcases, the men saw for the first time the rugged Cascade Mountains, which held the mines and challenged their destiny.

Kirk and Kellett registered with Seattle's Brunswick Hotel on September 9, 1886. Welcoming the Englishmen, Daniel H. Gilman (owner of the SLS&E) escorted them to a party at the home of Henry L. Yesler, founder of the city.[2] There they met Territorial Governor Watson C. Squire along with many business elites and other prominent people.[3] These Washington men saw in Peter Kirk "a very fine-appearing gentleman of the old school,—courteous and polished."[4] Some befriended him and found him kind-hearted as well.

Within a week, Kirk and Kellett arranged an expedition to the iron mines in the Snoqualmie Mountains with Gilman and the mine owners. Even though Kirk had brought four pieces of luggage and Kellett three, Kellett noted in his journal the two men needed to purchase canvas clothes "such as they use for life on the mountains" to spend a week investigating the mineral deposits.[5] Kellett further described their journey:

This morning we started at seven o'clock by wagon, for some distance to Lake Washington. Here, we got on board one of the small steamers, which ply on it and went across, about six miles. Then we got into another wagon to go over a mountain to Lake Issaquah where we got on board another small steamer in which we rode about 10 or 11 miles to the head of the lake. Here we had luncheon, after which we travelled about 20 miles on horseback to the Hop Ranch where there are about 800 Indian hop pickers working.[6]

"They are different tribes and are encamped in the neighborhood," Kellett wrote of the Englishmen's experience. "There are also about 120 whites employed here and a score or so of Chinese are employed in and about the kitchen and waiting at meal times. It is a strange sight to see the different races sitting down at the tables at mealtime. Everyone sits down at the same table and all are served alike."[7]

The hop ranch was near the present-day town of Snoqualmie. From there, the group traveled another 25 or 30 miles and camped in preparation to climb the mountain. The Englishmen marveled at the timber. Kellett spoke of "fir, cedar and larch trees 300 feet high and as straight as a line, with no branches for the first 150 feet."[8]

He noted that on the morning of September 15, the men readied themselves for the tramp on foot up the mountains. "It was a fearful climb of three miles, some parts almost perpendicular with no roads to guide us, fighting our way through the underbrush, but we found some splendid specimens of iron ore, marble, copper, silver and garnets. The country seems very rich in minerals. We later ate our luncheon in a rocky mountain gorge where snow lies, and then descended to our camp where we arrived at three o'clock. We at once yoked up and started back getting some ten miles on our way when darkness overtook us and we encamped for the night."[9]

Kirk's party collected about fifty rock samples, which Gilman carried out on his back.[10] The men traveled by Indian trails to investigate the coal prospects. Kellett noted they tested the samples for coking qualities and "found them excellent."[11] They could perform crude tests in the field but would also send samples to a laboratory for a better analysis. After several days, Kirk and Gilman proceeded to the mines of Francis M. Guye, while Kellett remained at Hop's ranch. The following week they all met with Mrs. Guye, who Kellett described as "an ardent and accomplished geologist [with] a very nice collection of minerals."[12] After a lengthy stay, the men went to Mr. Gilman's office to number, title and pack the rock samples for shipment to the testing labs. Upon their return to Seattle, the Englishmen toured Elliot Bay, Lake Union and the partially dug channel attempting to connect Lake Washington to Salmon Bay.[13]

The Englishmen not only had to investigate area resources for producing iron but also existing infrastructure and possible competition. They found Seattle a stark contrast to Workington. Established around 1852 with Henry Yesler's lumber mill and a small group of settlers, Seattle was younger than Peter Kirk by a dozen years. Scant industry existed besides logging, fishing, and agriculture. Even the territorial governor could not account for the resources produced in the territory. In a bleak report to the Secretary of the Interior, the governor noted that grain, salmon, and lumber found their way to market via Portland and Astoria, Oregon before he could obtain production figures.[14] Nor did the railroad reach Seattle; the tracks stopped in Tacoma, 30 miles south.

"Seattle has scarcely a factory, beyond a single railroad shop and one or two foundries and machine shops," lamented one local paper at the time, a glaring contrast to the heavy industry of Workington.[15] The only iron works in operation on the Pacific coast belched smoke at Irondale, near Port Townsend. A plant in Clipper Gap, California, had been abandoned. Near Portland, Oswego Iron Works had been the first iron works in operation west of the Rockies.[16] Its supply of local brown ore yielded about 40 percent metallic iron—far less than Washington ores.[17] Regardless, they had made quality bar iron, at the rate of 15 tons a day. However, they lacked enough ore to supply their own works, let alone any others. The managers imported pig iron from Tennessee, California, and Scotland to supply the mill, and they shipped in limestone from Tacoma.[18] They operated for about twenty years before shutting down in 1885.[19]

The Irondale works, launched in 1886 south of Port Townsend, claimed a capacity of 10,000 tons per year. Their advantage over Oswego included proximity to limestone quarries in the San Juan Islands and iron ore within three miles. They also received ore from Texada Island, British Columbia. They supplied some of the local machine shops with pig iron and sent the rest to San Francisco.[20]

Securing other business

Figure 4 Moss Bay rail
Rail from Kirk's Moss Bay steel works in England, located at the Northwest Railway Museum, in front of the historic Snoqualmie depot. (Photo by author, 2021.)

While Peter Kirk waited for the ore analysis results from his trek into the mountains, he forged alliances and negotiated sales. The Seattle Lake Shore & Eastern had already ordered several thousand tons of rails.[21] By November 1886, Kirk had also contracted with the Satsop Railroad Company to deliver 2,000 tons of steel rails for their Shelton to Grays Harbor line. General Sprague of the Olympia and Tenino Road ordered an additional 1,000 tons.[22] Later, Union Pacific ordered 15,000 tons.[23] Moss Bay, Ltd.'s yearend report credited Peter for the resumption of orders, "One of the managing directors, Mr. Peter Kirk, has been in the United States for some months and has obtained several rail contracts for the company."[24]

After seeing the ore and traveling extensively to speak with area professionals, Kirk relayed the information and his thoughts to his long-time business partner, Charles Valentine. In turn, Valentine went before the Moss Bay Ltd. board in November 1886 and reported, "Mr. Kirk was in Washington territory and strongly urged a branch works of the Company should be established in the territory. As he has no authority from the Company to act for them, he was acting on behalf of himself and Mr. Valentine, who would transfer their contracts to the Moss Bay Company without charge if the Company decided to proceed with this business."[25] According to family historian Geoffrey Kirk, who wrote about the Kirk iron industry, the Board agreed Valentine should join Peter in investigating the proposal despite concerns about powers to commit the company. Geoffrey Kirk stated that both men, later in January 1887, "made it clear they undertook financial responsibility." However, Peter requested the words "without charge" in the minutes of the November meeting be amended to "without profit,"[26] suggesting he would foot the bill but expected reimbursement for his efforts.

All along the Pacific seaboard, Kirk met with railroad executives, potential investors, bankers, railroad lawyers, engineers, and construction companies.[27] He inspected Irondale near Port Townsend, including its ore analysis to his growing list of possible sources.[28] As early as December, rumors in Port Townsend had alluded to "a syndicate of capitalists who proposed purchasing the property and erecting steel works there."[29] Kirk traveled frequently to the headquarters of the Northern Pacific Railway in Portland, attempting to purchase a portion of the railway's land holdings in the Snoqualmie Valley.[30] He also initiated negotiations with Arthur A. Denny for the Denny Mine iron ore, located about 50 miles east of Seattle in Snoqualmie Pass.[31]

By February, Workington newspapers had announced Moss Bay, Ltd.'s expansion in Washington Territory where "large ore royalties had been secured and arrangements in progress for the establishment of an iron works.... where an advantageous market was expected to be found in a region away from English competition."[32] Experts predicted steel could be made for half what it cost in England and sold for twice as much.[33]

Exploring mineral resources

Peter Kirk and Charles Valentine continued to trek into the hills, investigating potential claims of iron and other minerals. In a letter to his niece some years later, Valentine wrote about some of those adventures:

> I was a long way up the Cle Elum valley with a mining party, in the Cascade Mountains when I first went there say about 1887. A man, from a good feet elevation, showed me the valley, and the trend of the mountains, and he, and the other men, who were scratching in a gold mine they had found, told me <u>no</u> white man had traversed the ground I saw.

> At a later period, we had a mining gang hard at work, and while flour and meal was carried on horseback by the trail to the camp, the fish had to be caught and the deer shot. The trout were so simple-minded that a travelling friend of mine, when he and I were miles higher in the valley than our camp, caught between 30 and 40 lbs. weight of trout with a rod cut from a tree, and a line attached to it in about two hours' time. We had 'high jinks' for days, in the camp after that.

> At one time we ran short of meat. An expert with the rifle went out and brought back a mountain goat. Ugh! I don't wish to taste the flavor of another! The cook for the camp was a wide-awake, and so far as I could judge, a good sort of Scotchman. We had many a 'crack' together.[34]

After one excursion into the mountains collecting and testing ore samples, Valentine told the Seattle newspaper, "Many of your ores are practically worthless, but at the same time you have some which are valuable.

Those of the Denny mine seem to me the best for steel; and I have no doubt that you will have in time large concerns for making iron and steel."[35]

Peter Kirk and the other Moss Bay men were no strangers to the rigorous testing of resources and finished merchandise. One report noted, "The whole of the iron and steel products of [Kirk's] company are sold with a guaranteed analysis, with special reference to objectionable elements, such as sulphur and phosphorus, and as the results are invariably checked by buyers, accuracy is absolutely necessary and is attained. The minerals used by this company are subjected daily to the same rigid tests."[36]

The Denny iron mines were not the only ones in the region. Extensive claims were located at Cle Elum. There, the Englishmen collected "samples taken promiscuously from the bed at considerable intervals of a distance over a course of five miles. [This included] 18 sacks of ore taken at regular distances across the bed with a view to get a fair sample of the quality... [and] determine the actual value of the bulk of the ore for iron and steel making purposes."[37]

Concerning some of the coal samples, the men conducted their own tests in the field. A renowned metallurgist who conducted a survey of Washington Territory's resources found one such test. "An experiment of coking this coal in a small pit at the mouth of this bank was made by Mr. Kirke and his coal-bank manager, with as satisfactory results as could be expected from so imperfect a trial. I found pieces of the coke lying near, and saw better samples, which have been brought from here. While, of course, the coke thus made is not the best quality, it certainly promises well."[38]

Kirk did not depend only on Moss Bay's trusted chemists and other British professionals. He compared "hundreds of analyses of different specimens from various localities, such tests having been made of analysts of repute, both in the United States and in Great Britain. [They were] also favored with the results obtained by other chemists of less standing, which subsequent tests proved to be entirely unreliable."[39] More trustworthy results came from Washington Territory Governor's Report for 1885 and independent analyses from US professors at Columbia College, metallurgists William Courtis and William Ruffner, and others. One report concluded, "Washington has been eminently favored by nature as regards the distribution of those minerals which are necessary for the production of iron and steel of high character."[40]

No one disputed the quality of the Snoqualmie ores at the Denny mines, while the Cle Elum deposits required more explanation:

> In the Cle-Elum valley, a few miles almost directly east of the Snoqualmie Summit, lies an enormous deposit of iron ore, the bed being almost unbroken for a distance of about five miles. The peculiarity of this ore is, that while the proportions of sulphur and phosphorus are low, it usually contains a notable amount of chromium and nickel and cobalt, and that the percentage of metallic iron is less than that in the Snoqualmie ores…. The quantity above water level [is] eight million tons…. The Cle Elum ore is chiefly magnetic; some of it only slightly so, and carries with it the red oxide distinctive of hematitic varieties of ore.[41]

There were sufficient supplies of limestone in the San Juan Islands and the report noted deposits at the iron ore sites were "inexhaustible." Bituminous coal, suitable for manufacturing coke, was prevalent in the area. The report noted, "Experiments made on a practical, and indeed on a commercial scale, at Wilkeson and Fairhaven, have proved and are daily proving, without the possibility of doubt, that over a large area of the state the bituminous coal will supply excellent metallurgical coke, of purity and of hardness unsurpassed in the US."[42]

According to the report, deficiencies in raw materials could be countered with appropriate processing. "The chief drawback is that the coal contains an unusually large proportion of ash, which, however, can be easily eliminated by well-known mechanical methods. It is worthy of note that the percentage of sulphur in the coal is much below the average of that now used in the great iron and steel making centers of the world. With efficient washing, the ash and sulphur would be reduced considerably and the impurities would be eliminated to an important extent. In Europe, the necessity of doing this has compelled engineers to give it their special attention, and the result is that the operation is carried on both economically and effectually."[43] The report also suggested if manufacturers needed further reduction of sulphur and phosphorus in the blast furnace mixtures, charcoal would prove a good substitute for coke as the Irondale operation had demonstrated.

In an optimistic assessment, the report concluded that "practical men intimately acquainted with the subject [found] without doubt that Washington possessed all the minerals necessary [and that] the manufacture of superior metal is therefore only a question of scientific and practical manipulation."[44]

Shopping spree

A spending blast in the spring of 1887 ignited Peter's venture on American soil as he procured the resources for making steel. The Guye Iron Mine in Snoqualmie Pass cost Kirk $30,000 in April; meanwhile, he continued negotiations for the neighboring Denny Mines iron.[45] These were the best ores in the region, possibly in the US. William Ruffner, a metallurgist investigating the area's resources, compared samples from the Guye and Denny mines with samples from the Great Lakes region, and Iron Mountain in Missouri. He averaged the Guye and Denny samples together and found they exceeded the others in the quantity of iron while showing less in undesirable phosphorus and sulfur.[46]

The Cle Elum area, located about 35 miles from the Denny mines on the east side of Snoqualmie Pass, also interested Kirk. He secured bonds ranging between $1,500 and $10,000 to test several Cle Elum iron claims. Later, he purchased some of these claims for $10,000.[47] The Cle Elum ore deposits were extensive. As one expert said, "The ore appears rich, is magnetic, and is reported to assay from 56.5 to 66 per cent."[48]

For $28,000, Kirk secured 640 acres of coal land located between the Green and Cedar rivers, a few miles northeast of Franklin.[49] Situated within two miles of the Common Point, a location equally distant from Seattle and Tacoma, these mines already had access to the Northern Pacific Railroad. As Ruffner noted, "The Kirke coal, or at least a part of it, as judged by the eye, may be called bituminous coal, though not so much deoxidized as the Wilkeson [Carbonado]. The coals mined in this basin are firm, black and shiny; they burn freely, and make but little dust. There are five seams of from five to fifteen feet in thickness, one of them may be said to be over forty-seven feet in thickness, though not all good coal. A gang of miners was at work opening the beds, with the special view of testing their coking qualities in order to be used, if practicable, by the Moss Bay Company for smelting the steel ores of the Cascade Mountains."[50]

Alien sentiment

Peter Kirk quickly discovered logistics and ore samples were not the only problems to overcome. Land ownership enticed many immigrants to come to America, but it became a hurdle for Kirk. Continental expansion succeeded in part due to the Homestead Act of 1862, which allowed European immigrants to obtain 160 acres of land simply on the grounds that they had not borne arms against the US and would improve the property by building a dwelling and cultivating the land for five years. A shorter residency of six months and minimal improvements provided the wealthier immigrant with land for $1.25 per acre, purchased from the US government.[51]

Poor settlers felt threatened by prosperous immigrants, who acquired huge tracts of territory and had the potential to make them serfs again without ever becoming US citizens themselves. The year before Kirk arrived in America, newspaper articles echoed these misgivings. "Certain noblemen of Europe, principally English, have acquired and now own in the aggregate about 21 million acres of land within the United States," noted a Seattle newswriter. "A considerable number of emigrants, become tenants and herdsmen on the vast possessions of those foreign lords under contracts made and entered into before they sail for [American] shores."[52]

Revision of the immigration laws sprang from those fears. At the time, a proposed bill before Congress proclaimed, "American soil should be owned exclusively by American citizens…and absolutely prohibits citizens or subjects of other nations, so long as they adhere to and retain their allegiance to other powers, from acquiring ownership of American soil."[53] While Kirk was exploring options for building a new steel mill in the Pacific Northwest, the Payson Act of March 3, 1887 passed. The act restricted land ownership to American citizens and those who had declared their intentions to become citizens.

Kirk filed his intent to become a citizen of the United States on May 18, 1887.[54] The decision seemed hasty, but in fact, a Cumbrian reporter mentioned he had "several conversations with Mr. Peter Kirk upon the prospects of the English metal market, and the influence exerted upon it by the continuous up-rearing of the hostile tariffs of other countries."[55] Tariffs protected American manufacturers. The reporter went on to say he and Kirk debated the controversy of Free Trade versus Protection, where "Mr. Kirk gave proof of how German makers were unable to tilt successfully against the outer buttresses of English trade." Their discussions left him with the attitude, "Mr. Kirk was a great thinker, who had weighed out the position, so minutely, that he was resolved to seek the advantages which Protection in a rapidly-developing country like the United States can undoubtedly offer."[56]

Testing the merits of the argument, an auction of Bankfield's furnishings confirmed Peter Kirk's intent.

Seven—The Kirk Family Move to America

"Valuable modern household furniture for sale at Bankfield, Workington. Mr. John Jenkinson has the honour to announce the favor of instructions from Peter Kirk, Esq., who is going to reside abroad, to sell by public auction, on the premises, Bankfield, Workington, on Wednesday, Thursday and Friday, 22nd, 23rd, 24th of June 1887, the whole of his very valuable household furniture, etc."[1]

Whitehaven News, June 9, 1887

Following her husband's change in citizenship, Mary Ann Kirk packed the family's belongings and sold what she could. Provisions and preparations to relocate her family half a world away consumed her days. She knew the family would be living out of chests and crates for some time while the bulk of their household belongings were shipped around South America. One of the many necessary items that would travel with the family was a plank painted to resemble piano keys.[2] With this, the Kirk children would continue their practice until their own piano arrived in Washington Territory.

Mary Ann and her eight children departed Workington less than a fortnight after the household auction. They sailed first class aboard the *SS Servia* with twenty pieces of luggage among them. The Kirk's domestic servant, Margaret Hughes, traveled with them to help with the younger children. Moss Bay Ltd.'s young engineer, John Kellett, journeyed with them, in part to chaperone the older Kirk daughters.[3] Another Moss Bay civil engineer, William Anderson, accompanied the group as well. (The Kellett and Anderson families would later move to America too.) Interestingly, the Kirk family, Kellett, and Anderson all listed themselves as "immigrants" on the ship manifest while Miss Hughes identified herself as a "visitor" traveling with only one bag.[4] Perhaps she intended only to escort the family and help them settle in their new homeland before returning to England. If so, her plans would change.

The group's Atlantic voyage generated stories passed down by the tall, redheaded Scotsman, William Anderson.[5] He reveled in telling of "Mr. Kellett's difficulties in shepherding the young Kirk girls around, finding them dancing partners, introducing them, and generally riding herd on them. The three oldest girls were lively, vivacious, and generally enjoying themselves. Olive celebrated her 17th birthday on shipboard; the other two girls were older which brought them close to [Kellett's] age. Mrs. Kirk kept to her stateroom most of the time. Hers was quite a regal personality; almost imperious. The younger children were governed by Margaret, the maid they brought with them from England."[6]

Also onboard the SS *Servia* during the Kirks' crossing were the Hawaiian Island royals, Queen Kapi'olani and Crown Princess Lili'uokalani, and their entourage of lady's maids and military escorts.[7] The Hawaiian royals had been invited guests at Queen Victoria's Golden Jubilee celebrations and were returning to the Islands. Reportedly, three-year-old Arnold Kirk's playful spirit enchanted Princess Lil.[8] She was a renowned musician and composer of Hawaiian songs, and it is possible the Kirk family enjoyed her talents during the crossing.

While Mary Ann and her crew collected adventures on their voyage, Peter trekked across the continent to rendezvous with them when they landed in New York on July 11. The Kirk family's first steps on American soil came with some trepidation, later exposed by Anderson. "Mrs. Kirk reached the gangplank and noticed the steep angle it formed with the dock; she adamantly refused to put one foot on it. Her husband pleaded with her, the ship's officers tried to reassure her and finally, Mr. Kirk in desperation turned to [Mr. Kellett who] pointed out to Mrs. Kirk, as gently as he could; the only other way she could leave the boat would be in the baggage sling. One look at that and Mrs. Kirk sailed dignifiedly down the gangway."[9]

More adventures awaited as they learned life in North America differed greatly from England. From New York, the family made their way to Montreal, Quebec, where they boarded the Canadian Pacific Railroad (CPRR). Constructed during the years 1881-1886, the railroad stretched across Canada from Montreal to Vancouver, with separate lines linking Minneapolis, Milwaukee, Detroit, Chicago, and New York City. Like the ship the family had recently disembarked, the CPRR took a week to deliver them to their destination.

"It was so different to the English trains," recalled Aubrey Williams, son of Walter W. Williams, of his own journey crossing the American continent. His experience probably mirrored that of the Kirk family as he further described:

> The [North] American passenger cars were so much larger and you
> boarded them from either end. Whereas the English cars you got
> into on the side and the cars were divided into compartments and
> held about eight or ten passengers each. The heat was coal stoves.
> They sometimes had a dining car on, which was very welcome. Of
> course, the ride across the country was so interesting especially
> crossing the prairie country so big and the stops were frequent in
> those days. [There were] Indians at every stop selling buffalo robes
> & horns, polished to a high degree but no wild Indians, very colorful
> certainly. We kids had been told before leaving that we would be
> amongst wild Indians, black men and savages. The only black men
> we saw were the Pullman porters and they were good to us.[10]

The Kirk children had undoubtedly heard their father's tales of traveling across Canada and the US. As the Kirk family made their way to Washington Territory, they saw for themselves the northern border of Lake Superior, a lake one third the size of their homeland. They crossed the Canadian Prairies, so expansive, it took days. For the comfort of its passengers the CPRR had planted several "dining stations" along its route.[11] Reaching the extent of the plains, the tracks brought them to the Lake Louise station. The dramatic scenery surely captivated the Kirks with its deep blue waters contained by jagged peaks crowned with glaciers. Continuing west through the glaciated and majestic Canadian Rockies, the train meandered through valleys alongside turquoise streams fed from those tall mountains. Long trestles crossed deep gorges and mighty rivers, offering expansive views. The rails skirted huge lakes and tall waterfalls interspersed among hundreds of miles of uninterrupted stands of evergreen forests. Nearing the Pacific Coast, the family made another stop at the Glacier House, a Swiss-style chalet atop British Columbia's Selkirk Mountains.

After nearly a week crossing the great expanse of Canada's mostly virgin frontier lands, the Kirk family arrived in Vancouver. They probably stayed the night and then boarded the steamer *Eliza Anderson*, headed to Seattle. Ten days after arriving in New York, the Peter Kirk family reached Seattle, Washington Territory, and checked into the Occidental Hotel.[12]

Walter W. Williams

Besides John Kellett and William Anderson, Peter also convinced his trusted secretary of Moss Bay, Ltd. to relocate to Washington Territory. Born in 1850 in Wales, Walter Winston Williams joined the company early in its history. "[As] Mr. Williams was brought up in Mr. Kirk's home establishment," noted a reporter, "[he] is, therefore, a man of broad, practical experience." Indeed, he was "Kirk's general lieutenant."[13]

"Music was his life," remembered Workington residents of the formally trained musician.[14] W. W. Williams frequently conducted choirs in the area. Occasionally those choirs expanded to more than 150 voices when groups such as the Wesleyan Band of Hope and the Silver Star Brigade sang together.[15]

In addition to his conductor's baton, Williams brought with him a weapon. Before he left for America, Moss Bay, Ltd. employees, officials, and friends held a testimonial ceremony for Williams "as a token of their respect and esteem." At this event, he received "a very handsome Cape rifle, by the Braedin Armoury Company." The rifle included a silver plate with an inscription listing the contributors as "the employees and other friends connected with the Moss Bay Company, November 1887."[16]

Eight—Deciding on the Mill Location

"That Seattle, in said King County, W.T., shall be the shipping port for all products of said mines, the same to be shipped to and from that point; that the lessees shall agree that in selling the products of said mines that it will not discriminate against the iron industries of Seattle, but will sell as cheaply to the citizens of Seattle as in any other market or as to any other persons or corporations."[1]

Seattle Daily Post-Intelligencer, January 27, 1887

Peter Kirk secured the rich iron deposits in the Snoqualmie Mountains east of Seattle in the Cascade Range from Arthur A. Denny in January 1887. The details of the agreement included a lease of 48 years, with a graduated increase in the cost of ore tonnage from 12.5 cents to 50 cents over the first two decades. Obligated to purchase a minimum of 30,000 tons a year, Kirk had access to any of the limestone and marble removed from the mines at no charge. The deal would take effect within six months of the completion of the railroad within a convenient distance to the mine.[2]

The terms seemed suitable but came with a hitch. The Denny Mine agents made compulsory that Seattle benefit from the ore, not Tacoma. Seattle residents had felt cheated in the past by Tacoma and especially by the Northern Pacific Railroad. This contract helped ensure Seattle a winning hand in the longstanding rivalry between the two towns.

Having acquired the mines in 1869, Arthur A. Denny knew how the feud had started. Denny had the honor of reading a telegram in 1873 to a large, expectant Seattle crowd, announcing the Northern Pacific Railroad's decision for their Washington terminus. The frenetic era of America's rail expansion pitted every city and town against each other as community leaders sought links to the major lines connecting the East and West coasts. The railroads also fought bitterly for the best routes. After much posturing, bribing, and wining and dining of railroad officials, Seattle's citizens felt confident they would triumph over the little village at Tacoma. But they did not. When Denny read the telegram to his fellow citizens, it revealed that the Northern Pacific had chosen Tacoma as the terminus.[3]

To make matters worse, the Northern Pacific's financial woes prevented completion of the line. Not to worry, area residents reasoned. Plenty of railroads stood ready to pounce on their competitor's misfortune. Seattleites still wanted tracks of their own. They got a commitment, then lost it in another power shift in 1884 after which the Northern Pacific vowed, "A locomotive would never turn a wheel into Seattle."[4] Determined that Seattle acquire its own intercontinental connection, Judge Thomas Burke and Daniel Gilman made another attempt with the Seattle, Lake Shore & Eastern Railroad.

Denny witnessed the bitter battles and noted the painful setbacks. He understood that the Northern Pacific (and its surrogate city, Tacoma) held much sway over Seattle's prospects. Therefore, he promised, "the product of those [iron] mines will never find their way into the markets of the world through any other port except Seattle, as long as I live, and I will fix it so they will still be shipped from Seattle after I am gone."[5]

Peter Kirk had a dilemma: Denny owned the best iron and demanded transport through Seattle; Denny's opponent, the Northern Pacific Railroad, controlled the existing rail infrastructure, which terminated in Tacoma. Moreover, no lines connected the mines to any railway. Then another snag developed. Perhaps failing to understand Denny's intent on the extent of Seattle's role in the development of the ore, Kirk at one point asked for an adjustment to the contract.

"The intention [of the contract between Denny and Kirk], of course, was to have the ore shipped to Seattle and worked here, although this was not specifically mentioned," explained "a gentleman, who is in a position to have complete and reliable information regarding the entire subject."[6] Included in this reporting was the hope that Kirk and his investors would live up to the agreement as well as an assurance that if Kirk did not honor the pact, the Denny group would find other American capital.

Kirk tried to delay and re-negotiate the contract with Denny with no success. 1887 brought a series of maneuvers which positioned him at one point on a precipice, poised to lose all after having invested tens of thousands of dollars in coal fields, tests, bonds, travel, and moving his family. As he hesitated on accepting the terms of the iron lease agreement, Denny's group moved forward. In a move perhaps intended to force his hand, a group of Pennsylvania iron men "representing ample capital" headed to Seattle in August to investigate the mines. Reporting on the visit, a Seattle newswriter underscored the fact that "the terms of the [mine] owners will not be modified."[7]

Kirk reconciled this dilemma by changing the location of his proposed steel mill to the Sallal Prairie, four miles southeast of North Bend and 17 miles west of the Snoqualmie Pass summit. The area had the added advantage of being within 16 miles of Kirk's recently purchased coal lands, and Northern Pacific had already surveyed the route for the needed tracks.[8] William Ruffner, a metallurgist hired by the Seattle Lake Shore & Eastern Railroad to survey the mineral resources in the territory, came across Kirk's Sallal Prairie camp in November 1887. "We returned down the mountain and stopped for an hour at Sallal Prairie, where we found a large camp occupied by the employees of the Moss Bay Iron and Steel Company, of England, who expect to build iron furnaces on this admirable location."[9]

Located in Seattle's King County instead of Tacoma's Pierce County, the Sallal Prairie site satisfied that part of the Denny Mine Group's terms. Yet Kirk wavered. In his journal, Ruffner noted on November 11, 1887, "Returned to Seattle by way of Tacoma, where I met Mr. Peter Kirke, the partner and agent of the Moss Bay Company, who is preparing to erect a steel plant; but whether he intended to build at Sallal Prairie or at Cle-Elum,

I could not ascertain. In fact, I am not sure that he had then determined in his own mind."[10]

With Kirk's indecision, his competitors would publicly bicker over his proposed steel mill.

Railroads fought over Peter

Three major rail syndicates vied for Peter's attention in the spring of 1887. The magnitude of his project promised a high volume of freight, shipping raw materials in and finished product out. He might have anticipated annual resource usage of about 350,000 tons, like his England mill.[11] At that time, freight cars transported about 20 tons each.[12] To haul minerals from the mines, Kirk would need a fifty-car train every day of the year. He would also need tracks.

To link the iron ore deposits with existing roads, a railway would need to scale the rugged Cascade Range with 17 miles of track. Tacoma-based Northern Pacific Railroad (NPRR) had the most mileage in Washington Territory, with over 800 miles, and the NPRR already had a line in the area. The Columbia & Puget Sound Railroad (C&PSR), owned by the Oregon Improvement Company (OIC), had nearly 400 miles of track. A fledgling line with only about 90 miles of track, the Seattle Lake Shore & Eastern Railway (SLS&E) had the advantage of loyalty from the Denny Mine group.[13]

Each competing railroad voiced a willingness to add a route into the mountains. "There is no difficulty about reaching the [Guye and Denny mines] with spur railroads and inclined planes," suggested one engineer. "A narrow-gauge railroad might reach all of these mines, without heavy grades, by starting at the highest point of the Lake Shore [rail] road and following the divides from mountain to mountain."[14] With the volume Kirk projected, plus the opening of timber and agricultural lands, a line from pit to port seemed a sure bet.

Weighing the options, Kirk met with representatives from each enterprise. In early 1887, he traveled to Portland and met with NPRR, inquiring about land in the Snoqualmie Valley near the Denny Mines.[15] Not to be excluded, the OIC soon set to work constructing a wagon road from the Common Point to the Snoqualmie Valley, saying the access would strike the valley above Snoqualmie Falls. Explaining the venture, they said they felt compelled to build the road to protect themselves against Northern Pacific's overtures to Mr. Kirk.[16]

The OIC sent Kirk passes to consult with their officials, and he accompanied an OIC executive to San Francisco. Perhaps to divert attention from the business at hand, Assistant Superintendent, T. J. Milner claimed to be making the journey for health reasons. But following the usual practice of papers noting the travel of prominent businesspeople, a reporter discerned that Milner and Kirk landed in the same hotels, in the same cities, on the same nights in February.[17] He asked Milner if Kirk had gone south for his health, as well.

"Well, no, not exactly," explained Milner, "You see, these Seattle, Lake Shore and Eastern fellows are so busy they have no time to show Mr. Kirk about the country, and as I was going below, I invited him to accompany me."[18]

There were other secrets as the railroads jockeyed for position. As the fledgling SLS&E gained ground into the Snoqualmie Valley, OIC executives became nervous. According to the *Seattle Daily P-I*, a "thoroughly reliable" source leaked OIC's intent to lay track into the same valley.[19] The source claimed OIC had sent engineering parties on special trains, under cover of darkness, to survey the route in the dead of winter.

As Northern Pacific's attorney James McNaught reasoned, multiple lines covering the same routes were a bad idea. "If Kirke goes on with his enterprise, there will be two other roads built to his works," he said. (Railways were often referred to as roads.) "That will divide the business up so there will not be much in it for any one of them, and it will be a question of the survival of the fittest. Our experience in building through the Cascade Mountains has been a rather bitter one."[20]

The competition should have benefited Kirk with faster access and better bargains. In fact, the feud between Seattle and Tacoma, with the railroads at the head of each gang, obstructed his plans. Over the ensuing months, the groups publicly displayed their aggressive posturing, offering a peek into what Peter Kirk battled in the boardroom.

First, the signing of the Denny mines lease agreement was postponed because some of the claims needed re-surveying. Any delay was costly. As a former Seattle mayor made clear, "American capitalists of undoubted ability and large experience will only be so happy to take [Kirk's] place here and develop the mines in question."[21]

A member of the Denny Mines clique questioned whether survey issues were the real reason for the holdup. A year having passed since Kirk's initial inspection of the Denny mines, a reporter asked Judge Jacobs if the entrepreneur had made any move toward developing them. "No," said Jacobs. "After we bonded the mines to him, he got to hobnobbing with people interested in injuring Seattle and soon after that, he commenced to find fault with certain restrictions and conditions we had made [that looked] to the protection of Seattle's interest. Recently, he stated if some of those restrictions were not stricken out, he would cancel his agreement with the Company. We asked him to put that statement in writing, but he declined to do so, as he knew by so doing, he would relieve us from all responsibility in the matter." Jacobs added that as soon as the Kirk obligation expired, the Denny Mines group planned to sell the mines to the Seattle, Lake Shore & Eastern Railroad.[22]

Northern Pacific's land agent, Paul Schulze, chimed in for the Tacoma group. Speaking to the same reporter, Schulze acknowledged that he knew of Judge Jacobs' statements and Peter Kirk's plans. He then ascended his soapbox for a lengthy speech spanning more than two full newspaper columns. The Seattle team rebuked Schulze's grandstanding by arranging interviews with Arthur Denny and John Leary, proprietors of the iron mines, which spanned another two columns. Leary accused Schulze of interviewing himself. Schulze lunged in with his own rebuttal, pointing out that Kirk could save on expenses by using the shortest possible connection through Northern Pacific:

> Mr. Kirke and associates have abandoned the idea of buying or
> leasing the mines in the Snoqualmie Pass, and have practically
> decided to locate their plant in the Cle-Elum region [Kittitas
> County] where large deposits of different kinds of iron ore—
> some of them very rich—limestone and coking coal are found in
> close proximity, and where very little railway construction will
> be required to make them accessible. The establishment of blast
> furnaces and rolling mills in this region is no small undertaking
> and one that has many odds against it considering the high price of
> labor and material, the cost of bringing the machinery here and the
> sharp competition with Eastern and English manufacturers.[23]

Schulze bragged that NPRR had extended every incentive to Kirk, "in the most liberal spirit."[24] They were willing to build the road to the mines, offered coal and iron from their own digs at a low royalty, and would sell land at nominal prices. Northern Pacific asked only for a fair share of the shipping the steel works generated.

In response to the "Seattle Only Port" clause to develop the Denny ore, Schulze felt besieged "by the most unreasonable and un-businesslike restrictions and conditions."[25] Arthur Denny countered, saying, "We have no doubt some people connected with the road will make us trouble, and put us to expense if they possibly can. They would not be true to their piratical natures if they did not attempt it." Denny considered Schulze and others in the land-grabbing crowd all threats and bluster. He blamed Schulze for demonstrating "his usual recklessness in misrepresenting and misstating in order to get an opportunity to make a bling at Seattle."[26]

Denny also praised Kirk. "I have had a great many conversations with Mr. Kirke in regard to his enterprises, and I must say I believe he is acting in good faith with our people. Of course, we cannot expect Mr. Kirke to do much until transportation facilities are provided, but roads are being pushed toward the mines as rapidly as possible. I have talked with Mr. Kirke recently and notwithstanding the rumors, from Tacoma and elsewhere, I have no doubt but that he is acting in good faith and will carry out his agreement to the letter."[27]

Ignoring Denny's charge of recklessness, Schulze questioned the locations of the Denny and Guye mine, insinuating the claims were not legal.

"It's nothing but bluster," scoffed Denny.[28]

Former Seattle mayor John Leary likewise condemned Schulze's rhetoric as "mere bosh." He warned Schulze be careful with his attacks, saying, "Any attempt to stir up these matters might pull down the pillars of the whole edifice."[29]

Schulze accused Leary of being "as blind as Sampson if he thought he could tear down the pillars upon which the edifice of the N. P. R. R. rests."[30]

Leary retaliated. "Mr. Kirk has been heard to use some very strong expressions in regard to information given out from time to time by the Northern Pacific through Mr. Schulze, in which [Kirk] threw emphatic discredit on the statements emanating from that source."[31]

Schulze denied this, saying, "Mr. Leary draws on his imagination and maligns Mr. Kirk when he states that that gentleman has ever thrown out discredit on the statement emanating from an officer of the N. P. R.R. Personal abuse is invariably the last refuge of those who lack argument and have no facts to stand on." Then he switched track again, noting that the Denny and Guye mines sat at a high altitude and were covered with snow for five to six months of the year. He bragged that NPRR's Cle Elum mines stood "2,000-2500 feet lower than that of the Snoqualmie mines. The ore in every one of them can be mined all the year round without difficulty."[32]

Denny bit back, declaring, "The Snoqualmie Pass is at an altitude of about 3010 feet; the mines are a little this side of the pass, and about 500 feet lower. If, as Mr. Schulze says, the Cle-Elum mines are something like 2500 feet lower than ours, he only needed to add a hundred odd feet and he would have located them below the sea level."[33]

"It has always been a mystery to me to know from what source Schulze draws his information," Leary added.[34]

Schulze rejected Denny's figures and reiterated that the Cle Elum mines were at an altitude of 2200 to 2500 feet, while the Denny mines hovered at 4300 feet and the Guye summit mines at 5000 feet. Picking another fight, he also complained of the inferiority of the Denny ores.

Denny mocked Schulze's assertions. "Of course, if he has such an advantage in altitude and ore, equal, if not superior to ours, surrounded by coking coal, I am at a loss to know why the land ring or Mr. Schulze should want our mine at all; and shall expect them to voluntarily abandon the contest he threatens, and leave us in peaceable possession of our very undesirable property."[35]

Schulze hurled the last word. "The fact is the bodies of ore in sight of the Snoqualmie mines are limited and no regular veins have been found. The ore deposits there are pockets—large pockets to be sure, but nothing more. On the Cle Elum and Yakima, on the other hand, a number of well-defined veins have been found and traced for miles."[36] He had a point. The Cle Elum deposits were indeed far more extensive than the Snoqualmie ledges.

This bickering might have seemed to Peter Kirk as insignificant prattle, like flies swarming over a perfectly good picnic. He stayed out of the fray. As one reporter remarked, "Mr. Kirke does not like much publicity."[37]

Durham coal and the Pacific Investment Company

In late April 1888, Kirk signed an agreement with President Harris of Northern Pacific Railroad to develop his coal lands at Durham and to secure Cle Elum iron ore.[38] A few weeks later, NPRR's land agent Paul Schulze bragged, "My first work was to affect a complete contract with the Kirk syndicate, the conditions of which I cannot, of course, make known. Under it, however, the company will at once open their coal and iron mines and later begin the erection of the proposed large iron works. The latter will be on the line of the Northern Pacific."[39]

The NPRR/Kirk agreement stipulated that Kirk furnish the rails and fastenings to connect NPRR's main line with the Durham coal lands. He received credit for the rails to apply to future coal transport costs. However, he had to agree to ship all coal or coke on Northern Pacific's lines. The terms included leases for coal at Roslyn and the vast iron claims at Cle Elum as well as land sales for a mill site in the same area.[40] Cle Elum was on the Northern Pacific's main line crossing the Cascade Mountains in Kittitas County. The area supplied all the elements necessary for a large industry. There was ample ground to expand the town and erect a mill, and a large river fed by the Cle Elum Lake ran through the valley.

The contract addressed Peter Kirk's alien status and offered a retreat from the ironworks part of the agreement. "It is the intention of P.K. if, and when, the Act of Congress, approved March 3, 1887, shall be amended so as to allow aliens to acquire and hold mineral lands in the Territories of the U.S., to erect two or more blast furnaces and a rolling mill at some suitable point, east of the Cascade Mountains on or near the Cascade Division of the NPRR." If an amendment to the Alien Bill occurred within a year, Kirk was to notify the railroad of his "intention to proceed with the work of erecting said blast furnaces and rolling mill at the place agreed upon."[41]

Kirk's other terms to the agreement reflected a practical yet autocratic approach with provisions that read, "P.K. may give up the mine at any time if coal cannot be profitably worked therein…P.K. shall not be interfered with, or hindered in his operation, on any of the properties previously leased to him."[42]

Immediately, the Pacific Investment Company of San Francisco incorporated.[43] This company managed the iron and other mineral rights obtained by Peter Kirk since his arrival in Washington Territory.[44] The company later added more Cle Elum claims.[45] Kirk also applied for a coal patent with the Bureau of Land Management, augmenting the extensive coal lands he had acquired. He received patent No. 109 for 80 acres on the Green River, east of Black Diamond in King County.[46] Peter and Mary

Ann Kirk transferred their interest in the BLM patent acreage to the Pacific Investment Company for a $10 token payment.[47]

One of Peter's English colleagues visited the coal mines and gave an account on his return to England. He witnessed "the coal being excavated with but little effort from the open mountain side. One seam was 45 feet thick, 25 of which, was of the best quality. The remainder was of the quality of English cannel or rattler coal."[48] He described the coal as soft and possessing intense heat and suggested it was good for making coke and for household purposes.[49] Plans for developing the Green River land also included building a large firebrick works, coke ovens, and an ironworks.[50]

Within days after signing the NPRR contract, in early May 1888, Peter Kirk registered the coal lands. Days later, from his Tacoma office, he sought bids to clear trees on 20 acres of the Durham lands.[51] Many wondered if this meant he had selected the site for his great iron works. "Oh, no," Kirk said, "we have not yet determined upon the site. This only means a clearing for our coalmines on Green river. We have only just now come to terms with the Northern Pacific as to the iron mines, traffic, etc....The railroad company will begin to build the extension from Cle-Elum into the iron country at once."[52]

By the end of the year, the railway had graded its line up to Kirk's Durham workings. The mines put out 300 tons of coal a day, and Kirk proceeded to ship about 1,000 tons of it per week to San Francisco.[53] By year's end, Pacific Investment Company was a moneymaker. Moss Bay Ltd.'s annual report listed the Pacific Investment Company as an asset on its balance sheet, with an initial investment of £11,000.[54] The report also noted, "A considerable sum had been made, which had been placed to the credit of our company by certain members of the syndicate."[55]

Even with the obvious success, some criticized the effort. William Courtis, a mining engineer, evaluated some area coal prospects for making coke. These included Kirk's Durham mines. In his report, Courtis echoed the anti-British sentiment prominent at the time with scathing remarks about "the poor management of English enterprises in this country."[56] His analysis did not mention Peter Kirk specifically but criticized his methods in developing his collieries:

> Englishmen are poor managers as soon as they leave their tight
> little land and the customs of their grandfathers. Their managers
> are accustomed to the iron rule of a Board of Directors, even to the
> purchase of a few nails to keep a board in place. Let loose from this
> control, they seem to run wild in foolish expenditures and show
> no power of adaptation to the requirements of our country. They
> understand their business thoroughly, but need the control of an
> energetic, honest American management to direct their work. The
> Durham Coal Mines have suffered from just such management.
> Poor machines have been brought out from the old country, or
> bought of second-class dealers here at some great distance, passing
> by makers of standard machines nearer to them.[57]

Many hoped Moss Bay Ltd. would have direct interest in the Durham mines. But changes in the Alien Law had not yet happened, and so the clause in the NPRR agreement addressing this open-ended question remained in limbo. At the time of signing, Congress was debating a bill that would have allowed aliens additional rights to the public lands. A reporter asked Kirk if passage of the bill was necessary for him to proceed with his plans. "That bill passed the senate with a good majority, and I think it will pass the house," he answered with confidence. "However, if it should fail, it does not mean that our plans must fail with it." Furthering his long-sighted, targeted approach, he added, "It would only require us to secure capital in this country. That was not our purpose at all. We intended to get all the necessary capital from England."[58]

Nine—June 1, 1888 Headlines Around the World

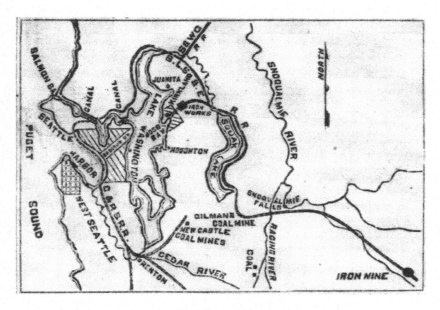

Figure 5 Map of steel mill location
Map used in a June 1, 1888 article announcing Kirk's steel mill would be
located on Lake Washington. His Durham collieries were located
near the Raging River at the bottom of the map.[1]

Three weeks after Kirk made these assertions, another announcement involving his prospects made news around the world. Despite the
earlier bickering between the Seattle and Tacoma railroad and mining
men, Kirk had brokered agreements with both camps. On June 1, 1888, as
documented with heavy front-page headlines and the flowing of much ink,
Kirk and his cohorts announced they would locate a Bessemer steel mill
on the northeastern shore of Lake Washington at a place recently christened Kirkland. Cradled between Puget Sound and the expansive forested

lowlands of the northeast corner in King County, this large lake's eastern shoreline had until now drawn little attention. Though the Northern Pacific had persistently tried to secure the location of Peter's iron works further south and had appeared to succeed with their recent agreement, reports noted Kirk "put aside all the inducements offered him to locate elsewhere and come to Seattle where no bonus was offered or required, was a fact of most striking significance."[2]

Explaining his decision, Kirk said:

I have been in the country nearly two years. I did not, you may be sure, determine upon the location at Lake Washington without full and careful examination of all the facts and considerations involved. In this work, I have occupied myself personally and have had the assistance of the secretary of my company, Mr. W. W. Williams. We have been over the ground thoroughly and have chosen the location near Seattle because in our judgment it affords more advantages than any other place. I may add that the advantages of this situation have been industriously kept before me by one of your citizens during the past six months.

I do not care to speak of details as yet, but will say this much, that the Works, which we propose, will be complete and extensive. Of course, we are doing this thing as a matter of business, and solely for business reasons, but it must in the nature of things, be a very important enterprise for Seattle. We shall lose no time in beginning operations, for I can assure you, we are anxious to be at work. I shall go with Mr. Williams immediately to the site selected and we shall begin work without delay. Of course, the work of getting ready will be very great, for the industry is new in the country and everything will have to be made from the beginning.[3]

Kirk had traveled to England earlier in the spring, attempting to raise more money for the American venture. In later years, he told friends he had indeed secured the necessary capital, but the source of the funds remains unclear since Moss Bay, Ltd. in England incurred losses the previous year.[4] The shareholders meeting in March 1888, which Kirk surely attended, included an announcement of these losses and a resolution that required each shareholder to contribute £2 for each share they owned to help the company through the tough times.[5] The board also announced that during the coming year they would invest in the recently purchased iron ore deposits at Woodend in Workington. Limited funds remained for Peter Kirk's risky frontier venture in America. Correspondence between Kirk and three other English associates signaled the company directors viewed the American prospects as "purely speculative" and risky, considering the Alien laws.[6]

Kirk later admitted he was induced to return to Seattle by Leigh S. J. Hunt, who had cabled him in England with promises of enough money to start the construction and operation of his proposed plant.[7] That would certainly have included land purchases. The June 1 announcement revealed a large tract of land already purchased and the venture ready to start. Conveniently, Leigh Hunt already owned a sizable piece of acreage in the proposed area.

Leigh Hunt

"Typically American in appearance," an Irish Parliament acquaintance surmised, summing up Leigh S. J. Hunt's lanky six-foot frame.[8] Blue eyes stood out against his dun-colored hair and colorless cheeks. A pointed nose punctuated his oval face and high forehead.[9] Hunt was soft-spoken, "slow and sparing in speech." His demeanor reflected a "characteristically American suggestion of quiet daring, boundless ambition, inexhaustible energy, with courage no difficulty could subdue."[10]

Jessie (Noble) Hunt saw in her Indiana-raised husband a "resourceful mind." Early on, she had perceived his "willpower, determination, unusual calm [and a] compelling presence." She viewed her husband as "rather frail" but "a natural orator, modest but with great charm of voice and manner…with unusual purity and delicacy of expression."[11]

Kirkland resident James Collins simply noted Hunt was "gifted with a silver tongue."[12] This surely assisted him in securing some top American investors for the steel mill. Collins further viewed Leigh S. J. Hunt as "a financier and business man of very unusual talents." Some historians credit Hunt for saving Kirk from the American Alien laws by buying land for the steel mill venture.

In the summer of 1886, Hunt was a newcomer to Washington Territory. Before journeying to the Pacific Northwest, he had served for a year as the president of Iowa State Agricultural College. Some cite the thirty-year-old's lack of experience and aggressive style of leadership as the reasons for his brief tenure.[13] Others later said Hunt was "a man of strong personalities who either hated or loved a man."[14] This trait may have hindered him in a role that demanded diplomacy.

Mrs. Hunt blamed the move to Washington on her husband's poor health and a doctor's orders to move to a milder climate.[15] Once in Seattle, Leigh Hunt quickly acquired two local newspapers. He merged them into the *Seattle Daily Post-Intelligencer* and threw himself headlong into improving it.[16] He worked long hours managing the paper, writing editorials, and double-checking every article.[17]

Hunt recognized the potential of Seattle's real estate market early on. "There are fortunes to be made here in real estate," he wrote a friend in December 1886.[18] By April 1887, he had incorporated a land company and a bank to facilitate his real estate transactions. Rumors hinted at underhanded dealings, including the use of other people's names in transactions.[19]

While Hunt was moving his family from Iowa and growing his newspaper and real estate businesses, Kirk was hiking into the mountains, collecting ore samples, and negotiating sales for thousands of tons of rails from his England plant. While Kirk was scouting locations all over the Tacoma/Seattle area, Hunt, in alignment with the Denny mine group, was determined to make Seattle the preferred choice. His newspaper pushed this agenda, claiming Kirk would build in Seattle over a year before the final decision.[20]

Likewise, Hunt's newspaper acted as his mouthpiece in promoting his political ideals. At a competing publication, an editorial writer noted that Hunt "was the political head of the Republican machine in King County" who made sure that county "always got whatever it wanted."[21] Hunt did not confine himself to politics on the county level. He was the guiding force for the Republican Party for all of Washington Territory.

Hunt's drive and ambition became hubris, however, and he soon overextended himself. Within months after starting his land company and bank, he suffered a nervous breakdown in July 1887. He took a leave of absence from the newspaper, turning it over to his manager. He rested for a few months at his Yarrow Point home on the eastern shores of Lake Washington before traveling to Hawaii at the end of the year to further recuperate.[22]

Hunt returned from Hawaii a few months later with renewed energy and a conviction to concentrate on real estate and steel.[23] In fact, he later told a reporter of his own newspaper, "I have but one ambition and that is to aid in building up an iron industry here at Seattle that will properly develop the great iron fields that are tributary to our port and market."[24] Hunt's talent for securing big-name investors like General Alger and Joshua Sears was indisputable. To convince such prominent capitalists, he offered the Denny ore analysis, listed other coal and limestone deposits in the area, and pointed to the dearth of such large enterprises on the West Coast. The expanding markets in China and South America were added incentive.

Hunt's return from Hawaii corresponded with Kirk's statement about one of Seattle's own citizens keeping the advantages before him for the past six months.[25] Hunt already had a sizable piece of land at Yarrow Bay and Hunt Point, south of the future site of Kirkland, which he had purchased a year earlier with his wife's uncle.[26] Perhaps it had been Hunt's dream all along to expand the area north of his property. At any rate, he bought hundreds and hundreds of acres.

On Hunt's recommendation, the Kirkland Land & Improvement Company (KL&I Co.) incorporated on July 12, 1888, several weeks after the mill location announcement. Hunt made almost two dozen land purchases with eastside homesteaders, totaling about $73,000. He transferred those holdings to the KL&I Co. for over $350,000. An item in the *Seattle P-I* exemplified these transactions: "Edwin M. Church to Leigh Hunt, bond for 70 acres in Sec 8, Tp 25 for $6440" then Hunt transferred it to KL&I Co., "assignment of the above mentioned contract, $14,850."[27]

Harry French, a local farmer in the area, mentioned in his journal that Leigh Hunt had bought "the DeMott and Nelson places for Peter Kirk of England for the Moss Bay Iron Works."[28] Multiple entries in the real estate column listed property purchased by others associated with the venture, including Peter Kirk. One day in September alone, ten land transfers in Kirkland (section 8, township 25 north, range 5 east) went to Peter Kirk, totaling almost 2,200 feet of waterfront acreage covering at least twenty acres.[29]

Kirkland

Before Kirk arrived, a large expanse of water and virgin forests separated the few scattered homesteads along Lake Washington's eastern shore from the 12,000 residents of Seattle.[30] For thousands of years prior to the homesteaders' arrival, the Duwamish Tribe inhabited both sides of Puget Sound in a great swath of varied habitats that extended thousands of square miles to the Cascade Mountains. The Duwamish had three distinct groups. Those from the Lake Washington area called themselves *hah-choo-AHBSH* or "People of the Large Lake." Several villages or "house sites" made up this group. Three settlements in or near the future site of Kirkland comprised the *TAHB-tah-byook'w* family group. One sat north at Juanita Creek, one to the south at Yarrow point, and one was in the future Kirkland area.[31]

The Duwamish lived in cedar longhouses with their extended families. They used long dugout canoes to navigate the region's myriad waterways in search of supplies and trade. Diverse and abundant resources filled the landscape, stretching from the ocean and tidal zone through temperate forests and across grasslands into lakes and mountains. Salmon and other fish, shellfish, ducks, deer, mountain goat, beaver, bear, and other mammals provided plenty of meat. The lake offered crayfish, freshwater mussels, and several varieties of fish. The forests provided salal, fiddlehead ferns, and all sorts of berries. The Duwamish pulled wapato (arrowroot) from sloughs and wetlands (like at Juanita Creek) and collected camas and acorns from the Garry oak prairies.

The Duwamish and many other local tribes signed the Treaty of Point Elliott with the United States within three years after Henry Yesler and his group of settlers landed at Seattle's Alki Point. The treaty provided the Duwamish with hunting and fishing rights and reservation parcels in exchange for 54,000 acres of their ancestral lands.[32] Some tribes received territory relevant to their homelands while others did not. Even though Chief Si'ahl (Seattle) was the first to sign the treaty, his Duwamish people received no land.

In 1866, the Bureau of Indian Affairs offered the Duwamish people land south of Lake Washington, near the present-day town of Renton. Local settlers, namely Arthur Denny and others, petitioned against the offer, and the proposal was withdrawn. The Government expected the Duwamish to move to reservations created for other tribes—even though those tribes were their traditional enemies, and the land was far from Duwamish villages and sacred places. After the US Army and other settlers burned their longhouses, many Duwamish made camps on Ballast Island, on the Seattle waterfront and eked out a living selling shellfish, trinkets, and working in the hop fields.[33]

As the US government opened Duwamish lands for homesteading, more white settlers arrived in the mid-1870s. The homelands of the People of the Long Lake and particularly the *TAHB-tah-byook'w* family groups eventually passed to men like Andrew Nelson, Harry French, Jay C. O'Connor, and E. M. Church and their families.

Clearing the land, these early settlers lived a hard life. Lacking the funds to support their families, some found work elsewhere while they built their homes and developed their farms. The men often traveled to Seattle to work for wages. The journey between jobs and homesteads was difficult, forcing them to live in Seattle for extended periods. They returned home periodically to work their land and see their families, who managed the homesteads during their absence.[34]

When the 1888 announcement of the location for Kirk's new steel mill hit the papers, the area was undeveloped wilderness except for a few farms. Eastside settlers contended with large and small predators getting into their livestock and gardens. Bears were a frequent nuisance and danger.[35] Deer ate their crops. Then, overnight it seemed, "The 100 or so settlers realized their forested hillsides dotted with patches of wild strawberries and woodland flowers might soon become a bustling city."[36]

To enlighten the many Seattle residents who had never ventured to the area, the *Seattle P-I* offered a description of the proposed townsite of Kirkland and its advantages. For one, there was enough land to support the large population needed to operate the mill. City planners put the iron works about a half mile inland on the hill, with the town proper intended for the former Nelson farm, closer to the lakeshore. The town would face west and south, facilitating spectacular views of the forests to the south and the expansive lake before it as well as Seattle's skyline in the distance and the rugged Olympic Mountain Range farther still. To the south, three forested points jutted into the lake and beyond that, the 14,000-foot glaciated cinder cone, Mount Rainier commanded a panorama surrounded by lowland forests.

Ten—The Ironworks Plan

"We have promised Seattle one of the best iron plants in America and have set about to make good that promise, and I assure you it will be done as fast as men and money can accomplish it."[1]

Peter Kirk

Expecting to employ thousands of men, Peter Kirk intended to build a sizable plant, mirroring his Workington plant, even in name. The American sister mill was called Moss Bay Iron & Steel Company. The potential market for the Kirkland mill's products included the western United States—Montana, Idaho, Utah, Nevada, Washington, Oregon, and California—along with China and nations on the Pacific side of South America, including Colombia, Ecuador, Peru, Bolivia, and Chile.[2]

Rumors circulated that the mill would manufacture plates for ship-building. Knowing they could save on freight and other charges, representatives of the great shipyards of San Francisco were already communicating with Kirk's syndicate requesting "the steel plate mills be put in operation at as early a date as possible."[3] However, the rail market—laying new track and replacing worn out ones—would ultimately comprise the bulk of the steel production in Kirkland.

The building of new railroads was sensitive to market fluctuations of shipping needs and local usage, but existing lines had a pre-determined formula for replacement track, expressed in rail tonnage per mile. For example, one executive with a prominent eastern railroad indicated his line required 240,000 tons of new rails each year for their 4,000 miles of railway. In all, 16,000 miles of existing track lay closer to Kirk's proposed steel works than to its eastern states' counterparts.[4] Per the formula, these rail lines would need an estimated one million tons of track for annual maintenance. The Kirkland planners also gauged the tonnage the mill might produce based on other iron and steel products imported into the western states. Information gleaned from newspapers put that figure at over 180,000 tons brought to the West from the eastern US and other countries—and that estimate was likely on the low end.[5]

One modern scholar studied the available statistics of rail expansion and rail replacement for the markets Peter Kirk sought in the years following the proposed completion date of the mill, arriving at a demand of 250,000 tons a year.[6] It is doubtful Kirk could have secured all the business in those sectors. Nevertheless, he planned an ironworks with the capacity of 6,000 tons a week or 312,000 tons a year. It is uncanny how closely the actual market demand matched Kirk's initial predictions.

Of course, Kirk could not have forecast the upcoming market crash that stalled further development in the United States. He could not have predicted the politics surrounding China's rail expansion which favored investors from countries other than America. He could not have foreseen that South American nations would never buy much US iron.[7] Only in the hindsight afforded by history would these facts become evident. How his prospects might have changed if the Asian and South American markets had performed as he expected remains impossible to calculate.

Figure 6 Kirkland steel mill building
Kirkland steel mill buildings during construction.
French Collection, courtesy of Kirkland Heritage Society.

Estimating the market as precisely as he could, Kirk designed the Kirkland mill so that workers could first complete half the project, then duplicate that half later. This plan would enable him to start production sooner than if he had waited for the completion of the entire facility. On the 120 acres set aside for the ironworks, the mill plan replicated Workington's facility, with four large blast furnaces, each 75 feet high with a capacity of producing 1,500 tons of pig iron a week.[8] To operate these huge furnaces, the plant would need two engines 84-feet long powering twelve 30-foot boilers.

Once made, the pig iron went to a cast house twice the size of the engine houses. The rolling mill, including the trimming and working rooms at each end, extended the length of a football field, as did the ore bunkers for storing raw materials. Ancillary departments each encompassed over 5,000 square feet. The pattern rooms, blacksmith, and machine shops, and a smaller foundry for making 30-ton castings was part of the early construction. These shops would facilitate the building of the mill. The planners knew it was not possible to make all the equipment and procure all materials on site. Items such as blast furnaces, firebrick, and clay had to be brought in from other parts of the US as well as Scotland and England.

"We will not bring the machinery we intended," Peter Kirk explained. "It will all be new. Some of it may be ordered in this country, as I think we can secure part of it at least, cheaper."[9]

Building the town

The Kirkland Land & Improvement Company managed the details of buying, clearing, and platting the land as well as the building of the town proper. Kirk served as president, Hunt as vice-president, W. W. Williams as secretary and manager, the Puget Sound National Bank as treasurer, and Harold Preston as attorney.[10] Almost immediately, allegations spread that the project was a land speculation scheme under the ruse of a steel mill.

As railroads expanded throughout the country, land booms ran rampant. Speculators rushed in and bought land cheap when railroads announced plans to put in a line here or there. The more unscrupulous ones sold this land at inflated prices to unwary settlers. A similar dynamic played out in some business speculations. Opportunists would announce a grand idea, securing investors who they abandoned as the scheme mysteriously collapsed.

While Kirk was negotiating for the Denny Mines ore early in 1887, the city of Tacoma had fallen prey to such a ploy. Arriving in town, a certain William Selover raved about mineral deposits in the Coeur d'Alene area hundreds of miles away. But because he "loved Tacoma for itself," he claimed he would build a smelter there. Of course, he needed to acquire land and capital. Tacoma's citizens ponied up $10,000 and property on the tidal flats. Selover scurried around the country looking busy. All the while, "the yearning gaze of all Tacoma had been steadily turned toward those tide flats for the first faint movement of the smelter. It only rained drearily, and the tide came and went every day."[11] In the end, Selover blamed his eastern partners and tried to weasel another chunk of money from Tacoma, but by then, his investors had wised up.

Comparisons to Kirk's venture were inevitable. "This is no Selover smelter racket," volunteered a local businessman who had met Kirk, "but is a bona fide enterprise, being carried on quietly by a man of vast experience and plenty of capital."[12]

A rare interview with Kirk also served to counter suspicions that his project was a land boom racket in disguise. The reporter pointed out there was, "an effort to discredit [Kirk's] enterprise at Lake Washington as a side affair, subordinate to a great enterprise that was to be established somewhere on the line of the Northern Pacific."[13]

With typical British pragmatism, Kirk assured the reporter and his readers the land company remained incidental and subordinate to the iron business. With steeled entrepreneurial confidence, he also challenged doubters:

I don't feel called upon to answer talk, which has no sort of effect upon me, or my plans. I have expected these attacks from certain sources. There are always some people who know more, and who are always willing to tell more, about a man's business than he does himself. If I recognized any responsibility to the public for my actions or purposes, I should, without doubt, have something to say in answer to the slurs, which have been put afloat by interested parties; but I have no such responsibility.

Neither myself nor those who are with me have asked anything in the way of subsidy or assistance. We have made our own contracts for materials, a large body of land for our works, town site, etc. We have done our own business, in our own way, and shall continue to operate upon the same plan quite indifferent to talk, which does not concern us.

But, to those of your community who are interested in our work, I will say that they would be wiser to judge of us by what we do, by results, rather than by rumors put afloat in a spirit of criticism.[14]

Asked if he could provide more details on the steel mill's progress, Kirk hedged only a little:

Yes, although it seems a little premature since the matter has not yet gotten into complete legal form. The iron company is composed of men living in Seattle, in the Eastern states and in Europe. I may say that the bulk of the capital comes from England, from men with whom I am now and have been for many years connected in business. The capital stock will be $5,000,000, and every dollar will be subscribed; in fact, arrangements are already complete for placing the stock.

It seems to worry many people that we should own our own town site. Since our works will without doubt, create a large community, we shall provide a place for that community to live. We shall, after a while, have residence and business property for sale, but not till, by our own industry and development, we have created a legitimate demand for such property. This we presume we have a right to do. The purpose in setting apart a town site was to protect our workmen by furnishing them homes at reasonable cost, but if by our own efforts we honestly create values which do not now exist we ought not to be blamed if we get some share of them. But the original idea will be strictly maintained. The first consideration is to provide homes for our own people. We hope to have a town in which each workman shall own his own home.[15]

When the reporter asked if the Seattle, Lake Shore & Eastern Railroad had located a spur line, Kirk maintained the project was a work in progress that would undoubtedly see completion:

We have been at work ever since the location at Lake Washington was decided upon. You must know that everything has to be made from the beginning, and it is no small work to make plans. We are now doing the general preliminary work of planning, surveying and engineering. I saw in the paper of last Tuesday or Wednesday, I think, a statement which, to say the least, was premature. We have been running several survey lines, but the location has not yet been made and will not be till we have definitely located the reduction works. Only this much is certain, that the terminus on the lake will be at Moss Bay, as originally planned.[16]

The Kirkland Lumber & Manufacturing Company organized in the fall and immediately built a lumber mill large enough to handle the huge trees of the heavily forested area and the demands of the extensive construction about to unfold. Given that the Pacific Northwest was famous for lumber exports, the mill being ranked among the largest in Washington was significant. Steam engines operated 58-inch saws, fueled by a modern design in which sawdust from the milling of the logs automatically fed the boiler's fireboxes. The mill was also fully equipped with "the thousand and one things known only to sawmill men." With a capacity of cutting 75,000 board feet a day, it kept "about forty men answering the whistle, morning, noon and night [because it found] it hard to keep up with orders."[17]

The lumber mill was initially the heart of Kirkland, pumping energy into the building of the town by milling the lumber for the multitude of workshops, bunkers, homes, and other buildings needed for the virgin enterprise. Supplying it, lumberjacks systematically cleared thick forests for the future ironworks and town site. They cut more timber than was needed, and the excess was burned. Multiple news reports noted that Lake Washington's eastern shore remained shrouded in thick smoke, sometimes for many days.

Priority went to platting the town as developers recognized the workers' need for adequate housing and services. In this, Kirkland would give Kirk the opportunity to build a town from scratch. Before arriving in Seattle, he had traveled America in search of a place to expand his English business. With his keen eye for innovation, he noted the organization of other mill towns. Thus, Kirkland would utilize "the best features of the manufacturing town of Pullman, near Chicago with proper reservations for municipal, religious, and educational purposes."[18] City planners also expected to establish a modern industrial school.

Kirk's engineers, Anderson and Kellett, designed a "diamond-shaped city center terminating in a town square."[19] The whole project re-created Moss Bay Ltd., so place names echoed the connection to Workington, England. Anderson and Kellett platted streets west of Market Street at an angle, allowing every lot a view of the lake.[20]

Following Kirk's penchant for expert workmanship, the detailed drawing of the city plat drew attention from the auditor's office when the company recorded it. Containing more than 5000 lots, it was the largest plat ever recorded in King County at the time. The recorder praised the survey work, hailing the plat as, "accurate to the minutest details, clearly and cleanly drawn, and [if any mistakes exist] they are so small that they do not amount to more than four or five inches in the whole area. Even the fractional lots can be sold without further measurement, the figures so correct that no dispute can arise."[21]

Travel across Lake Washington

Getting to and from Kirkland in the early days usually meant crossing Lake Washington. The other water route was via the Black River, beginning at Elliot Bay and passing through Renton at the south end of the lake. Only during times of heavy rain or snowmelt could a small steamer navigate this shallow river from Puget Sound to Lake Washington.[22]

With limited demand on the lake in the early days, travel to Kirkland was slow and restricted to only a couple sailings a day. The *Laura Maud*, a scow with two single steam engines and a boiler, was the main means of transport. Eastbound passengers boarded at Lake Union for the three-hour sailing to Kirkland, traversing through a glorified ditch to Lake Washington before the canal was built.[23]

As Kirkland and the nearby communities grew, so did demand, and more ferries were put into service. Before long, passengers crossing Lake Washington could choose from several steamers, including the *Laura Maud*, *Elfin*, *Kirkland*, *Edith E.*, and *Mary Kraft*. The scow *Squak* primarily hauled logs for its owner, the Kirkland Lumber Mill, but it also ferried passengers at times. By 1890, cable cars on Madison Street, Yesler Avenue, and Jackson Street linked passengers to different routes on Lake Washington, the fare to Kirkland being 25 cents.[24] The *Edith E.* advertised five eastbound departures daily, beginning at 6:45 am. Her captain left the Leschi dock every two hours for points along the lake, with the last sailing at 4:30 pm.

The *Kirkland* had a unique design as a sidewheel steamboat. At a length of 96.5 feet and a beam of 19.4 feet, many considered her the prestige vessel on the lake and praised her speed. The steamer's owners advertised passage at a competitive roundtrip fare of 15 cents as an "inexpensive, healthful and pleasing recreation to journey from Seattle to Kirkland."[25] The popular excursion listed seven scheduled departures from Yesler Avenue each day. Starting at 7:00 am, departures left about every hour and forty minutes, with a final crossing from Kirkland at 6:30 pm.[26]

While building the town and mill, company executives also had a yacht at their disposal. Peter Kirk bought the *Aquilla* from James McNaught, general counsel for the Northern Pacific Railroad. Once owned by William Randolph Hearst of San Francisco, the 48-foot steam launch transported steel mill executives, investors, and other dignitaries. Apparently, the *Aquilla* was extremely fast and earned the moniker of "Greyhound of the Lake."[27]

She was not fast enough, however. Early one summer morning in 1893, the *Aquilla* tried to cross in front of the *Elfin*, her captain grossly misreading the distance. The *Elfin* struck the *Aquilla*, smashing several planks and nearly sinking her. Expecting repairs within a couple days, the owners discovered a different fate awaited the *Aquilla*.[28] She sat for months at the Williams' family dock at Juanita Bay until she was eventually sold for the Bartsch family ferry service.[29]

Extensive travel

While woodsmen felled forests and engineers platted lots, Kirk signed a new contract between SLS&E and Moss Bay Iron and Steel Company of America for 20,000 tons of rails valued at $1 million. The contract dictated a strict delivery timeline between July 1, 1889 and January 1, 1890.

Reporters wanted to know when construction would commence. Pressed for time to catch a train, Kirk tersely responded, "Just as soon as we can get at it."[30] He further explained:

> One of the provisions of the contract signed today is that we are required to manufacture the rails at Lake Washington. Now, since that is part of the contract and delivery must commence in less

than 11 months from this time, you will readily perceive that there can be no delay in getting our works established and turning out steel rails. It will be impossible to fill this order from our own mines. We must import the raw material for the first installment of 20,000 tons, but shall be able to fill the next order with King county material. We shall have our blast furnaces ready by the time the road is built to the iron mines.[31]

By August, SLS&E had begun work on the proposed Kirkland branch line, and Kirk had made plans to go East for machinery. When asked if he expected to buy all the machinery there, he said, "No, we will buy only such as we cannot make ourselves. A considerable part of the machinery will be made at Kirkland in our foundry which is very soon to be erected."[32]

Newspaper tidbits and ship manifests during the initial launching of the ironworks revealed Kirk's extensive movements across and around the continent. He visited the West Coast ports of Portland and San Francisco, seeking contacts for the enterprise. He also traveled to Eastern states to talk with investors. At times, Kirk was accompanied by his British business partner Charles Valentine who described what one might expect on such journeys:

> Travelling in America was in many ways nothing like so comfortable as it was in this country, while in some instances it was even dangerous owing to the railroads not being fenced in. Cattle often strayed onto the railroads, and it was no uncommon thing to run down a cow or a horse, in which case it was ten to one that some of the carriages got off the line. Going from Portland to San Francisco, the train ran over a horse, and mangled it. The railroads, too, did not appear to be so well made as they were in [England], the cuttings being in some instances so narrow that parts of rock, getting displaced with rain, fell on to the rails causing a serious smash when a train came along. In other parts railway travelling was anything but pleasant owing to snow blocking up the lines.

Sometimes they were snowed up for about a week. In one place, we had to pass under 40 miles of snow-sheds with narrow openings here and there and it was not very nice riding there.

The Pullman cars in America were very nice in summer, but in winter were heated to such a degree that they became intolerable, and to get a window open and a breath of fresh air was no easy matter. They were generally heated to 70 or 80 degrees, and the colored man who attended to the heating apparatus kept it up to that, whether the passengers liked it or not. Travelling for six days at a stretch like this was no light work.[33]

Peter traveled so often that at one point he went missing. A shipment of rails arrived in Port Townsend but could not be moved to Seattle until the duty was paid. Among the three entities sharing the cargo was the Seattle, Lake Shore & Eastern Railway, whose auditor tried to pay the railroad's share so the ship could proceed. But officials required the full duty. The frustrated SLS&E auditor was able to track down one of the parties, but not Peter Kirk. "No one knows where to find him and telegrams have been sent in all directions in the hope one of them would reach him," the auditor said. "These telegrams announce the arrival of the vessel and contain a request that he arrange as soon as possible to pay his portion of the duty, so that the ship can proceed to Seattle and discharge."[34] Apparently in transit, Kirk arrived in Seattle at midnight on a switchback train six days after the ship arrived.[35] The duty was paid, and the cargo unloaded at Seattle's Ocean Dock.[36]

Kirk's excursions included extensive tours to England, as well. He was still a director of Moss Bay Ltd. with duties to fulfill in addition to starting the American venture. He spent more than a month just in the roundtrip commute between Seattle and Workington. The journey, 7,000 miles each way, began with ferry passage from Kirkland and a steamer ride from Seattle to the Canadian Pacific Railroad's hub in Vancouver, British Columbia. Kirk then spent a week crossing the continent to New York, where he boarded a ship to Liverpool for another week's voyage. Manifests from the *Majestic, Umbria,* and *Germanic* all list Peter Kirk traveling first class. His train, ferry, and lodging arrangements likely involved similar comfort.

In 1888-9 alone, Kirk traveled to England several times.[37] At least one trip occurred in conjunction with Moss Bay Ltd.'s board of director's meeting and included a visit to his brother, Tom, in Stockton, presumably to ask for his help with the American project.[38] Kirk also escorted his older daughters to Florence, Italy, to attend school.[39] On another excursion, he accompanied his cousin George Seville Kirk and his new bride, Jane, to Kirkland as George joined the Kirkland ironworks.[40]

George Seville Kirk grew up in the iron industry working in the same foundry as Peter and his brothers. Born in 1864 to Thomas and Fanny (Seville) Kirk, George was considerably younger than his Kirk cousins. George and Jane made their home in Kirkland. Two sons were born to them there, Joseph and Thomas. George's function within the Kirkland enterprise remains a mystery.

Eleven–Family Life

Figure 7 Mrs. Kirk and children
Photo from the French Collection, courtesy of Kirkland Heritage Society;
earliest known photo of Kirk family when first arrived in Kirkland:
BR-Fanny, Margaret Hughes (maid), Peter Jr., Marie;
FR—Clara, Mary Ann holding Arnold, Jessie. Circa 1887-90.

The Kirk family stayed in Seattle only temporarily after their July 1887 arrival, occupying an average-sized house on a large lot, including a carriage house, that Kirk purchased at 1202 South J Street in Tacoma.[1] He kept an office nearby at No. 10 Chamber of Commerce Buildings.[2] But to manage the building of his great ironworks from Tacoma would involve an inconvenient commute to say the least. Kirk needed to relocate his family again.

"Mr. Peter Kirk will move with his family to Kirkland on Lake Washington within the next few days," reported the *Seattle P-I* two days after the big announcement. "In selling his farm upon which the town will be built, Mr. Andrew Nelson reserved the right to remain in possession of his dwelling until September 1st. But as Mr. Kirk was anxious to bring his family immediately Mr. Nelson generously volunteered to vacate the house."[3]

Andrew Nelson received $13,600 for his land and his house at Nelson Bay (the future Moss Bay), located on the lakefront near an old steamboat dock.[4] Three weeks after the steel mill plans went public, Kirk moved his family from Tacoma to the Nelson house.[5]

"I find it a pleasant place to live and my family are delighted. We could not wish a more charming place of residence," Kirk noted after the move.[6]

Fir Grove

Figure 8 Fir Grove
Fir Grove, Kirkland, about 1889; photo courtesy of Kirkland Heritage Society

The Kirks continued to live in the Nelson house until Peter selected over a dozen lots in block 6 of Kirkland to build a family residence.[7] Situated between streets Burlington/Ports and Bond/Waverly Way, the lots fronted the lakeshore.[8] Peter hired a 52-year-old Swiss emigrant, John George Bartsch (or Baertsch), as the contractor and builder. Known for his European designs and quality work, Bartsch worked on a few projects for Kirk. It took over a year and $6,000 to construct the three-story, shingled-roof, frame house for the Kirks.[9] The family named the grand residence "Fir Grove," possibly due to an original stand of fir trees remaining in the yard. A picket fence encompassed the house and its elaborate garden landscaped with fruit trees, roses, and wild strawberries. A large veranda on the elegant home commanded sweeping views of Lake Washington, Seattle, and the mountains beyond when the weather allowed.[10]

Fir Grove easily accommodated the large Kirk family, some now teenagers, along with a domestic servant and guests. A host of Quirks, Kirks, Valentines and Dixons came to see what their cousins were doing in the American Far West, making long stays of their visits. Many professionals from England were entertained at Fir Grove as Peter sought their advice or investments.[11] Within an easy stroll from dock to doorstep, the Kirks and their guests might board a steamboat and cross the lake to Seattle.

Life at Fir Grove surely replicated much of what they left behind in Workington, just as the street names leading to their door did. Once at Fir Grove, Peter's wife, Mary Ann, probably greeted her guests in the parlor. The room furnishings were "especially lovely, Victorian in style, and brought from England."[12] Mary Ann often sat in a large, upholstered, custom-made chair as if holding court over her brood of eight children, ranging in age from five to twenty. Her dark hair pulled back from her round, attractive, but stern face; her short and stout physique; and her elegant demeanor reinforced the resemblance to England's monarch. Describing her as regal and "almost imperious," the Kellett children recount how the younger Kirk children referred to their mother as "Queen Victoria." The Kellett children did the same, the youngest of them recalled, but of course, "You may be sure, Mrs. Kirk was never called 'Queen Victoria' to her face."[13]

Family help, Margaret Hughes

Mary Ann surely needed help with such a large family, and Margaret Hughes supplied it. The Fir Grove kitchen provided her a domain as the family's domestic servant. It was large enough to have one stove dedicated to cooking a leg of lamb or a large beef roast and other dishes. A separate stove provided a means to cook food for the numerous large dogs kept in the back yard.[14] Margaret managed those two stoves with their roasting haunches and ensured Mary Ann's household ran efficiently. The multitude of her duties surely meant long hours: getting up before the rest of the household, working all day, retiring after her final duties for the family in the evenings. At the time, many domestic servants lived in the house of their employ, often in a room in the attic or near the kitchen area. Many of these women devoted themselves to their charges, often delaying or foregoing a family of their own. This seemed true for Margaret.

Before she came to America at age 33 in the service of the Kirks, little is known of Margaret's life except that she was born in Wales.[15] Petite in frame and short in stature, she kept her brown hair pulled away from her face and tied neatly in place. Still, errant wisps escaped, hinting at curls perhaps difficult to control given her busy schedule. Worn over a dark dress, her white apron, perfectly pressed and clean, belied the duties of her profession. Her face appeared stern, affirming family lore that her Kirk charges "were in no doubt as to their punishment if they disobeyed her."[16]

Though Margaret listed herself as a visitor to America on the SS *Servia* manifest, she remained with the family for many years. Her employers brought her into the fold as one of their own. When one of the Kirk daughters became ill, Kirkland's newspaper gossip included Margaret on the sick list for the household as well, more like a family member than an employee.[17]

Peter's dream for the town that "each workman shall own his own home" included his household staff too.[18] Margaret eventually owned a small lot a few blocks from Fir Grove.[19] Although the large Kirk family undoubtedly demanded a great deal of work, there was levity in Margaret's life. She attended social functions with the older Kirk children, perhaps as their chaperone.[20] She also traveled with the family, undoubtedly to care for the younger children.[21] The family enjoyed visiting Salish Sea destinations to the north of Seattle, where Margaret later found time for courting of her own.

Family pastimes

"The love of music was always there in the family," remembered Kirk descendant Barbara Dickinson, "and the Kirk girls were each required to play an instrument. The family would congregate around the piano while Peter Kirk played, Fanny, of course on her violin."[22] The parlor probably staged those musicals, which may have included melodies composed by some of the Kirk daughters: Florence, Olive, and Marie. Olive sketched out one piece of music on a sheet of the Moss Bay Iron & Steel Company of America letterhead.[23]

Fanny Kirk said her father "was a skilled pipe organist; that when the regular organist was absent from church he substituted for him; that he was in the habit of improvising his own voluntaries, and when asked, 'What was that voluntary you played?' he couldn't tell, nor play it again."[24] All the Kirk family's musical talents were cultivated in the church where Fanny played violin, Clara sang in the choir, and Florence played the organ. The choir even met for practice in the Kirk home.

The Kirks attended the Episcopalian church. The first church was in Houghton, built on land donated by the Kirkland land company. Peter Kirk, Jr. and his sisters Fanny, Clara, Mary (Marie), and Florence joined the Episcopalian First Church of Christ by confession of their faith with twenty-two other Kirkland townspeople. Besides the musical aspects of their church membership, the family held different positions on the church board over the years. Certainly, church activities encompassed a large part of their social life. The congregation put on various dinners and entertainments to raise money for the church. Kirk family members probably helped in these endeavors. The congregation also held a Christmas program in the early years of the township. In the evening, "the little church on the lakefront began to assume a lively appearance and was packed to overflowing.

A Christmas tree was hung with presents. Candies and sweet meats were handed out. A literary and musical program provided the entertainment."[25]

As Kirkland grew, residents started another church. The teenagers from both congregations formed the Endeavor Society, a shortened name for the Young People's Society for Christian Endeavor. Members held discussions on different topics, with leaders assigning them to different departments, such as Spiritual, Literary or Social. Peter's son Arnold was associate member of Endeavor society.[26] Fanny was active in the group as well. The number of members attending the meetings in Kirkland averaged forty. They also had outings, considered "quite the event in those days."[27] For instance, Society members took a moonlight excursion on Lake Washington and a trip to Snoqualmie Falls to attend Camp Endeavor.

In their early years in America, the older Kirk daughters continued their education in England and Europe. Florrie and Olive, ages eighteen and seventeen, respectively, when they immigrated, returned to attend English and European private schools, where they were educated in music, art, and languages.[28] Presumably, Marie and Fanny followed this pattern when they reached the proper age.

The younger Kirk children, however, went to the local school in Kirkland. The typical single-room, little red schoolhouse sat behind the Kelletts' house, well within walking distance of Fir Grove. Attendance was irregular; as one of their peers mentioned, they only went when there was a schoolteacher.[29] It is possible they were homeschooled at other times. Many of the schoolchildren came from the families who immigrated with the Kirks to build the new steel mill, including the Williams, Kelletts, and Andersons.

The English immigrant families probably found their common culture a comfort in the new land. Young and old, they socialized on occasion beyond church functions and gatherings. The young people attended parties, at times making the society page. The young people in Kirkland also planned their first ball.[30] Held at the Hotel Calkins in East Seattle, it was lauded as "one of the great social successes of the season." Attendance was quite large, the guest list including many familiar names of the area, among them Kirk, DeMott, Church, Kirtley, Bogg, Williams, and Bartsch.

On the same day, Mrs. Kirk and Mrs. George Kirk attended a tea at Yarrow Bay given by Mrs. Leigh Hunt. The Kirkland enterprise ran a common thread among the guests, namely: Mrs. Jacob Furth, Mrs. A. Fiskin and Mrs. D. H. Gilman. Mrs. Hunt entertained frequently, yet this seemed a rare gathering with the Kirk women. In fact, many connected to the Kirkland project rubbed elbows at Seattle society events: The Nobles, Struves, Hunts, Heilbrons, and Gatzerts, in addition to the others listed above. From these Seattle events, the Kirks remained absent. One of the Williams' children remembered the Kirks as "rather a strange lot [who] did not mix generally."[31]

Twelve—More Difficulties for the Venture

"I don't think Mr. Mallalieu will buy American land bonds at any price because he does not consider it a good security in the present state of the Alien Law and this will be our greatest difficulty here with the other people."[1]

Letter from J. Ellis to W. W. Williams

Meanwhile, across the seas, the Moss Bay parent company in England continued to fret over the American land laws. The board of directors' report in March 1889 for the previous year stated, "It had been the intention of the directors to secure a direct interest in the undertaking, but so far the operation of the Alien Law had prevented this. The territory in which the property is situated had very recently been admitted into the Union as a State, and it was believed the restrictions which prevented foreigners from owning real estate would now be mitigated or repealed."[2]

In fact, statehood did not mitigate the problem. Washington's State Constitution complied with the national standard, allowing aliens to buy land only after meeting eligibility standards to become citizens. But the English investors took hope in the new state Constitution's Article 2, Section 33, which stated, "the provisions of this Section shall not apply to lands containing valuable deposits of minerals, metals, iron, coal, or fire-clay, and the necessary land for mills and machinery to be used in the development thereof and the manufacture of the products there from." Nonetheless, the final statement of the provision upheld the federal immigration standard and dashed their hopes. It read, "Every corporation, the majority of the capital stock of which is owned by aliens, shall be considered an alien for the purposes of this prohibition."[3] Kirk's steel mill in America would need to be funded with a majority of American money

108

to prevent the tariffs charged to companies backed with a prevalence of foreign money.

The Alien Land Laws were not the only problem. The depression in Britain's iron market had continued since Kirk arrived in America due to market saturation and lost production to American companies. Kirk's Moss Bay works in England were more efficient due to improvements made in years past, but the company could only secure orders at very low prices. They sustained another year of losses, albeit in the small amount of £323, restricting additional investment in the American prospect.[4]

With problems of their own, Moss Bay of England directors saw the company's survival on a different path than Kirk, grumbling that the company should confine its efforts closer to home since the earnings were so paltry.[5] Rather than invest in the US venture, they intended to develop their local Woodend coalmines and build a private harbor. Both efforts would improve the company's bottom line, with the harbor project alone projected to save over £6,000 annually.[6] Kirk remained adamant about the potential for his Washington mill. But a black cloud hung over the project, poised to snuff out his pioneering efforts.

1889 Great Seattle Fire & 1890 restructure

If members of the Kirk family were at home on June 6, 1889, their fine veranda at Fir Grove would have provided an unimpeded view of the horrific fire and smoke-engulfed skies as Seattle's entire business district burned. Ignited inadvertently in the basement of a building at the corner of Madison and Front Streets and fueled by dry weather and the town's abundant wood buildings, the blaze burned for hours, engulfing all the major structures of the city as it razed twenty-five city blocks. Damages estimated at $17 million were almost equally split between business and personal property losses.[7] Among the many homes destroyed was the residence of Peter's good friend and colleague, W. W. Williams.[8]

Kirk's business partner, Leigh Hunt, suffered even more, losing the newspaper operation. Remarkably, some of his *Post-Intelligencer* staff were able to save cases of type and a small job press before flames destroyed the building.[9] Hunt jimmy-rigged a foot-operated press and put out a small paper the next morning from a tent.[10] Within days of the fire, his newspaper was encouraging residents to rebuild or, if they could not afford the construction costs, to sell:

> Holders of real estate who are unable to rebuild at once can render a great service to the city by parting with their holding at reasonable prices. Those who cannot build should come to terms at once with those who are ready to build if they can find suitable locations. Seattle must be rebuilt, and that at once. It is the duty of every citizen to do all within his power to further [the city's] rebuilding, even though he must part with some cherished piece of real estate in order to do so. No man who cannot improve inside property should hold it, so long as those who can improve are willing to pay a fair price for it. No citizen of Seattle should clog the wheels of progress now.[11]

To prevent another destructive blaze, the city leaders passed ordinances making the downtown area a brick-only district. They took the opportunity to repair some of Seattle's infrastructure, widening and straightening streets and correcting waterfront problems. To address the huge financial outlay for businesses to rebuild, civic groups raised money. Provisions and funds came from around the nation. Even Tacoma citizens put their rivalry aside and collected $15,000 for their sister city, further promising, "They would send money, food, clothing or anything else as long as they had anything."[12]

The banks guaranteed loans to anyone willing to rebuild. Shortly after the fire, Governor Ferry told citizens gathered at the armory, "Now let me say that those who wish to build bricks can get funds of the banks here, and when they run low we can get all the money we want in San Francisco." A local banker added, "The banks of Seattle do not wish to make money upon the misfortunes of its citizens. Reasonable security is all they will ask."[13]

Seattle's Great Fire marked a turning point for Seattle and consequently for Kirkland, which suffered in the aftermath. Many of the capitalists interested in Kirkland had suffered heavy losses in the blaze, and steel mill funds dried up in the flurry of activity that favored rebuilding Seattle over investment in Kirkland.[14] Neither would there be help from England as Workington's Moss Bay Ltd. continued to be strapped for cash following several years of strained finances, bad contracts, and rising costs for raw materials.[15]

In fact, in the months before the Seattle fire, Moss Bay Ltd. had begun officially weaning itself of the American venture. At a shareholders meeting, the board of directors announced a vacancy on the board.[16] By mid-April, board minutes reflected a decision, "that Mr. Kirk be requested to send in for the consideration of the board particulars of any claim he may have against, or any amount he may consider due to him from the company."[17] From this, it seems the board was interested in cashing him out. Yet Washington newspapers reported Kirk returned from Europe at the end of April "with unlimited English capital, to commence the construction of the largest steel and iron works on the Pacific coast."[18]

Whatever capital he brought to Kirkland was not enough. By year's end, lack of funds had stalled the Kirkland enterprise, causing work to suspend for some time.[19] A simple balance sheet for Moss Bay of America dated December 31, 1889 lists cash deposits from Hunt for $5,000 and Henry A. Noble for $2500, with Peter Kirk matching their funds, totaling $15,000. The expenditures listed for the brick works, offices, supplies, Kellett's house and salary, and legal expenses totaled $15,032.27, thus overdrawing the company's account at Puget Sound National Bank of Seattle, operated by mill investors Bailey Gatzert and Jacob Furth.[20]

By the following summer, in 1890, the directors dissolved the Moss Bay Iron & Steel Co. of America and incorporated a new company called the Great Western Iron & Steel Company (Great Western). Signaling a defeat for Peter Kirk, the new company stacked the deck with a full house of American investors including General Russell A. Alger of Detroit,

Joshua M. Sears and P. T. Tyler of Boston, H. A. Noble of Des Moines, and J. L. Norton of Chicago as well as Edward Blewett, Jacob Furth, and Bailey Gatzert of Seattle. "New interests have been identified with the enterprise," Hunt reported, "and new men have been brought into it. Indeed, so great has been the change in the personnel of the company that it may fairly be regarded as a different organization."[21]

Figure 9 Kirkland steel mill, 1891
Depiction of Great Western in *King's Handbook of the United States*.[22]

Leigh S. J. Hunt became president of the new organization while Peter Kirk took on the office of Manager of Operations. The articles of incorporation allowed each of the managing directors an annual salary of no less than $5,000 ($140,000 in 2020 dollars).[23]

When asked by a reporter from his own newspaper what caused the collapse of the previous effort, Hunt deflected the questions, saying, "The effort to locate this great industry at Kirkland has never failed. We have never ceased to labor in behalf of the enterprise and have never despaired of success. If you mean to inquire for the causes of delay and those which induced the reorganization of the company, I can only say that it would be neither interesting, nor profitable for the public, for me to enter into a discussion of this subject."[24]

To entice new capital when things did not go as planned, it was a common business practice to liquefy and then incorporate anew. During America's railroad boom, banks and other companies were eager to extend credit. Kirk's English venture had operated the same way, periodically by overextending and then overcoming the shortfall by re-inventing the organization.[25] During his early business years, a hearty British market helped him stay one step ahead of the game, and he likely thought he could weather the current difficulties in the same manner.

Even with restructuring into Great Western, one problem remained: the directors failed to demand immediate payment from the investors.[26] Instead, they extended credit to their stock subscribers. Kirk—and probably other directors—also took out stock on credit.[27] There was a constant struggle with cash flow. A remark to Walter Williams by Joseph Ellis at the England ironworks concerning shipment of rails and iron works supplies revealed how capitalists had funded each step of the venture piecemeal. Ellis wrote, "You must try to get subscriptions for the duty...but we shall do our very best here to find money for steel work machinery because this job must go on to completion."[28]

Loathe to shirk on commitments, Kirk tackled the problems with persistence. One reporter noticed and remarked that he "labored early and late with absolute faith and loyalty. Delay did not discourage nor defeat dishearten him."[29]

Thirteen—Peter Kirk Forges Ahead

"A person stationed upon the hill overlooking the clear, smooth waters of Lake Washington, looking eastward across the lake, could have seen day by day during the past year, a forest gradually disappearing and in its stead a town spring up as if by magic—not a town of cheaply constructed buildings, but a town which contains brick business blocks and residences that would be a credit to a city of greater pretensions. That town is Kirkland. Here are now about 150 new buildings that cost on an average nearly $1,500 each."[1]

Seattle Post-Intelligencer, January 1, 1891

The city skylines progressed on both sides of Lake Washington after the Great Fire. The infusion of new capital evidenced in the restructuring of Great Western Iron & Steel advanced a feverish rate of construction on a large cookhouse and bunkhouse to accommodate a crew of over 110 men.[2] However, Kirkland had no electricity or gas engines; work was limited to steam-powered machinery and the sweat of men.[3]

The fledgling towns of Kirkland, Houghton, and Juanita soon boasted two public schools and two churches, Congregational and Methodist, in addition to a Baptist society and an active Women's Christian Temperance Union. Kirk completed his lavish residence and Leigh Hunt enlarged his own fine residence at Yarrow. Co-investor Charles Cummins (Mrs. Hunt's uncle) also built a new home near Yarrow. Stores supplied the needs of tourists and residents alike. A large new wharf was built, said to compare with Seattle's waterfront, and a second new wharf replaced an older one.[4]

The Kirkland land company built a new brickyard near the ferry dock. It made bricks for the commercial block and four executive houses as well as the boiler installation at the steel plant.[5] Three main buildings made up the business sector on Market Street, each named for a major investor: Sears, Kirk, and Jackson. A reporter once asked Peter Kirk what he planned to do with the millions of brick made in Kirkland, to which Kirk said, "Pardon me, sir, if in reply to this question I ask you to come and see a month hence." He added, "As soon as the Sears building…is completed, our people will open a bank, and our company is also preparing to organize a building and loan association that will enable all to build and own their own homes. In fact, we will render every assistance that can be given to people who make Kirkland their home."[6]

Figure 10 Planking a roadway in Kirkland
Photo courtesy of Kirkland Heritage Society, circa 1890.

"There was no railroad of any kind at or near the brickyard," Aubrey Williams (son of Walter Williams) later recalled. "All work was done by manpower and help was cheap in those days, except a dollar was worth 100 cents." Williams described early Kirkland streets as "old wagon roads before the turn of the century. Market Street was the only graveled street with wooden sidewalks, but Piccadilly Street was a roadway to the Steelworks on Rose Hill…[On] Piccadilly Street [was] Brooks Grocery Store, which supplied the needs of Kirkland from horse collars to toothpicks as well as meat (when they had any), flour and feed."[7]

The public kept a cynical eye on Kirkland's progress, and the media pursued every chance to detail each step. When development halted on the building of the ironworks before the company reorganized, some said it proved true the claim that Kirkland was nothing but a land boomer racket. Hunt, vice-president of the Kirkland Land & Improvement Company, tried to quiet these rumors with a bold and generous guarantee: The company would refund dissatisfied investors of their full purchase money plus 10 per cent interest and cost of improvements.[8] Even with this promise, the boomer conspiracy persisted, partly due to others trying to jump on the coattails of the project. Opportunists regularly advertised (at inflated prices) land for sale near Kirkland. These lots were located miles away, with no roads to the area or services available.

Approached often for interviews, Kirk would grow irritated, as evidence in this exchange with a *Seattle P.I.* reporter:

> "What more would you have me say," Kirk challenged, "for is it not best, if we are to take the public further into our confidence to wait until this promise is fulfilled? If I were to tell you the half that we propose to do for Kirkland some fellow who has not been sufficiently 'let in,' or who is sorry for other reasons that we are succeeding, would bob up and say that I was booming town lots."

> "Did you ever know, Mr. Kirk, of a successful enterprise that did not have jealous enemies?" countered the reporter.

> "Well, that is true," Kirk conceded, "and I would not have or imagine that I seriously consider them, for so long as we are responsible to those whom we lead our way and keep faith with the public, those croakers can do us no harm, and themselves but little good, yet it makes me indifferent as to whether I give the public news of our progress."

> "I see you have put your land upon the market," said the reporter.

> "No, sir, we have not. We are in no way responsible for those additions to Kirkland which you see advertised; many of them are

miles away from what will be the town of Kirkland and the people who invest in them do so upon their own responsibility and hence cannot hold us blamable if they should sustain losses."

"Will you put your property on the market?"

"We have instructed our land commissioner, Mr. J. Compton, to put a portion of the lots upon the market July 31, [1890]. This we are compelled to do in order to give our friends, who believe in us, a chance to link their fortunes with Kirkland at a time when prices are reasonable, and to give those who want to make improvements an opportunity to do so at once. If there are any who doubt our good faith we will give them such a guarantee as will certainly satisfy them."

"Do you hope to have any other manufacturing industries located in Kirkland?"

"We do. Believing that we can offer better advantages than almost any other locality, and knowing that it is the disposition of the land company to be very liberal, I feel justified in saying that we will give all rivals a lively competition, for we are determined to make this a manufacturing center."[9]

The reporter did in fact go to Kirkland and witnessed for himself the progress. He described the work at the plant as "being pushed vigorously and without interruption."[10] The reporter noted the foundry, machine shop, and pattern shop were already completed.

Peter went East and acquired 275 tons of machinery to outfit the mill's various departments.[11] But delays of material from Great Britain and the lack of railroad facilities prevented further progress on the foundations of other important buildings.[12] The arrival of the *Cromartyshire* in early 1891 doubtless quelled land-boom suspicions among the naysayers.

Various machinery and 2,270 tons of blast furnace firebrick filled the ship. The machinery included plate rollers and heavy machinery for manufacturing fire and silica brick.[13] Unloading the *Cromartyshire* cargo at Smith Cove coalbunkers required nearly a month, and 125 rail carloads were needed to transport it all to Bothell for storage until SLS&E finished the road to Kirkland.[14] That did not happen until later in the summer of 1891, adding extra handling and expense to the project.[15]

Another large vessel, the *King Malcom,* arrived from England in August carrying another 2,000 tons of firebrick and cement to construct 200 coking ovens, steel heating furnaces, lining for ladles, converters, and cupolas. At the same time, forty-five rail cars arrived from the East on the Northern Pacific with two blowing engines, plates for construction of the blast furnaces, and stoves.[16] The shipment included machinery for the foundry machine and pattern shops and added to other shipments from Chicago and Cincinnati containing drills, boring machines, and planers.[17] According to one report, Kirk had stockpiled 5,600 tons of machinery and material for the construction of the steel works.[18]

The mine owners and railroads were also making progress. In January 1891, the *Seattle Post-Intelligencer* reported:

> A force of men is now engaged in opening up this mine, and a contract has just been let for the extension of the Seattle, Lake Shore & Eastern from Sallal prairie to the mine. The Northern Pacific is likewise building from Palmer on its main line to the mines. The Lake Washington belt line is graded from Renton to Kirkland, and will be extended thence to connection with the Lake Shore road near Redmond, giving railroad communication from Kirkland to the mines, and also with the Northern Pacific railroad.[19]

President Benjamin Harrison visits Seattle

As rail cars loaded with the *Cromartyshire* cargo were being transferred to Kirkland in April 1891, United States President Benjamin Harrison was embarking on a train excursion from Washington D.C. to the West Coast. Though interested in expanding America's port infrastructure, Harrison stopped in Seattle for only one day, May 6. A reception committee planned and organized the president's visit. Not surprisingly, Kirkland advocates filled the committee, among them A. A. Denny, L. S. J. Hunt, Jacob Furth, Mrs. D. H. Gilman, Mrs. H. H. Heilbron, and Judge H. G. Struve.[20] As part of his port infrastructure expansion, the president favored constructing the canal. His stopover was a great opportunity for Kirkland investors to encourage the building of the canal through Lake Union, a preferred method for moving steel mill products to overseas markets.

The canal project predated Peter Kirk's enterprise. Various groups discussed and even started digging the canal long before Kirk arrived. Thomas Mercer talked about it on a 4th of July celebration as early as 1854. Harvey Pike took matters into his own hands in 1860 when he took up a pick and shovel and dug a ditch between Union Bay and Lake Union.[21] This ditch proved inadequate, and residents continued to rely on access to Lake Washington from Elliott Bay via the shallow Black River slough and the Duwamish River. Controversies over the canal route prevented construction during the following decades. Efforts persisted, though, and citizen groups periodically rallied to the cause. Yet the project's trajectory mirrored the skipping of a stone on water's surface—fits and starts, fits and starts, until the money ran out. Citizens hoped President Harrison's visit might change all that.

The Seattle committee greeted the president in Tacoma, as did other personal friends of the president, namely D. B. Jackson who was currently building one of the brick buildings in Kirkland's business district.[22] The planning committee invited Leigh Hunt to host a luncheon for the president's party at Yarrow Bay.[23] Instead, Hunt volunteered the services of the elegant *Steamer Kirkland*, owned by one of his enterprises. Decorated with flags, ferns, and flowers, the *Kirkland* greeted the presidential entourage for a tour of Lake Washington on an overcast and perhaps rainy day.[24] En route, the dark clouds cleared slightly, producing a contrast that enhanced the view. Onboard, the president, "who was familiar with the lake's beauties, called the attention of the ladies of his party to its distinctively characteristic picturesqueness, and invited those on board to meet with him. Presentations were made and old acquaintances renewed."[25]

Intending to highlight the development of Kirkland, the committee utilized its namesake steamer and paraded the president past the fledgling town to inspect the mill site before the ferry landed at Madison Street dock.[26] Peter Kirk likely joined the other Kirkland investors of the committee onboard, as he would have been most knowledgeable to explain the enterprise to the president. At the very least, he would have joined the prominent businesspersons in Washington and British Columbia invited to hear the president's speech. Thousands of people of all ages attended the event at the University of Washington fairgrounds.

President Harrison spoke about the differences he observed since his visit six years before. Reminiscing, he said Seattle had good prospects in those early years, which he described as a "period of expectancy rather than of realization."[27] He recognized Seattle citizens were now attaining their aspirations. Speaking of his wish to expand Seattle ports, he said:

> I fully appreciate the importance of this great body of water upon which your city is situated. This Sound, this inland sea, must be in the future the highway, the entrepot, of a great commerce. I do most sincerely believe that we are entering now upon a new development that will put the American flag upon the seas and bring to our ports a largely increased share of the commerce of the world. I believe the great patriotic heart of our people is stirred, and that they are bent upon recovering that share of the world's commerce, which we once happily enjoyed. I will have a watchful

observation of the needs of your state, of your harbors, for defense, improvement and security.[28]

President Harrison's speech surely heartened Peter Kirk and other promoters of Kirkland and the canal. Within a year, a $500,000 appropriations bill passed the Senate for work on the canal, further encouraging the investors.[29] Seed money for the canal also encouraged other business prospects. Construction of a woolen mill was underway and proposals for a large shingle mill and woodenware factory were announced.[30] Also making the news at this time, many from the steel mill enterprise, including Kirk, incorporated the Kirkland Brick Company.[31] Kirk's dream of an industrial complex in Kirkland was taking shape.

Fourteen—Establishing the Mitchell Bay Homestead

The positive atmosphere President Harrison left in Seattle may have given Peter confidence to set down more roots and establish a vacation home. He and his family often cruised to Victoria, British Columbia, on Vancouver Island, passing by the beautiful San Juan Islands and likely found the area compelling. Kirk also spent time on San Juan Island investigating the Roche Harbor Lime Company, an alternative lime source for Kirkland's steel mill. In the fall of 1891, he purchased two large adjoining pieces of land on San Juan Island at Mitchell Bay for over $5,000. This initial purchase gave him 334 acres, including almost all the northern shoreline of Mitchell Bay.[1] In subsequent years, he would continue to add to the estate, buying various-sized parcels from his neighbors until he owned most of the peninsula.

Covering the distance between Kirkland and the islands took the better part of the day or more. The journey began with a ferry ride across Lake Washington and then a buggy or cable car transfer to the Seattle docks. Another ferry conveyed passengers north on the Salish Sea through Puget Sound and across the Strait of Juan de Fuca, making stops along the way.

The mail steamer *Lydia Thompson* made the run to San Juan Island ports at a roundtrip fare of four dollars.[2] By spending a little more for a stateroom, island-bound passengers could enjoy a more comfortable journey since they had to board in the middle of the night.[3] Returning to Seattle meant leaving San Juan Island in mid-afternoon and arriving in the evening. Ferries to Kirkland stopped running by dinnertime, necessitating an overnight stay in Seattle.

Landing in Friday Harbor after several hours at sea, the Kirk family reached the Mitchell Bay property by crossing most of San Juan Island on a wagon road connecting Friday Harbor to Roche Harbor, a journey of a few hours. Docking in Roche Harbor, they faced a shorter buggy ride, but ferry schedules did not always accommodate the extra stop. As an alternative, a separate launch could shuttle them directly to Mitchell Bay from either port on San Juan Island.

The large waterfront acreage at Mitchell Bay encompassed rolling hills of white and Douglas fir, alder, cedar, maple, and oak. Rocky ledges left parts of the hills exposed. Salal, mosses, maidenhair, and sword ferns covered the forest floor.[4] Where the sun broke through the dense timber, prickly wild rose took over. Beaches dotted the extensive rocky shoreline. Peter Kirk commissioned John George Bartsch to construct a sizable house for the Kirk family at Mitchell Bay. In May 1892, newspaper chitchat noted, "Peter Kirk has a beautiful cottage under way at Mitchell's bay."[5] After completion at the end of summer, the family visited regularly, mainly in the milder seasons and often for months at a time.[6] Because of all the deer roaming the property, the family named it Deer Lodge.[7]

Figure 11 Deer Lodge at Mitchell Bay
Kirk children at Deer Lodge, circa 1892. *East Side Journal,* July 7, 1966, p. 13.
Caption states photo was submitted by Vivian Middleton.

Quiet and secluded, Deer Lodge marked a stark difference from the relentless cacophony of Kirkland construction. The gabled cedar house graced a point of land near the head of Mitchell Bay overlooking Canadian waters. Bartsch elegantly designed it with elaborate features of English architecture, including oversized rooms and five fireplaces for heat. A novel design joined the drafting of the five flues into only two chimneys.[8] A later occupant of Deer Lodge described the house as having a total of eighteen rooms, some quite large. The house had big windows with stained glass panes above each. The dining room alone contained five huge windows.[9]

Massive sliding doors divided two large rooms on the main floor of the house. When opened, these revealed a grand space for entertaining. Island old-timers remembered the Kirks as cordial neighbors who occasionally hosted festive parties.[10] The family enjoyed frequent visits by friends and family from Seattle, England, and elsewhere, sometimes extending for weeks at a time. Of course, music filled the evenings in the luxurious home.[11]

Kirk's estate at Mitchell Bay eventually included three and a half miles of waterfront property. With limited island roads, access by water proved advantageous. The family had skiffs for rowing around the long, narrow bay, as it was faster to row across the narrow bay to call on neighbors than it was to go overland. Mitchell Bay was sheltered enough to allow even the younger children to row around the little coves in the undulating rocky coastline. Navigating to Deer Lodge by land or sea simply entailed locating the large wooden water tower standing near the house.[12]

Figure 12 Fishing party at Mitchell Bay
Photo from French Collection, courtesy of Kirkland Heritage Society. Members of the
Kirk family after some impressive salmon fishing. L to R: Peter Kirk, Olive, Fanny;
Clara, & Arnold in skiff; two unidentified men. Circa early 1890s.

Modern as it was, the Kirk retreat did not include electricity.
Telephones did not reach their part of the island until after the turn of the
century, and only rudimentary wagon roads and horse trails connected
the home to the rest of the island. During the winter, these inconveniences
often caused discomfort for the family, particularly Mrs. Kirk, as she found
it difficult to get around on the country paths and so preferred being at
their Kirkland home during the rainy and sometimes snowy seasons.[13]
Likewise, winter storms put vessels sailing across the Salish Sea and their
passengers to the test.

The Kirks had access to two main villages on San Juan Island, Roche
Harbor and Friday Harbor. Roche Harbor boasted closer proximity to the
Kirk property, but it existed only as a mill town for the limestone works,
with limited businesses. With a population of about 1,500, Friday Harbor
enjoyed the distinction of being the county seat for San Juan Islands
County. The number of inhabitants remained relatively stable beyond an
immigration wave associated with the 1859 Pig War and another increase
that occurred in the early 1890s, including the Kirks.

Part III: Dreams Become a Nightmare

Fifteen—Mill Failure

"My father, Peter Kirk, had great faith in it [steel mill] and Kirkland and it was a hard blow for him when things did not go on."[1]

Jessie Kirk Charlton

The Kirk family carried on their routine of traveling between Deer Lodge and Fir Grove while Kirkland grew with each season. Prospects looked good for the fledgling town. In the summer of 1892, nearly 900 people called Kirkland home.[2] The woolen mill had commenced operations with seventy employees.[3] Plans progressed for a woodenware factory.[4] Owners of the steel works had already spent a hefty sum towards their goal, and backers remained hopeful it would be completed within a year.[5] The seasonal steel works construction shut down for the winter in September that year, not knowing it was permanent.[6]

"It came almost overnight," recounted a later resident. "In Kirkland all work stopped, all investors lost heavily."[7] The Seattle Lake Shore & Eastern Railroad went into receivership the next summer and so did the Northern Pacific. Money dried up for Kirkland. General Russell Alger defaulted first on his $20,000 subscription.[8] Others followed, and rumors circulated.

Gossip aside, signs forecasting a nationwide recession or even a financial panic already existed. For decades, railroads encouraged an unprecedented bubble of expansion across the country. It was the Gilded Age when men only need think a scheme and it could be so. Corruption and conspicuous consumption marked the Gilded Age, and with it, unfettered capitalism. Even though many railroads and businesses overextended, banks continued their eagerness to offer loans. Significant profits muted the occasional losses. But when the Reading Railroad conglomerate succumbed to receivership in early 1893, the fuse was lit. Soon after, the repeal of the Sherman Silver Purchase Act pitted the previous gold-backed currency against one of silver. Without the guarantee that the US government would buy certain amounts of silver, prices fell. Lack of confidence in the economy sent citizens and capitalists rushing to the banks, detonating the fragile financial system.

National banks, private banks and savings institutions failed in a fireball that swept the nation, growing as it spread west. Other businesses followed suit. Unemployment skyrocketed. Railroads across the nation went into receivership, representing almost 20 percent of US rail mileage.[9] 15,000 bankruptcies and 500 bank failures earned the Financial Panic of 1893 its place in US history as the worst recession ever.

Kirkland faced a crisis. After Great Western Steel shut down, townspeople left in search of work. "The flourishing community was deserted," noted one account. "There were no jobs so families moved away leaving empty houses and closed businesses behind. The steel mill dream faded."[10] Of the hundreds of streets in the original town and mill site plan, only a few had materialized. Instead of the population of thousands projected by the steel mill developers for Kirkland, only a few hundred remained.

"People were desperate," a resident said. "All there was to show for an iron works was a ship load of fire brick, two or three warehouse type buildings and a few holes where excavation had been started. The firebrick [remained] piled in long rows adjacent to the site of the furnaces. Some of this material was intended for the coke ovens, which were never built."[11]

Much speculation exists to what factors caused the project to fail despite the intellectual capital of Kirk, Kellett, Williams, Valentine, Hunt, and the multiple other captains of industry who backed the Kirkland Steel Mill. Some blame the lack of a ship canal. Some fault the absence of a suitable approach to the Denny mines. For others, the quality of the coal for making coke made the project untenable. In any event, the Panic of '93 seems to have been the straw that broke the camel's back.

What if the resources were better?

Early on, the steel mill based its prospects on the nearby "mountain of ore and valley of coal."[12] Of the quality of the iron ore in the area, little doubt remained. The Denny Mines contained the cream of the crop, albeit in small amounts. Cle Elum and the other deposits offered lesser quality but were extensive. Cle Elum had the added advantage of accessibility with the nearby Northern Pacific Railroad. Combining the two grades of ore at certain ratios worked in the Bessemer process, but it was imperative to have the higher quality Denny ore for the mixture.[13] A rail line to Denny's iron mountain was therefore essential.

Some investors questioned the quality and usefulness of the area's coal to make coke for steel production. William Ruffner, the metallurgist hired by SLS&E to survey the local resources in 1887, noted Kirk's field tests of coal in quantities sufficient for his needs had yet to yield, "the heating power or coking qualities of the Wilkeson coal."[14] However, another mining engineer, W. M. Courtis of Detroit, also tested many collieries in the region, and while he found many substandard, he offered a way to improve them: "So far as I have tested, all the coals of Washington must be washed before they will make a coke fit for smelting Bessemer Pig-iron for steel making."[15] Courtis predicted the collieries would work out these quality issues in adjusting to the market when the Kirkland blast furnaces were complete.[16]

If only there was a ship canal...

One aspect favoring the Kirkland iron mill was the transportation infrastructure, which included ample railroad transportation to the interior markets. Additionally, steamships already connected the western American continents with cross-Pacific markets. Still, getting the steel to the coast for shipment would have proved problematic. Without a canal from Lake Washington to Salmon Bay, the product from Kirkland's iron mill would have to have been loaded onto trains and then transferred to ships, adding an extra layer of handling and cost.

The Kirkland project certainly added vigor and expediency to the ongoing campaign to construct a suitable channel connecting Lake Washington to the sea. Proponents believed President Harrison's visit and stamp of approval would surely get it done. But Harrison did not win re-election, and the political winds shifted in other directions. Many Seattleites opposed "Kirkland's Ditch" as unnecessary.[17] Residents of other Washington cities worried canal funds would only benefit a few residents and businesses, leaving scant monies to address their communities' needs.

The delayed canal project was not for want of trying, though. Ironically, Northern Pacific had acquired the Seattle Lake Shore & Eastern Railroad, linking their success with Kirkland's plans. Others who had previously battled for Kirk's favors likewise joined forces to further the canal. James McNaught, NPRR's legal counsel, championed the project. Early in 1893, before The Panic swept the country, McNaught wrote to D. H. Gilman of the need for lobbying: "If you cannot go to Washington yourself, I think it advisable for you to telegraph all your friends in the House to use every effort to secure the passage of the Canal Bill this session. I am writing all my friends today."[18]

Politicization of the project choked further progress of the canal. The lack of a good water route to Seattle thwarted prospects for both the Kirkland steel mill and the potential of other industries to fulfill Kirk's vision of a manufacturing center.

What if there was access to Denny's iron?

The availability of the iron ore remained critical to the enterprise. By 1892, neither SLS&E, nor Northern Pacific had built the necessary 17-mile line to the Denny mines. With the mill lacking raw materials for production, proponents of the ship canal lacked credibility despite the blast furnaces, machinery, and firebrick already onsite at Kirkland.

It was rumored "the shipment of ore from the Denny Mines was impractical and the reason why the railroads delayed putting in the line."[19] One scholar proposed, "Had the financial panic of 1893 not occurred, there is a strong possibility that the Seattle, Lake Shore and Eastern Railroad would have had the capital to complete its line to Spokane and the capitalists backing the steel project would have been able to purchase the Kirkland steel mill stock for which they subscribed."[20]

It is impossible to know if better resources, access to the Denny mines, or a ship canal would have been enough to save the operation. In the end, the mines remained without means of transport, and the steel mill remained unfinished. The enterprise was heaped on a slag pile before the mill could even create one.

Sixteen—Grappling with the Aftermath

"Some people were inclined to criticize Mr. Kirk for being a part of the land development (and its subsequent failure). I know personally, however, that Mr. Kirk (himself) was the greatest victim of the promotion."[1]

James W. Collins, former Kirkland resident

On May 26, 1894, Peter Kirk ferried across Lake Washington to protest hearings concerning the delinquent taxes of the Kirkland Land & Improvement Company and the Great Western Iron & Steel Company. Later, he and fellow ironworks directors Henry Noble and Walter Williams signed a confession of judgment filed against Great Western in favor of KL&I totaling almost $50,000.[2] A sheriff's sale commenced within a week, and most of the mill equipment and hardware sold to an Ontario company.

A grim newspaper notice marked the end of the Great Western Iron & Steel Company. In stark contrast to the grand announcement a few years earlier trumpeting the launch of so great an enterprise, these few lines seemed a mere whisper: "A shipment of ten car loads of engines, boilers and other machinery has been made to the Philadelphia Engineering Works at Hamilton, Ontario, which has bought it, the entire consignment going through by fast freight."[3]

The exodus of the mill machinery did not absolve Kirk of trouble. On the contrary, as one of the executives, he had the responsibility of completing the dissolution process. He also had another issue to deal with concerning Great Western. Like General Alger, he owed the now defunct corporation for stock subscriptions he took out on credit. Complicating the situation, Kirk had not received his salary as a director since before the Panic, if in fact he had ever received a salary at all. The company needed cash to settle its indebtedness, and when Kirk pushed the clause on directors' salary, the company demurred. The directors disputed whether his salary was warranted since the venture "had not been actively engaged in any business or in the prosecution of its corporate enterprises and by such reason thereof, the duties of its managing directors have not been burdensome."[4] To settle the matter, Kirk exchanged $15,000 ($460,000 current money) in past due salary for the unpaid stock subscriptions. He signed the agreement for the plaintiff as president of the company and himself as the defendant.

Moss Bay sues

In addition to contending with the problems relating to the mill failure in Kirkland, Peter Kirk also had to deal with the backlash of its connection to the England Moss Bay entity. Long before rumors of American railroad receiverships and the Panic of '93, Moss Bay of England had troubles that cast a dark shadow over Kirk. Claiming an arrangement with Kirk in June 1888, the month the Kirkland steel mill announcement hit newspapers, England Moss Bay directors Joseph Ellis and John S. Randles sued him. Their pact called for the two directors to extend "financial advances to enable [Kirk] to carry through the formation of the American Company and meet calls on certain shares in English companies, including those he held in Workington's Moss Bay ironworks. The value of the American shares, which were to be transferred, if they could, was $250,000, and a very large sum was due for the advances."[5]

The contract called for Kirk to repay the amount of these advances with interest and shares in the Kirkland Land & Improvement Company. If the directors could not hold the shares due to the Alien laws that prevented British nationals from holding shares because the American company had exceeded the allowable percentage of foreign investment, they would have the cash value instead.

Kirk launched a defense and a counter claim, but the judge denied these, citing Kirk for default in answering the interrogatories. This left Ellis and Randles with the win.[6] The court failed to list the final figure since they had yet to determine the Kirkland shares' value and account for advances.

This all happened before the Panic of '93; before creditors made a run on the Kirkland assets. The England directors had no way of knowing the US would suffer a financial crash so soon after the judge made his determination. The difficulty surfaced during Moss Bay of England's 1890 liquidation. Bankruptcy papers referenced 500 debentures of £100 each, "constituting a charge on the [company]," conspicuously dated June 6, 1888, just days after the big announcement.[7]

The company's red ink provoked shareholders and residents alike. For decades, Moss Bay of England had been a stalwart industry benefiting investors and other businesses in the area. Finger-pointing and rebukes dominated shareholder meetings. Investors demanded an investigation into past management, and newspapers echoed their concern. Some blamed "one of the directors of the Moss Bay Company who paid protracted visits to the Pacific coast of America, presumably in the interests of the shareholders."[8] It is unclear if they were referring to Peter Kirk or Charles Valentine, the latter still in the role of managing director. However, others hailed Kirk and Valentine for the decades of success under their leadership.[9]

Peter Kirk visited the Workington area in 1890, supposedly waiting for the general shareholders meeting, before returning to America.[10] He still owned shares, but whether he attended the meetings is unknown. Surely, he followed the status of his old company. The newspapers reported the investigative committee finally determined the cause leading to liquidation. Moss Bay of England took a heavy loss on a sizeable sleeper contract, which amounted to £25,000.[11] The company had bought materials at an inflated price and was forced to sell the finished products at a loss due to the sagging market. Before this, and coinciding with Kirk's move to America, the board of directors had elected some new individuals. Some believed "those gentlemen ruined the concern."[12]

To save Moss Bay of England, the committee determined to raise part of the money for the restructuring "by selling the mines and the share in the American property near Seattle, which it estimated would realize £50,000."[13] They also called up the remaining £3 per share held by investors in the old company. These decisions may have contributed to the Ellis v. Kirk lawsuit. Moss Bay of England believed they held shares or value in the American property. The 1888 contract provided payment if any "call" on Kirk's shares in Moss Bay of England occurred. Even as late as 1891, Joseph Ellis and John Randles communicated with Kirk concerning the sale of his Moss Bay shares.[14] Possibly, Ellis and Randles had to pay thousands of British pounds to cover the call in 1890 on Kirk's shares, leading to the 1893 suit against him.

Whatever liability resulted from the suit strained Kirk's already fragile finances. He may have known he was fighting a losing battle with Ellis and Randles. A couple months before the judgement against him, he tried to raise cash with his rolling mill patent. He signed an agreement with Julian Kennedy, one of the superintendents of the Carnegie steel conglomerate in Pittsburg. Kennedy, a mechanical engineer and contractor, would act as agent for the patent and share one-half interest with Kirk. Failure by Kennedy to sell it after one year would cause the patent to revert back to Kirk.[15] Likely no revenue resulted since the men signed the agreement in January 1893, just as the Panic hit.

Mary Ann's treasure chest

After the crash, Peter Kirk may have been bankrupt, but he remained bankrolled. A letter arrived from her nephew, Louis Dixon, detailing Mary Ann's earnings from the Quirk and Gibson estates, a treasure chest of inheritances from her mother and aunt.[16] The timing suggests the family needed the extra income following the steel mill failure. Peter and Mary Ann supported a large household at two separate residences. Even without a mortgage, they paid taxes and upkeep. They held large amounts of property in Kirkland, these investments now threatened if they could not pay their taxes. They also supported their third estate in England. Bankfield had been mortgaged many years earlier and attempts to rent it proved difficult.

Wealthy in her own right, Mary Ann's legacies buoyed the family through the lean years that followed the collapse of the Kirkland project. The estates of her mother, Hannah (Gibson) Quirk, and her aunt Mary Gibson included the Whitehaven sailcloth business and land holdings of their father, Peter Gibson, following his death in 1865.[17] Mary Ann's mother had also taken over her husband's currier business and kept it going until her own death in 1871.[18] Hannah Quirk's heirs sold her Whitehaven and Workington properties, which included a dozen dwelling houses, some with attached shops, and two tenement buildings.[19]

The Gibson and Quirk estates yielded lump sum payments and ongoing annuities. Louis Dixon, also a benefactor of the Quirk/Gibson estates, explained these in the 1895 letter to Mary Ann.[20] Her initial inheritance totaled about a half of a million dollars in today's money. She also received an annuity that was worth about $23,000 in current values. She had not cashed in those annuities for years, which left her account balance worth over $140,000 in today's figures.

Mary Ann's portfolio flourished over the years. One holding in a Cumberland mining property grew 350 percent. The portfolio included ongoing rents from properties in Carlisle. Mary Ann also held stock in many companies, including British cotton spinners, a brewery, and many railroads in England, Scotland, and Argentina. These investments alone were valued at hundreds of thousands of dollars (in 2020 dollars) and provided dividend earnings.[21] In later years, she netted over $15,000 annually (2020 values) from those stocks alone.[22]

Mary Ann's inheritance supported the large family and their holdings in Washington, but it was not enough to save Bankfield Mansion. As the remnants of Peter's steel mill dream rode the rails to Ontario, the Yorkshire Penny Bank conveyed their beloved Bankfield in Workington to the Iredale family. It had been a rocky road for the estate since the family moved to America.

The troubles began as early as 1888 when Joseph Ellis wrote W. W. Williams of the progress—or lack thereof—in the planned sale of Kirk's Moss Bay, Ltd. stocks. Other directors tested Ellis' patience as he admitted, "they make my temper boil over sometimes." In response, he "gave Capt. Robinson a biting letter which [he] meant for Mr. Liddelow as well about the treatment served out to Mr. Kirk about the house at Bankfield."[23] Kirk may have tried to sell the house or use it as collateral for another loan.

No records exist indicating how long Bankfield remained vacant after the family moved to America. In the summer of 1889, Kirk had it painted and rented it to a wine and spirit merchant.[24] His sister and brother-in-law, Ann and Charles Valentine, continued to live with their family in the other half of Bankfield. Even with tenants, Kirk's interests in Workington diminished. In the fall of 1891, administrators struck him from the list of claimants who sought freehold claims, a position of status for landowners. An objector to Kirk's position noted, "Mr. Kirk has parted with his qualification, and now has no beneficial interest in the property. He now resides in America."[25]

Any rents Kirk received did not sustain the mortgage, and he lost Bankfield to foreclosure in 1895. The bank sold the estate for £5,000.[26] Undoubtedly heart wrenching for Kirk, the sale portended further doom for Bankfield, which would bump around between private and public organizations.

Kirk disappeared from the headlines but not Kirkland

As Kirkland pioneers adjusted after the financial panic, they realized their "boomtown had not become a ghost town."[27] Many workers left when the steel plant was shuttered. However, the sawmill, shingle, and woolen mills remained. Many of the families who settled the area stayed.

Mary Ann's earnings may have kept the family afloat, while Kirk pursued other ways to support their family. He and others from the Kirkland Lumber Mill started a new venture called the Seattle and Kirkland Ferry Company to operate ferry boats on Lake Washington and its tributaries.[28]

A lot of competition already existed on the lake, and with people leaving the area in droves, the viability of the company was questionable.

Kirk also went back to the drawing board and initiated another patent for a machine to produce compressed steel. As with many of his other inventions, his idea stressed quality and efficiency of labor, process, and materials. "The special object of this machine," he said, "is to produce steel rails and bars &c., direct from the molten metal and of a superior quality, dispensing with blooming mill, roughing rolls, reheating furnaces, and the saving of the labor and wear and tear involved by same; also reducing the waste of steel and crop ends to a minimum."[29]

He further explained, "This machine is designed for casting steel into bars or billets under pressure from centrifugal force, regulated by the speed at which the machine is driven." His idea saved the large expenditure needed "by the usual method of working down large ingots through blooming mills, etc." He added, "It also admits of the manufacture of such bars in much longer lengths than is obtained in the ordinary methods, and the bar leaves the machine hot enough to roll to finished sections without heating—in fact this machine allows of great latitude in the amount of steel used per cast and the length of bar produced."[30]

Found among his papers passed down through the generations, but not at the US Patent Office, the patent was never registered. The typed description does not include a date, witnesses, or any hint of how Kirk intended to use the new technology.

Others find work

Peter's English associates also had to find employment. After making ends meet by working for a time in 1893 as a "watchman" for Great Western Iron & Steel, engineer John Kellett secured work at the Walla Walla penitentiary. He then found other engineering jobs before acquiring a position with Julian Kennedy in Pittsburgh, a firm that employed others from the failed mill project.[31]

Kellett and William Anderson both involved themselves in a Ballard enterprise called the West Coast Iron Works Company, incorporated before the crash.[32] Their names were also associated with the Ellensburg Foundry and Engineering Company.[33] Pacific Investment Co. awarded a contract to the Ellensburg venture for the purchase of 35 tons of iron plates for its firebrick works.

William Anderson did not linger in Kirkland. The Scot took his family and engineering skills to the Kootenay region of British Columbia and gained employment with the railroad.[34] He later moved to Vancouver, British Columbia, and advanced to head partner in the engineering firm Anderson, Wilkin, and Warden.[35] Anderson was Consulting Engineer for the city of Vancouver and laid out the city's new waterworks and power plant. Highly respected, he worked with the city of Port Alberni as a consultant when they upgraded their water plant.[36]

After the Crash hit Kirkland, W. W. Williams brought his family back from England, where they had gone for the children's education.[37] The Williams family struggled after the crash as did many. Walter finally found work in Seattle as a mining engineer, and the family moved from the East Side.[38] He later became secretary at a steel and equipment company. Williams remained Peter Kirk's business assistant even after the Kirkland enterprise dissolved. Letters between the two referred to banking duties in which Williams proved instrumental to Kirk.[39] It is unknown why he hesitated to complete his citizenship for another decade.[40] His activity with the British-American League may have played a part. Hundreds of people met with this group to hear speakers and sympathize with the Brits, who were engaged in the Boer War. Williams often sang for the organization's meetings, receiving much applause.[41]

Leigh Hunt leaves then returns

Millionaire Leigh S. J. Hunt suffered heavy losses during the crash and had to sell the *Seattle Post-Intelligencer*. His bank failed and creditors took over his other holdings, leaving him "a financial wreck."[42] Borrowing money for his personal expenses, Hunt left Seattle in December 1894, seeking opportunities to recoup his wealth. He pursued railroad concessions in Japan and China but was unsuccessful. He learned of Korea's fledgling gold mining operations and set off to try his hand, finding adventure, opportunity, and a fortune.[43]

He returned from his Korean mining interests to Seattle several years later.[44] Upon his arrival, gossip spread about him having made more money in Korea than during his glory years in Seattle. According to the rumors, he had "wrested $50,000,000 from gold diggings in Korea."[45]

Hunt celebrated his homecoming by paying off all his former indebtedness, said to amount to nearly $1.5 million. "Not yet content," the newspaper endeared, "he hunted up everyone he could find that had invested any money in his undertakings while in Seattle and lost thereby, and returned them their investment money with seven per cent interest."[46] Hunt even "looked up a number of accounts and notes against him that were outlawed" and paid them off with interest as well. One anecdote told how Hunt gathered many of these creditors at an elaborate banquet, placing a bank draft beneath each plate to reimburse whatever amount the individual had invested (and lost) when his bank failed.[47]

Hunt attempted to buy back his former newspaper, the *Seattle Post-Intelligencer*, but the owners refused. He then turned his energy to starting a new morning paper, intended "to wrest political prestige from the *P.-I.*"[48] He and some friends incorporated a firm, established an office, and ordered a press and other machinery from the east.[49] He even threatened the Associated Press with a lawsuit to compel it to furnish him with the morning correspondent service.[50] The entire venture collapsed in short order. Hunt's close friends, labeled "the faithful" in one account, hosted a bon voyage dinner in his honor two weeks after his 1901 return.[51] He left with excuses of poor health and unfinished business in his Korean mines.[52]

Leigh Hunt's quick trip and busy itinerary may have caused him to forget one other creditor. The day after his bon voyage dinner, Hunt was subpoenaed to King County Superior Court in response to a suit Peter

Kirk filed against him.[53] The limited details in the case fail to answer why Kirk brought the lawsuit or his initial demands. Hunt's response hinted that Kirk had surpassed a time limit and failed to offer sufficient evidence to support his claim. A month later, the lawsuit was dismissed. Yet, a separate correspondence from the Court, not included in the court documents but found in Kirk's papers, referenced an out of court settlement requiring Hunt to pay Kirk $10,000 and convey certain unspecified lands.[54]

Seventeen—Family Affairs

The media turned its gaze from Kirkland, and newspaper ink went to matters other than Kirk and his family's activities. Two of Peter and Mary Ann's daughters, Marie and Florrie, married during the hectic Panic years of 1893-4. The repercussions of both marriages affected the family greatly with one moving back to England and the other marrying below her station. Concerning Marie's nuptials, a rare news clip noted a trip East by Peter, Mary Ann, and their younger children. Awkwardly, their travel brings into question whether they attended Marie's wedding. No one could have imagined a more unlikely couple than her and her husband, James Bell, separated by nationality, class, and education. Even more unlikely was the exodus of the entire Kirk family from Kirkland, an event that would occur when James and Marie eventually separated.

Marie & James Bell

In 1890, Mary Gibson (Marie) Kirk and James Bell both lived in Kirkland. Seventeen-year-old Marie lived at the Fir Grove mansion with her family.[1] James, a twenty-year-old laborer, answered the work whistles at the Kirkland Lumber Mill and slept in its bunkhouse.[2] In what amounted to organized chaos, lumberjacks had cleared the forests around Kirkland, and construction had started on the huge buildings needed for the steel mill. Born in Belfast in 1869, James belonged to a large family who would emigrate a few at a time from Ireland.[3] He joined relatives in Pittsburgh about 1885. Perhaps learning about Kirkland's proposed steel mill when the big announcement hit the papers in June 1888, he headed west before the rest of his nuclear family immigrated to Pittsburgh a few years later.[4] Entering the United States as a minor, James needed witnesses for his naturalization papers. His employer, Orin Kiteley, president of the Kirkland lumber mill, signed with a firm hand; James Bell signed with an "X."[5]

A small town in those early years, Kirkland was separated from happenings across the lake in Seattle. Plenty of opportunity existed for James and Marie to meet and see each other at social gatherings and church. With many other Kirkland young people, both attended Kirkland's first ball.[6] Their romance was likely fraught with misgivings from Marie's parents. After all, he was an Irish laborer and she an English maiden born into privilege and opportunity. Her education included fine schools in Europe, whereas his was limited. Social pressures would have suggested she marry someone of her own class or better. Once she reached the age of majority, however, she no longer needed her parents' permission.

Six weeks after Marie turned twenty-one, the couple filed a marriage license with the King County Auditor's office.[7] The following day, November 15, 1893, Marie married the Irishman in Fairhaven, Washington, near Bellingham.[8] Marie's sisters Florence and Fanny signed as witnesses. Oddly, the marriage record for Whatcom County lists James' residence as Seattle and Marie's as San Juan Island. Two weeks later, a clerk inserted an unusual hand-written certificate into the Whatcom County record book.[9] This document lists James and Marie's residences in Kirkland and states that they married in the parsonage of the Fairhaven church. It is striking the couple traveled all the way to Bellingham to say their vows when Kirkland had its own churches. San Juan Island offered another beautiful venue as well, and pastors there were familiar with the Kirk family. One can only guess the couple chose Fairhaven for anonymity and distance from watchful eyes.

An uncomfortable span of time lingered between the wedding and a *Seattle P-I* clipping, which reported, "Mr. and Mrs. Peter Kirk, Miss Clara Kirk, Miss Jessie Kirk, Master Peter Kirk and Master Arnold Kirk of Kirkland, returned from the East on Saturday and are at the Diller [Hotel]."[10] (Margaret Hughes, their domestic help, traveled with them.) Travel to the East in those days included at least six days on the train and a few nights' hotel stay in each direction to facilitate transfer between various ferry and rail connections in Seattle, Vancouver, and New York. The Kirk family returned to Seattle December 2, seventeen days after Marie and Jimmie Bell married in Fairhaven. It is unlikely Mr. and Mrs. Kirk and their young entourage departed right after the wedding, went East, and back in that period. Of course, they might not have gone all the way to the East Coast either.

Even so, the couple veiled more than their residences from the marriage officials. Cloaked beneath the ruffles and gathers of Marie's skirts was a six-month baby bump. James and Marie's first child, Vivian Primrose Bell, arrived exactly fourteen weeks later in Kirkland.[11]

Florence & Arthur Dixon

Soon after the baptism of Peter and Mary Ann's first grandchild, Vivian Bell, church bells rang again for a Kirk daughter. Marie's oldest sister, Florence, married Arthur Llewellin Dixon in Victoria, British Columbia.[12] Louis, as many called him, was the son of Mary Ann's sister, Hannah, who had married Thomas Dixon, Peter's former business partner, in the early days of his career.

The two young people may have found affection for each other during Florence's educational sojourns in England. Louis was also a guest of the Kirk family in 1891.[13] By this time, the United States had outlawed first cousin marriages, so the couple married in Canada, which followed England's practices. Not long after their nuptials, Florrie and Louis returned to England and took up residence in Stockport, where he worked with his brother in a tea and coffee dealership.[14]

The Kirk family looked forward to packages sent by Florrie with Dixon tea. The Kirk sisters often shared music and little trinkets with each other as well. Correspondence with the family reveals a happy life together despite challenging financial times.[15] Florrie revealed her resilience by learning to sew and cook. Louis worked hard, but as Florrie made evident in letters to her mother, he suffered from the strain of it, laboring six days a week from early morning until late at night. Florrie filled pages of letters with gossip and small talk. The weather, Sunday strolls, and Louis' health were common themes, along with family gossip: "Is Olive really engaged? I would like to hear all about it. Ask her to tell me."[16]

Margaret abandons her post

Another marriage and shift in the Kirk household occurred in 1895. Margaret Hughes, the Kirks' domestic help, became the subject of correspondence as Florrie wrote, "Fanny tells me that Margaret is going to be married, is it true? Is a joke? Surely, she is not going to marry that young fellow. Is she going to Alaska with him? I was much interested in the launching of the schooner; [Fanny] sent me the cutting from the paper. Clara wrote me a grand account."[17]

A recent German immigrant, Peter P. Floy, captained the ship Florrie mentioned.[18] "Schooner Floy Burg was launched, at Mitchell's Bay, the last of the week, in the presence of quite a large number of people," announced the *San Juan Islander*. "Miss Kirk broke the bottle of wine amid cheers and christened the new schooner the 'Floy Burg.'"[19] Within weeks, more newspaper gossip predicted another voyage for Floy and his schooner, complete with cargo and a new bride. According to rumor, they would head for Alaska.[20] At age forty, Margaret had married "that young fellow," Peter Floy (twelve years her junior) soon after his ship was christened.[21]

Margaret's contact with the Kirk family after she married is unknown. Only one obscure entry in the *San Juan Islander* suggests she might have contacted them after Mary Ann's death: "Mrs. P. Floyd and son, of Kirkland, are visitors at Deer Lodge."[22]

Mary Ann sails to England

After many years away from her homeland, Mary Ann decided to visit England and intended to bring her daughter, Fanny, with her. Florrie had certainly missed her family and expressed it in her correspondences. She wrote an animated letter, excited about her mother's upcoming travel but also intimating a change in the Kirk family's financial status. Mary Ann planned to travel in November, but this worried Florrie. "Rather than you should have a stormy passage in November I would rather you put your visit off until spring, because I do want you to have a nice sea trip. Are you coming by one of the best boats? I would like you to; you will have a shorter time on the sea, & be more comfortable, too…. Are you going to travel tourist? It is very comfortable indeed, & you can bring as much food from home, which makes it nice."[23]

Mary Ann heeded Florrie's advice and rescheduled for the spring. Florrie was eager to see her mother and Fanny and share her new talents from the dressmaking and cooking lessons she had attended. She made elaborate plans for their stay: violin lessons for Fanny, card parties and gatherings with her neighbors. The "Aunties" (Mary Ann's sisters, Martha and Emily) planned coordinating vacations.[24]

Mary Ann further postponed her departure until the summer due to illness.[25] The only clue to Mary Ann's actual travel date was her stay with Peter at Seattle's New England Hotel in June 1898.[26] The following spring, Mary Ann was still in England.[27] She may have extended her visit after learning Florrie was expecting her first child. Undoubtedly, Mary Ann spent considerable time assisting her daughter through her first pregnancy and preparing the nursery. Florrie's daughter, Florence Lucile, arrived in March 1899.[28]

Mary Ann probably visited her sisters, family, and old friends at afternoon teas in grand halls or in perfect English gardens. The sisters may have also sailed to the European continent for a holiday. Mary Ann might have even called on Peter's sister and husband, Ann and Charles Valentine, at their London home.

Of course, this English lady enjoyed being back in her homeland. A decade earlier, she had left the cobbled and familiar streets of Great Britain for the muddy tracks of a frontier. Forsaking the fine life at Bankfield, replete with gardeners, cooks, and other domestic help to trek halfway around the world to Washington Territory, Mary Ann revealed her true-grit spirit.

Only a few farms existed around Kirkland when the Kirk family moved in. A large lake separated them from the nearest metropolis, Seattle. The area proposed for the mill was still raw wilderness, uncharacteristic of the cultivated woods of England, which were long bereft of beasts save for red deer, fox, and small mammals. Beyond Fir Grove's fence, wolves, coyotes, and mountain lions stalked the timbered shadows. Incidents involving bears plagued Kirkland's farmers even years after the racket of mill construction pushed the forest back from the water's edge.[29]

A year after Mary Ann's departure from Washington, the San Juan Island newspaper noted, "The fine Kirk place, on Mitchell's bay is reported to be for sale, because of Mrs. Kirk's desire to remain in England, where she went last year to visit a married daughter and other relatives and friends."[30]

Another problem loomed for the Kirks and their Mitchell Bay property. Part of the massive estate qualified as a homestead in 1892; in 1899, it was time to "prove up" on the property. To complete the process, Peter needed to be a naturalized citizen. A dozen years before he had filed his intent to become a citizen, but the legal naturalization process remained incomplete. The entire family's immigration status depended on him, as did the homestead section of Deer Lodge.

Mary Ann had carved out a life in a rugged frontier likely not by her own choosing, but by her husband's. Their dreams of prosperity dashed upon the shores of Lake Washington; she kept the family afloat. Her hard-working husband traveled frequently, experimenting with various business ventures to support their family. Mary Ann may well have longed for their earlier life.

Peter may have felt similar longings. Possibly he considered returning to England to work again with his brothers in the family business, a haven for many generations of Kirks. However, his own ambition and pride prevented him from going back to England. Peter's friends later expressed he was "so disappointed over the failure of his plans that he did not care to face his former associates in his native country, when they were ready to help finance a plan, which met with lamentable failure."[31]

Therefore, with Mary Ann having sailed to England to join Florrie, and Peter holding down the fort with their other children in Kirkland; Deer Lodge, "the fine Kirk residence at Mitchell Bay," was rented out.[32]

Eighteen—Pioneering a New Future

"We invested $300,000 in building the iron works in Kirkland, in Seattle suburbs, years ago; but the outcome for any profit is buried in the womb of the future," Peter Kirk lamented as he grappled with the challenges at the end of the century. The circumstances of his wife's return to England, the possibility of selling his beloved Deer Lodge, and his immigration status swirled about him. The financial climate had improved, however, and capitalists reignited the idea of building a steel mill in Seattle. Invited to go see the proposed site, Peter voiced his reluctance, "With my experience before me, I tell them I'll wait and see what the result will be, as my enthusiasm is pretty well gone."[1]

Fervor for the Klondike Gold Rush descended upon the Seattle area, breaking the gloom of the Panic of '93 and possibly offering Peter a catalyst as well. The newspapers of the day contained articles and ads spotlighting the Gold Rush and other gold strikes in Alaska and the Yukon. Thousands of people from around the world passed through Seattle daily, leaving for the gold fields with a ton of goods and high expectations. Kirk likely witnessed the long lines at the ships as he made his way along the Seattle waterfront. The increased production at the Kirkland woolen mill was obvious as the northbound stampeders geared up with long johns and blankets.

The enthusiasm caught hold of Peter Kirk. As the Klondike rush ebbed in 1899 and miners struck off for Nome, he registered his patent for hydraulic dredging improvements for gold mining. His opening remarks explaining the device addressed the conditions of the Klondike, the interior Alaska region along the Tanana River, and the beaches at Nome, but also suggested its use could facilitate projects closer to home, namely in digging the ship canal. "My invention is in the nature of a new machine designed to dredge rivers for gold-bearing gravel or sand covered by water or other-wise, and is also adapted for ordinary harbor or channel dredging."[2]

A decade had passed since Kirk's last registered patent, suggesting he was not involved with any other manufacturing-type industry after trying to build the Kirkland steel mill. His previous patents were always associ-ated with the iron business. Filing and registering patents took capital, yet the company had previously absorbed those costs as it utilized the ideas. Kirk's intentions for this new patent remain unknown. Available papers fail to indicate if he developed or planned to employ the dredge within an enterprise of interest to him or if he just wanted to sell the idea to the gold seekers heading north. However, an interesting clue surfaced in a letter from his daughter Florrie in the months after the Gold Rush hit Seattle. "I did not know Mr. [Williams] was intending to go to Alaska."[3] She referred to Peter's good friend and business ally, W. W. Williams, but the letter offers no other information.

The new century brought resolution to a host of Kirk's difficulties. He took the oath of US citizenship in November 1899, then immediately proved up on the homestead piece of the Mitchell Bay property.[4] The date of Mary Ann's homecoming from England remains unknown, but she was counted with the rest of the family in June 1900 when the census taker knocked on Fir Grove's door.[5] In the ongoing pursuit of supporting his large family, another patent idea landed on Peter Kirk's drawing board, and with it, a new business project.

A good steer

Kirk entered into an agreement with A. J. Pidgeon regarding a precious metals smelting operation in Arizona.[6] The bitter sting of the Kirkland mill failure had left an indelible mark, evident in that the con-tract called for Pidgeon to pay all Kirk's expenses and take responsibility for raising the needed capital. Kirk also received a generous amount of the company's shares. In return, he agreed to provide intellectual collateral, the new patent, and his time and expertise in constructing a working smelter.

In response to the deal, Peter Kirk registered a patent for a combined ore roaster and smelter suited for smelting silver, lead, copper, and gold. He reasoned in the patent application that these ores required roasting before smelting because they sometimes contained high amounts of sulfur. In typical fashion, he was introducing a new way to roast and smelt the ores "in a practically continuous way with a great economy of heat and labor."[7] To do that, he intended to replace coke as the fuel with crude oil.

"The furnace is more or less an experiment," Kirk explained, "since none exactly similar has before been tried."[8] He jotted in his pocket notebook concepts he worked out for the patent development, including diagrams of certain machinery, calculations for barrels of crude oil, and methods for determining the temperature in open-hearth furnaces. "Place an iron rod 0:31 inch diameter through a hole in the door into the furnace, let it remain 26 seconds, withdraw quickly. If the furnace is very hot, the end of the bar will be at a white welding heat throwing off sparks. If the furnace is cold, the rod will be red or yellow."[9] In a later interview, he explained the process for the new smelter. "The ore is dumped in by a hydraulic hoist directly over the furnace into towers 30 feet high by 8 feet across. This will constitute the roasting apparatus. From these towers, there being two, the roasted ore drops into the furnace, where the fusion is taking place. Oil and steam are forced into the charge for fuel. The slag is tapped out occasionally as the smelting proceeds, and the bullion tapped whenever the hearth is full."[10]

In the spring of 1901, with Peter Kirk as general manager and Pidgeon as one of the directors, the Phoenix Reduction Company incorporated.[11] Once again, Kirk worked with cutting-edge technology, designing and building machinery. But this time, someone else took the financial risk. Prospects looked promising as area resources contained an abundance of precious metals. The downside for Kirk was spending much of his time in Arizona, away from his family. As manager, he supervised everything from ordering machinery to plant construction.

As the smelter site, company officials selected Benson, Arizona Territory, strategically located at a railroad junction near the Mexico border.[12] The little town lay 24 miles directly north of Tombstone and 45 miles east of Tucson. The nearby Dragoon mountain range was rumored to contain enough ore to keep the plant running for years.[13]

Within a year, the company reorganized into the Empire Smelting Company. Kirk's partner, A. J. Pigeon, briefly described the enterprise in February 1902: "Our plans call for a 500-ton plant, but we will make a start with a capacity of 100 tons [per day]. The estimated cost of this plant is $50,000. We expect to be in operation within sixty or ninety days."[14] Optimism pushed machinery orders from Pittsburgh, and the company secured an old smelter with the help of the townspeople who helped raise funds. The ninety-day projected timeline for the smelter construction extended into the summer. By July, Empire Smelting had prepared the buildings for the new custom plant.[15] They had 25 tons of castings on the ground, with fifteen more en route.[16] September brought more machinery, including an engine, two boilers, and castings.[17] After the delivery of the fourth rail car of machinery, a local newswriter reported, "As rapidly as possible, the machinery will be installed and the plant will be ready to blow in the latter part of December."[18]

More equipment arrived in October along with a delay. Construction halted while the smelter's managers determined the plant's exact location. Only then could the Phoenix and Eastern Railroad make their final survey for the rail line. In the meantime, Empire Smelting contracted with mine owners for a steady supply of ore needed to keep the smelter running when it became operational. In addition, the Southern Pacific Railroad constructed an oil tank at Benson with a capacity of 1.5 million gallons.[19]

The following spring, Peter Kirk submitted an accounting of expenses incurred on behalf of the Arizona plant for the previous eighteen months. These included patent fees of $330 ($10,000 in 2020 value), smelter site, machinery, freight, wages, and various other expenditures. The bill also reflected his expenses for travel, hotels, telegrams, and even postage stamps, amounting to almost $6,000.[20] In May, bank drafts signed by R. A. Boggess and payable to Kirk began rolling in every two weeks until August, totaling $11,000.[21] It is not clear what the extra payment was for.

Kirk also signed a new pact with A. J. Pidgeon concerning the ore roaster patent and his shares in the Empire Smelting Company. The agreement reduced Pidgeon's half-share in Kirk's patent to 1/5 in exchange for 100,000 of Kirk's shares in the company, with Kirk retaining 150,000 shares.[22]

The initial ninety-day construction period had elapsed many times over. Finally, in the early months of 1904, the 100-ton furnace neared completion. However, executives at Empire Smelting decided to erect a second furnace with the capacity to process 200 tons daily. The company employed a force of men to clear the area in preparation for delivery of the 200-tonner being constructed in San Francisco.[23]

Kirk had labored on the smelter for two years. "We expect to be turning out 75 tons of high grade matte near the first of March," he told the *Arizona Republican* in February 1904.[24] His prediction failed to materialize. By July, the smelter company once again reorganized under the new name of Southwestern Smelting and Refining Company, with Riley A. Boggess as president. Kirk attempted to extradite himself from the company before it restructured. The previous fall, Boggess had agreed to buy Kirk's 150,000 Empire shares for $5,322.[25] Days before the smelter company reorganized the following summer, Boggess signed a promissory note with Kirk. He put up 25,000 shares of stock in the Imperial Quicksilver Mining Company as collateral for a $2,500 loan from Peter for one year at seven per cent interest, a debt he would ultimately fail to pay.[26]

Kirk's commitment to cash out and complete his obligations with the smelting company was evident in correspondence between the two men. In 1905, he inquired about the funds owed him, but Boggess hedged. "I note that you are depending upon the ultimate payment of the notes referred to, and I can assure you that they will both be taken up. I note your kind offer to extend the first one, providing I can assure you that the security is alright." Boggess added excuses, changed the subject, and suggested the land alone was "so valuable as to assure its security."[27] Ultimately, he begged for Kirk to extend the note a bit longer.

Boggess ended the letter on a peculiar note. "I might add that I have not forgotten your desire, at our mutual convenience, to be allowed to complete and test the oil smelter, and I assure you that you will find me ready and willing, at the proper time, to meet you half way."[28] The over-flowing words, while politely acknowledging Peter's wish to test the smelter, insinuated a threat. The ninety-day project had extended beyond four years because of delays, smelter add-ons, and multiple re-organizations by the directors. Kirk could not fulfill his part of the contract until he tested the smelter.

Ultimately, all the infamous smelting company produced were headlines. Years after the project's inception, an article in an Arizona paper noted, "Smoke has never belched forth from its stack. It is not running, nor has it ever been blown in. According to some, who assert they are creditors of Promoter Boggess, it served as a good steer to rope in investors."[29]

"RILEY A. BOGGESS IS A BANKRUPT," announced the *San Francisco Call* in 1906. The article contended that Boggess had been "concealing valuable assets from his creditors with intent to hinder, delay and defraud them."[30] Boggess had $250,000 in outstanding obligations with little security. Among these was over $6,000 owed to Peter Kirk.[31]

Lawsuits ensued from multiple parties. Peter Kirk, former manager of the smelter, found himself witness at one of the proceedings for judgment against Boggess. In his deposition, Kirk, who had also served as the company's treasurer, affirmed he had indeed ordered machinery for which Boggess still owed him thousands of dollars.[32] Kirk held an interest in the Benson property but soon relinquished it to the Phoenix and Eastern Railroad.[33]

"Bankrupt man attacks creditors...calls them 'chicken hearted,'" the *San Francisco Call* reported two years into the proceedings. Rebuking his detractors, Boggess asserted, "All debts would have been paid long ago if creditors had not instituted court proceedings, which ruined the possibilities of the projects."[34]

Kirk continued efforts to collect on the debt, though these ultimately proved futile. He lost money in the smelter operation and in the stock Boggess had offered for the $2,500 loan. In 1909, Kirk's bank was still attempting to resolve the debt on his behalf. "Referring to your stock in the Imperial Quicksilver Mining Co.," they advised, "we have received the enclosed letter from [their bank]. You will notice they are having difficulty in locating the proper transfer officers of this Company. It would be best for your interests to secure the transfer of this stock in some other manner than that indicated by them."[35]

Around the same time, Kirk's former partner, A. J. Pidgeon, found himself mixed up in another sordid affair. Charges levied against Pidgeon included misappropriation of funds. Investors also maintained that for several years he kept the companies he managed idle. Unsurprisingly, he had sold his house and moved to Louisville around the time the trouble began. As to the accusations, Pidgeon stated it was a mistake.[36]

In one respect, Kirk had been smart to escape the farce when he did. Perhaps he saw things unraveling for the bogus Riley A. Boggess and did not want to be a pigeon any longer. His involvement seemed minimal, and he was never accused of misconduct concerning the smelter business. He was a victim like many other creditors. Yet, his intelligence and experience come into question: Was Peter Kirk culpable or just gullible?

Later statements from Kirkland residents suggest the latter. "As to Mr. Kirk's personal character, every word I have heard or read of him was in his praise. One testimonial was to this effect: 'He was so honest and honorable himself that he could not comprehend how anyone could be otherwise; and unscrupulous persons sometimes found him an easy mark.'"[37]

Nineteen—Meanwhile, Back at the Ranch

Another mystery surfaced during the early months of the Arizona smelter when Kirk was busy traveling between the Southwest and the Pacific Northwest. In March 1901, he had sent a telegram from Phoenix to his lawyer, C. S. Preston, in Seattle. The cryptic message said, "Amount twenty-five thousand will accept half cash half Kirkland Stock writing."[1] Since he sent this from Arizona, the $25,000 in cash and stock might have been a payment from the smelter deal. The time frame also coincides with Kirk's lawsuit against Leigh S. J. Hunt that was settled out of court. In any event, Kirk had funds to invest following the steel mill demise. Some went toward the purchase of more property adjacent to Deer Lodge and the conversion of some acreage into a sheep ranch. Kirk purchased 100 ewes from his neighbor, Isaac Sandwith, and by October 1901, four rams had arrived from Victoria, British Columbia.[2] Kirk brought in woodcutters to clear a portion of his property for pasture and crops. The cut timber also provided income.

The Roche Harbor Lime Company needed large quantities of timber to fuel their kilns. To fulfill contracts with the limekilns, woodcutters canvassed local property owners to cut stands of timber on their land. The abundance of coastline on Kirk's property appealed to the woodcutters since logs could be hauled on a scow to the lime works' dock.

In one agreement, Kirk received 25 cents per cord stumpage fee, totaling about $177 (over $5,000 in 2020 dollars).[3] In another deal with the same man and his Japanese hands, another 500 cords were cut. The Mitchell Bay property had many varieties of trees, from spindly alder to monstrous Douglas fir. Mature fir trees have bark several inches thick. Kirk received earnings for several cords of bark produced from this deal.

After the arrival of the sheep, Kirk hired a caretaker, Edward Botsford, from Kirkland. (Botsford had a homestead near Kirk's steel mill site.[4]) He safeguarded and worked the ranch for four years, covering Kirk's time in Arizona.[5] The two men drew up a detailed fifteen-article contract resembling a tenant farmer agreement.[6] Kirk provided tools, land, and a house, and he paid the taxes on all the property. Botsford could farm, grow crops, and raise his own livestock. In return, Kirk received one-half of the proceeds generated from his property, including the shearing of sheep and woodcutting. (The woodcutting contract might have been part of this agreement.) Kirk expected the custodian to keep ample books, available for his review at any time, with an accounting made each September. Maintenance responsibilities fell on Botsford for all houses and outbuildings. Living on site, the tenant and his family protected Deer Lodge when the Kirk family was absent.

Robert Jackson story

Acquiring more land for the sheep ranch took an unusual turn. During the difficult financial years following the Panic of '93, when bankruptcies and foreclosures kept Kirk busy and seemingly broke, he loaned his neighbor to the north $600. Robert Jackson, in return, pledged his 171-acre Garrison Bay homestead as collateral on the loan.[7]

In the summer of 1900, two Kirk young people took this 86-year-old neighbor some cookies. Sadly, they found the old-timer dead, with his faithful dog lying beside his bed. They summoned Doc Capron, who surmised, "It was probable that the immediate cause of death was an acute attack of indigestion, occasioned by improper food and lonely manner of living."[8]

Robert Jackson died with considerable provisions in his little cabin but without an heir and without having paid a dime on the Kirk loan. Kirk filed a lien on Jackson's estate for almost $1,100 for the debt, which included principal and interest for five years. At a sheriff's sale held to liquefy the holdings and settle any liens, Kirk was highest bidder, purchasing the Jackson property for $1,230, which satisfied his initial investment and legal fees.[9] This gave Kirk an almost continuous shoreline along the north coast of Mitchell Bay and southern shore of Garrison Bay, encompassing nearly the entire peninsula of the area today known as Yacht Haven.

Fanny marries Dr. Capron

After the sheep arrived, the family returned in 1901 to the mainland, where they celebrated the marriage of daughter Fanny to Victor Capron at their Kirkland home.[10] Dr. Vic Capron was a recent arrival to San Juan Island. In 1898, he had taken a position as company physician for the Roche Harbor Lime Company. Few physicians practiced in the islands, so Capron expanded his medical practice to the citizens on San Juan Island and neighboring islands.

He was a bit of a character, teased in the local paper for his mishaps but also lauded for his medical skills and for often going beyond expectations to help his neighbors. At one point, he rigged a mobile X-ray machine to his automobile to expedite treatment for rural patients.[11] His political views were no secret: In support of the theory of a one-tax system, he eventually drafted his own ideas on the topic in a small booklet.[12]

Capron demonstrated energy and smarts. He entertained many ideas for improving life on the island, and he had the means to achieve them. Early in 1900, he received the permits and gathered the materials to build San Juan Island's first telephone system.[13] He later expanded service to neighboring Lopez and Orcas islands. This project was well underway when 34-year-old Vic Capron and 27-year-old Fanny Kirk married in October 1901. The couple enjoyed a short bridal trip and then returned to Roche Harbor, occupying the doctor's home behind the Hotel De Haro, a residence provided by the lime company.[14]

Loss of a friend

After Fanny and Vic's nuptials, Peter returned to Arizona.[15] Not long after, in February 1902, sad news reached the Kirk family. Peter's friend

John G. Kellett died at age forty-six of a cerebral hemorrhage. Kellett had developed his own plans to kick-start the iron works again, intending to use scrap iron in a re-smelting mill. From the start, he had thought this would be more successful in the area than the full reduction plant Peter Kirk had envisioned, but he was overruled. Kellett worked at the Bremerton Navy Yard to raise money for his venture. According to his family, he finally told his wife of his plans the evening before his stroke, saying he planned to begin work on the project immediately.[16]

John Kellett's death had to have been a huge blow to the Kirk family as he was considered one of Peter Kirk's right-hand men. He escorted the Kirk family to America. Their families regularly visited each other. The Kirk, Kellett, and Williams children often intermingled and at times dated one another. Yet sad as it was, the loss failed to compare to what would soon befall the Kirk family.

Part IV: Retirement

Figure 13 Kirk family

Circa 1894-7. This photo of Peter and his family is the only one known showing so many members of the family together. Seated on her white cloud in the center, only Marie looks directly at the photographer, holding eye contact.
In what seems a premonition of her premature death, she engages in the moment while her family, in sync, looks to a future in which they will proceed together, without her. Photo courtesy of Kirkland Heritage Society.

Twenty—Derailed

"Peter Kirk and family of Kirkland, and San Juan Island, Washington state, are spending the winter at Blennerville, Esquimalt road, corner of Head street."[1]

Victoria Daily Colonist, November 19, 1904

Peter's first known trip to Victoria, British Columbia, occurred in October 1886, soon after he arrived on the West Coast. He stayed at the Clarence Hotel, but there is no indication of the purpose of his trip. In the years that followed, Victoria became a favorite destination of the Kirk family. They may have spent time there after emigrating and before setting up their household at Tacoma, and it may also have served as a summer retreat before they built Deer Lodge. When in the San Juan Islands, the family continued their forays to Victoria and other parts of Canada, such as Harrison Hot Springs. Only a short boat ride away, Victoria offered a pleasant British reminder of home with the grand architecture of the parliament buildings, Christ Church Cathedral, and Craigdarroch Castle.

The Kirk family getaway in November 1904 was hastily planned and uncommonly prolonged. The Kirks needed to escape Kirkland, and winters proved difficult for Mary Ann at their San Juan Island home. Even with frequent postal exchanges between the American Kirk family and Florrie in England, one of Florrie's postcards, addressed to her sister Olive at Fir Grove, had to be forwarded to the Blennerville house in Victoria. Beginning November 1, Peter rented this elegant and oversized residence for $52 a month for a total of four months.[2] However, they extended their stay well into the spring.

Fanny (Kirk) Capron and her toddler, Marjorie, frequently traveled to Victoria from Roche Harbor to visit the family. Throughout the winter, Peter adjusted his work schedule to coordinate visits. In May, a San Juan local went to Victoria and conveyed the Kirk family to Mitchell Bay.[3] In a letter, Mary Ann's sister Emily agreed with her sister's sentiments about leaving: "Yes, you will be sorry to leave Victoria, but still, you will enjoy the summer at your island home."[4] Retreating to Deer Lodge, the Kirks would never return to Fir Grove in Kirkland.

The previous summer had held hope and promise for the Kirk family, wrapped in the familiar shawl of routine. Peter was determined to wrap up the Arizona smelter project while the family went about their seasonal shifts between homes. The Kirk children were grown, and even the youngest, Arnold, had completed two years of college at Acme Business College in Seattle.[5] Several grandchildren filled the ranks and kept everyone busy.

Three of the grandchildren belonged to Marie (Kirk) and James Bell. Despite his ignominious admission to the clan, Jimmie, as the family called him, found a place in the group working as a land agent collecting rents on Kirkland properties. Gone were the sweat-stained, saw-dusted work clothes of a miller. Marie's love and guidance had starched the blue-collar right out of him. James Bell served as Justice of Peace for the Kirkland Precinct and secretary for the Kirkland School District where their children attended.[6] For a man who had signed his naturalization papers a decade before with an "X," these were significant accomplishments.

In 1902, James and Marie moved their family to a small cottage on Rose Hill next to the Congregational Church. "She and her husband, James had been so happy in their new home next door to the church. Although busy with three small children, she still found time to write music," wrote a church historian.[7] James provided well for his family and made sure Marie had domestic help for their home, giving her time to compose.[8]

Like her father, Marie was an accomplished musician. "James Bell, being protective of Marie when she was composing her music, kept all the children out of the house when she was at the piano," recalled Barbara Dickinson of the stories told by her mother, Charlotte, the youngest of the Bell children.[9] In 1903, Marie G. Bell published "Bonnie Scotland."[10] A man's name accompanied Marie's on the music, necessary she was told, in order to publish it. Charlotte assured her descendants Marie had composed the music and written the lyrics herself.[11]

The next summer, the Bell family had a new well dug at their cottage. Tragically, typhoid bacteria contaminated it. Typhoid spreads when people unknowingly ingest fecal material from an infected person or a carrier. Carriers can live for decades without knowing they have the disease. An infected neighbor's sewage likely leached into the Bells' new water source. Symptoms of the disease took a week to manifest, affecting the family members in varying degrees. Marie and her children, aged seven to ten years old, all fell ill with typhoid fever.[12] None had been vaccinated against the disease, and no antibiotic cure existed. The children miraculously recovered, but Marie languished with the malaise, diarrhea, and lack of appetite.

"Sunday school was held during the summer but the church bell was not rung as a courtesy to Mary Kirk Bell. Suddenly, she became gravely ill...and lay ailing for many weeks," wrote a church historian.[13] The illness persisted until September 16, when beloved and gifted Marie succumbed.[14]

Mary Gibson Kirk Bell's family and friends buried her two weeks before her 32nd birthday, in the Kirkland cemetery her father helped organize in 1888. Jimmie, possibly overwhelmed by the sudden burial expenses of preparing her body and purchasing a casket, plus fees for the wagon, cemetery plot, and digging, did not place a headstone on her grave. Family stories divulged that Jimmie, proud despite his grief, refused to allow his father-in-law to purchase one.[15] Consequently, Marie's grave went unmarked for nearly a century. Heartsick, Jimmie Bell had all copies of Marie's song "Bonnie Scotland" pulled from the market, suggesting that if he could not hear her music, no one would.

Jimmie remained in Kirkland as the Kirk family departed with their grief. His inability to call a doctor when Marie fell ill from typhoid troubled him, compelling him to install Kirkland's first telephone service.[16] He probably had help from his brother-in-law, Dr. V. J. Capron, who had initiated the phone system on San Juan Island a few years earlier.

Twenty-one—New Life in the Islands

Despite their loss, Peter Kirk and his family went on with life on San Juan Island, making alterations and repairs to Deer Lodge now that it was their permanent home. Peter commissioned a local boat builder to construct a new 28-foot gasoline launch.[1] "The Kirks, when they lived on the island, always had a boat; first the *Constance I* and later the *Constance II*, named after Clara Constance Kirk," recalled members of the Kellett family.[2] As opposed to the ferry, these boats provided fast, easy access to destinations in the San Juan Islands and all around Puget Sound, including Seattle. From the Deer Lodge dock, Victoria lay across Haro Strait and to the south. The Kirk family often took friends on excursions, many from Kirkland.[3] The beauty and wildlife of the San Juan Islands remain exceptional. On outings, the Kirks may have seen pods of orcas and porpoises cruising along or seals bobbing in the waves or sea lions that had hauled out on sun-warmed rocks. Whales migrated to and from their Alaska summer grounds through the waterways of the Salish Sea. Migrant and resident sea birds also passed by.

Life on San Juan Island slowly came to include modern technologies. Telephone lines traced the island's road system after the turn of the century, and electricity followed. As early as 1905, automobiles cranked and sputtered over island roads.[4]

The Kirks' social fabric was likely interwoven with church. The Methodist pastor performed services in Friday Harbor and Roche Harbor each Sunday. The family probably joined the closer Roche Harbor services. They attended dances and celebrated weddings and other special occasions. Involving himself with the politics of the island, Peter attended the Republican convention as a delegate with Dr. Capron in the fall of 1906.[5]

The Kirks visited with neighbors and Kirkland friends. Fanny and her daughter Marjorie lived close by. Jimmie Bell escorted his children to Mitchell Bay to visit their family when his busy schedule as a single father allowed. One postcard suggested the Bell children were guests at Blennerville during the family's grieving.[6] In one letter, Florrie expressed her hope that Jimmie was doing well in the telephone business, but she wondered if he was making much money. "I often think of the three little children," she wrote. "I wish I could do something for them, it is as much as we can do now to pay our own way."[7]

As Vivian and Clarence Bell approached their teen years, they became active in the Kirkland school and held offices in the Literary Society.[8] Florrie wrote, "I would like to think of dear Marie's little children being educated nicely. Have a talk with Jimmie & see what can be done. It is so important."[9]

The recipient of Florrie's letter is unknown, but the message got across. Mary Ann Kirk loaned James Bell $520, which coincided with an expansion of his telephone business to Redmond after his connection with Seattle's line the previous summer.[10] Another loan followed the next year for twice the amount. These loans and others—some never repaid—would cause tensions between Bell and his father-in-law in the years to come.[11]

Peter pioneers a life without Mary Ann

Earlier in the summer of 1907, happy news from England announced the birth of Florrie and Louis' son, Maurice Emil Dixon. But happiness was short-lived. Later that summer, days after Mary Ann celebrated her 67th birthday, an affliction that may have begun as a cold turned to catarrh, a severe case of sinus congestion. Her symptoms worsened in September, and her son-in-law, Dr. Victor Capron, attended her at Deer Lodge. Mary Ann's ten-year battle with heart problems contributed to her decline. The inflammation in her lungs soon turned chronic, and Peter hired a nurse to look after her. On September 29, four days after pneumonia set in, Mary Ann died, leaving the family grieving again.[12]

A San Juan maritime breeze blew away the pleasant fall weather of Mary Ann's last day. A cloudy, cooler climate, befitting the pall of grief at Valley Cemetery, moved in. The Methodist pastor officiated at her burial "to a large number of friends and acquaintances who extended a last sad tribute to her memory." Her obituary also noted, "Mrs. Kirk was very fond of the place [Deer Lodge] and loved to entertain her friends there. She was most highly esteemed for her amiable qualities and kindly disposition."[13] A Kirkland resident described her as "a woman of pure motherliness, a lady of the finest character."[14] She had lived a littoral life by the sea. Waves of happiness and sadness crashed upon her shores. Storms blew into her life with Peter; she cast them off with a royal flick of her wrist.

Mary Ann and Peter were blessed with nine children. With the seven who survived her, he now had to find his way without her. The family's grief may have been particularly sharp since they had lost Marie Bell in September three years earlier. Life must have felt tuneless and discordant, accented only by visits from friends and family.

In the months that followed, Peter tackled the details of her estate. At the time of her death, her personal assets included huge tracts of land in Kirkland, Ballard, and Mitchell Bay; stock in the Kirkland Development Company and Kirkland Land & Improvement Company; and a small amount of cash and loans.[15] She also had £5450 left in her England estate, totaling nearly three quarters of a million dollars in 2020 dollars.[16]

Mourning for Mary Ann softened in the New Year with the arrival of another grandson for Peter. Victor James Capron, son of Fanny and Vic, arrived in January, a welcome distraction from sorrow.[17] The Bell grandchildren continued to live in Kirkland with their father, Jimmie, but that would soon change.

Peter occupied himself with farming duties at the expansive Deer Lodge estate. He arranged for more land clearing and fixed fences. He planted hay and hired locals to do the threshing, bailing, and other specialty jobs. He tackled the tedious but necessary chores of buying new equipment and replacing livestock.[18]

Demise of Fir Grove

In the years after moving from Kirkland, Peter struggled with what to do with Fir Grove, their home in Kirkland. Long before Mary Ann's passing, he had signed a contract with a buyer, Douglas Ross to buy the mansion, but in 1906, he suddenly canceled it.[19] Mary Ann's death may have pushed Peter more firmly to sell it. Within the year, he wrote in his pocket notebook, "Aug 22nd I offered on the Kirkland house with 16 lots to Judge Windsor for $7800."[20] The Judge did not accept, and no other records of negotiations exist.

Residing at Deer Lodge, the family traveled often to Seattle for business and to visit friends, but there is no indication they stayed at Fir Grove. Instead, the Kellett family often hosted the Kirks, as did the Williams family and other Kirkland friends.[21] Being such a large house, Fir Grove was likely too expensive to keep ready, or if rented out, it was unavailable to the family.

Tenants were infrequent, and prospective buyers complained Fir Grove was a bit run down despite the paint, fencing repairs, and tree-pruning Kirk arranged. His property manager, C. L. Parrish, complained people "did not want to pay anything for it." He added, "I have had an awful time to keep the place from being destroyed by cattle and boys. I have nailed the gates all up and put signs on the place to keep out."[22] Even though Kirkland promoters hoping to attract Seattle professionals billed the town as a quaint bedroom community, Parrish found it was "certainly hard work to sell that class of property in these times." He noted, "I am satisfied that I could have sold it long ago if the house had not been so large."[23] He tried to sell the property to a doctor for use as a sanitarium, but that also fell through.

Peter Kirk would own Fir Grove until his death years later. At that point, Peter Jr. and Arnold inherited the Kirkland mansion and sold it. The new owner tore it down and built three new houses from the salvaged material.[24] Perhaps Peter had held onto the house knowing the ship canal was finally under construction. Congress had finally agreed to nearly $2.3 million for the locks to connect Salmon Bay to Lake Washington.

This may have prompted land developers Burke & Farrar to buy the Kirkland Development Company, which held all the land for the Kirkland town site—and much of Kirk's faith in the future. Expecting to infuse life into the quiet Seattle suburb, the developers purchased the entire 2,000 acres encompassing Kirkland, including its two miles of lakeshore.[25]

For Kirk's part, the details of the transaction are unclear and incomplete. A June 1910 letter from E. Cardin of the Kirkland Development Company to Peter Kirk mentions the deal included 140 acres sold at $150 per acre.[26] Burke & Farrar put down $10,000 and agreed to pay Kirk six percent on the balance. A subsequent letter from the same person stated Burke & Farrar agreed to pay Kirk $30,000, more than the $21,000 sum of the previous figures. Details of the final transaction are vague, but it clearly did not include all of Kirk's holdings in Kirkland, perhaps involving only the Kirkland town site and mill site.

Twenty-two—Changing Times, Changing Life

In semi-retirement at Deer Lodge, Peter remained busy welcoming guests, managing properties, and seeing to farm duties. He organized his life around his children, several of whom lived with him. Life in general and current events kept everyone busy. The summer of 1909 brought fresh entertainment with Seattle's Alaska-Yukon-Pacific (AYP) Exposition. Deer Lodge became a revolving door as Peter's granddaughters took up residence and more of his children married.

The AYP world's fair highlighted the development of the Pacific Northwest, including British Columbia, particularly during the gold rush era. The fairgrounds later became the University of Washington campus. Over the course of the four-and-a-half-month exhibition, all the Kirks attended the must-see exhibition, sometimes staying in Seattle for weeks. Peter traveled to the city during the Expo's June opening.[1]

Within two weeks of Peter's Seattle excursion, the gossip column noted that his granddaughter, Vivian Bell, visited Deer Lodge.[2] Peter may have accompanied her to San Juan Island when he returned from the AYP Expo. Jimmie Bell escorted his youngest daughter, Charlotte, to the estate a month later.[3] The Bell children often were guests of their Kirk relatives, but this time seems different. Earlier in the spring, the Kirk aunties went to Seattle to check on Vivian during her hospitalization for an undisclosed illness.[4] Now, the local San Juan newspaper increasingly indicated Marie's daughters, ages fifteen and twelve, were staying with their Aunt Fanny and her Capron family in Roche Harbor and with their other Kirk relatives at Deer Lodge.

While their aunts Clara and Jessie attended the AYP Expo, the Bell sisters accompanied their uncles to Victoria for the day.[5] Into the fall and winter, they visited their grandfather often at Mitchell Bay.[6] December brought a flurry of social calls to Deer Lodge among the Kirk, Bell, and Capron families.[7] According to the local newspaper, Vivian and Charlotte re-entered school shortly after.[8] Too old for the Mitchell Bay school, Vivian must have attended high school in Friday Harbor. Right before Christmas, Fanny's husband, Dr. Capron, bought the Stoliker residence on Blair Avenue in Friday Harbor.[9] Vivian and Charlotte Bell moved with the Capron family to Friday Harbor a few months later.[10] Marie's son Clarence remained with his father, who had moved from Kirkland to North Bend, where he managed the telephone service.[11]

One can only speculate as to why the Bell daughters moved in with their Kirk relatives. Letters from Florrie had expressed concern for the children's wellbeing and education after Marie died. Other records hint at the financial strain on James Bell as he took out loans with his Kirk in-laws. Peter wrote one draft to "James Bell, Guardian" suggesting that he supported his grandchildren even after his granddaughters moved to San Juan Island.[12] Peter also set up a trust account putting the Bell children's inheritance from their grandmother under the supervision of the court lest James Bell "dribble it away."[13] In spite of the apparent tensions between the two men, Jimmie visited his daughters in the San Juan Islands and they made trips to North Bend for extended retreats with him.[14]

Jessie & Ralph Charlton

Another addition to the family came in mid-November when the youngest Kirk daughter, Jessie, married Ralph Charlton, a first for both.[15] The newlyweds set up housekeeping in Ballard. A skilled machinist and boat builder, Ralph became partners with his father-in-law, Peter Kirk, in the Charlton & Kirk Machine Shop.[16] Strategically located on Salmon Bay, the company handled general repairs of gasoline engines and was a complete machine shop.

Within months of the Charlton's nuptials, Peter had another beautiful new gasoline launch, possibly built at the Ballard workshop.[17] San

Juan's newspaper, the *Islander*, lauded it as "the finest pleasure launch in the county," and further described her as being "ten net tons burden, equipped with a 10 h.p. eastern Standard engine."[18] The new *Constance* made the Seattle trip in a speedy seven hours from Mitchell Bay. Soon after acquiring this "fine power yacht," Peter added a boathouse to the Mitchell Bay estate.[19]

Peter's youngest son, Arnold, often captained the family launch around local waters. "He had always been fond of boats, so much so, his nickname was 'Cappy,'" remembered a family friend, adding that he sometimes worked on small boats plying around Puget Sound.[20] He loved working on the water and later told his family, "This is just like being on a cruise."[21]

Current events

The walls of Deer Lodge surely soaked in the rousing debates sweeping the nation on alcohol prohibition and women's suffrage. No records indicate how Peter Kirk felt about these issues, but his Wesleyan upbringing would have inclined him toward temperance and support for women's right to vote. His father's involvement with the Band of Hope, an organization encouraging children to embrace a life of sobriety, likely influenced him too. In addition, Peter's brother and brother-in law were involved with the Temperance Union in Workington and often gave speeches.[22]

Before the national prohibition of alcohol sales, communities voted individually to discontinue licensing saloons. For a small island village, the effects may have been felt more keenly, with friends or neighbors losing their livelihood. Nevertheless, Friday Harbor went dry May 10, 1910, by decision of a special local election. By an overwhelming margin of 87 to 36, the town favored abolishing the town's saloons.[23]

The women's right to vote was also a hot topic and often tied to the alcohol debate. Proponents of temperance claimed too many men, seduced by the jingle of coin in their pocket on payday, stopped at the pub and drank, leaving the family with scant resources until the next payday. Men voted on the issue of prohibition, yet women, greatly affected by the outcome, were left without a say.

The enfranchisement question was first addressed locally. By 1910, only four western states in America had voted in amendments to their state constitutions. Rousing debates occurred all over Washington. Friday Harbor hosted its own debate early in 1910 and the argument favored a women's right to vote.[24] San Juan County voted 2 to 1 in favor of enfranchisement. The state followed suit, and Peter Kirk's daughters, along with all Washington women, finally received their right to vote in 1910.

Halley's Comet

The Kirk family enjoyed the company of many friends on their beach in May 1910.[25] Surely, the crowd discussed the impending arrival of Halley's Comet and the Doomsayers' prediction of world devastation. "A hundred million miles away and coming this way at 40 miles a second!" warned a *Tacoma Times* story in the months leading up to the comet's arrival.[26] Historically, Halley's Comet had fueled myths it brought war, fire, pestilence, and changes in dynasties. The beachgoers might have discussed folklore about the comet, including the idea that "the close approach of a comet to the earth affects and disturbs men's brains, so that men are inwardly stirred with warlike impulses."[27]

Impending doom was predicted for May 18 when the comet traveled between the earth and the sun. Alarmists shared superstitions and concerns over the earth passing through a tail containing potentially dangerous gasses. The local newspaper regularly broadcast the comet's progress. Thankfully, San Juan Island's weekly journal arrived on May 20 with the headline "Halley's Comet Speeding Away," suggesting the world had escaped Armageddon: "Halley's comet passed between the earth and the sun without causing any known convulsions of nature or apparent atmospheric disturbances. On that day, the earth was enveloped in the comet's tail for a few hours and passed through, or across, about one million miles of it."[28] A clear night over San Juan Island afforded residents a good view of both the comet and tail, part of a spectacular celestial double feature.[29] A few days later a total lunar eclipse occurred as well.

More Kirk children fledge

Plenty of opportunities occurred for the Kirks to socialize. The Roche Harbor Club House hosted regular dances, as did neighboring islands. Family friend Peter Kellett (son of John Kellett) had a shipyard at Cowichan Bay, near Victoria, enticing the young people to make frequent forays across the channel.[30] They attended grand events at the John McMillin home, where two more of Peter's daughters may have fallen to Cupid's arrow with employees of McMillin's lime company.[31]

The first was McMillin's personal secretary, Pearl Morrill, who was beguiled by the older, but decidedly beautiful, Clara Kirk. Befriending the Kirk siblings, he joined Clara and her brothers on trips to Victoria in the *Constance*.[32] In 1911, they married at Jessie and Ralph Charlton's home in Ballard.[33]

Correspondence hinted Clara's father, Peter, and sister, Olive, might not have attended. Days before the wedding, Peter wrote to his friend Mr. Williams, "I don't want to leave home till the weather is warmer."[34] In fact, it was snowing and just above freezing a few days before the wedding when brothers Arnold and Peter Jr. arrived from Mitchell Bay in the *Constance*.[35] The temperature barely broke 40 degrees on the cloudy day of the Morrill wedding.[36] Olive might have stayed to care for their father, indicated by a postcard Arnold sent to her two days after the wedding to let her know they had a good trip down the sound.[37]

Olive Kirk was her father's main caregiver after Mary Ann's death. The last of the Kirk daughters to marry, she remained a spinster into her 40s and never bore children. Her husband, Frank D'Arcy captained the Lime Company's tug, the *Calcite*. Olive may have joined Frank on the *Calcite* when it took a crowd to Bellingham to hear Reverend Billy Sunday as the Earth passed through the tail of Halley's Comet.[38]

Family stories told of Peter Jr. courting Cora Scribner by rowboat across Mitchell Bay.[39] The couple married in the Friday Harbor Presbyterian Church in February 1914. A letter from Florence to her father speaks to a hasty marriage: "I was surprised about Peter's marriage, especially as I did not know he was engaged. I must write to him and wish him happiness. I think it much better for Peter; it must have been uncomfortable for the boys alone [at Deer Lodge]."[40]

Peter Jr. and Cora took over the sheep ranch at Mitchell Bay after they married.[41] It proved a difficult venture for them, forcing them to borrow money from his father. Writing with a payment, the son explained, "I enclose your check value $60.00 in payment for one half the interest due on the house. Arnold & I will fix up the other half later. I am doing my harvesting now and have to meet labor & thrashing machine expenses, & I find it very hard to collect any money that is owing me."[42]

Generosity to his children

In fact, all the Kirk children borrowed from their father at times. Besides the loans to James Bell after Marie died, Clara and Pearl received help with their homestead in Coronation, Jessie and Ralph with their Ballard machine shop, Olive and Frank with a house in Friday Harbor.[43] Peter also helped Fanny and Vic secure their Cady Mountain ranch.[44] It must have grieved Peter not to have an ironworks to pass down to his sons and employ his sons-in-laws. The 100-year legacy he had enjoyed with his brothers and cousins was no more.

Instead, his vast land holdings were his legacy to his children. He willingly paid the taxes on the Kirkland property bequeathed them by Mary Ann. Florrie wrote to her father thanking him for his help: "Many thanks for offering to attend to our tax papers. It is most kind of you to trouble yourself over them. I was hoping to be able to sell some of the land, but from what Clara says there is no chance yet awhile, so must wait. I thought if some of the land could have been sold, then you could keep the money in payment for the taxes. After all these years, we must owe you a lot of money."[45]

Jessie and Ralph found finances difficult during their early years also. Ralph wrote to Peter, "Jessie & I have talked it over and we think it will be better for you to foreclose on those lots as it is impossible for us to pay the assessments in time. I have tried to collect some debts but can not."[46] Peter did not let them give up so easily. A month later, another letter indicated a new deal had been struck, and ownership of the lots remained intact.[47]

Twenty-three—Dampening Down the Furnaces

Sometime before his son's wedding in 1914, Peter Sr. moved from Deer Lodge, possibly prompted by ill health. As early as 1911, Peter's debility popped up in newspaper gossip and family correspondence.[1] The illnesses ranged from severe, lasting several days, to seasonal colds that crippled him.[2] The winter months confined him indoors during the harshest weather. With his daughters married and living away, there was no one to care for him except the domestic help. He employed a husband-and-wife team, Mr. and Mrs. Kawasaki, to help with the housework and outside duties, such as maintaining the large garden at Deer Lodge.[3]

Increasingly, Peter visited Fanny in Friday Harbor, eventually moving in with her and her family. During the early months of 1914, Vic Capron attended a six-week post-graduate medicine course in San Francisco.[4] His absence may have compelled Peter to move in to help Fanny but concerns over Peter's health could have also factored into the decision. Fanny and Victor's full and active house, with their two children and the two Bell nieces, stood in stark contrast to the quiet emptiness of Deer Lodge. The young ladies hosted parties. Vivian Bell gave piano lessons and entertained a suitor.[5] Fanny was a charter member of the Women's Study Club, which rotated meetings among the members' houses.[6] The Caprons also entertained friends with card parties. Dr. Capron entered politics, suggesting there must have been lively debates and campaigning at the home.[7] Before leaving the busy household, Peter's oldest granddaughter, Vivian, married Alfred Middleton. Peter played the wedding march by his favorite composer, Mendelssohn, for the September ceremony at the Capron house.[8]

Earlier in the summer, Peter Kirk bought over an acre of land in the same block as the Capron household, paying $440 in gold coin to J. L.

Blair.[9] The property sat along Park Street near its intersection with Blair Avenue. Peter proceeded to build a modern bungalow with the help of J. A. Scribner, an early pioneer of San Juan Island.[10] Scribner was a highly acclaimed carpenter and grandfather to Cora Scribner, Peter Jr's new bride. By the end of August, Peter's new house neared completion. "It will be one of the finest residences in the city [which will] embody the latest design in bungalow architecture," hailed the local paper.[11] The craftsman-style house included the graceful, curved rooflines of Japanese-style architecture popular at the time.

The modest two-bedroom cottage suited Peter. Its stately design sported 11-foot ceilings, stained-glass windows, dark wood beams, and a granite fireplace in the living area. A large kitchen adjoined a wood-paneled dining room containing another fireplace. A separate little office occupied part of the wrap-around deck.

Figure 14 Peter Kirk home in Friday Harbor
Peter Kirk's bungalow in Friday Harbor, circa unknown. It is a bed & breakfast, located at 595 Park Street. Photo shared by Doug & Roxey Kasman.

"I am enclosing you a picture of your new house that Cora took before we left Friday Harbor," wrote Peter Jr. to his father after he moved in. "We showed it to Dr. O'Connell & he likes it very much. He has a nice picture, an enlarged photograph of the Parliament Buildings in Victoria he is going to have framed & sent to you to put up in your new house."[12]

Always an important part of Peter's life, music filled his new home. A piano or organ may have occupied space near the south-facing bay window. Peter had a proclivity for modern devises, and he probably placed the elegantly crafted graphophone he purchased after Mary Ann's death in a corner of the living room. He shopped the Sears & Roebuck catalog for other items for the new house.[13]

Living in Friday Harbor, Peter had access to the local piped water system. Telephone service was available as well. He made regular payments to Friday Harbor Packing Company for fish, to R. Bowler for groceries, and to Ed King or the creamery for his dairy products. He paid San Juan Agricultural Company for chicken feed. He may have had a home garden, perhaps with fruit trees and strawberries like his other homes.[14]

He paid Miss Lillian Rethlefsen a regular salary as his housekeeper, but she would not have been the only one helping Peter since his family resided nearby. Fanny lived on the same Blair Avenue block; a stone's throw away. His granddaughter Vivian and husband Alfred also lived close by, at the corner of Blair and Reed, after they returned from their honeymoon.[15] For a time, Clara and her toddler, Fanny, resided with Peter, while husband, Pearl, traveled.[16]

Peter's sons-in-law may have visited only occasionally, as they were often busy. Fanny's husband, Dr. Capron, had served as a Friday Harbor councilman, then its mayor. Expanding his public service to the state level, he became a legislator soon after Peter moved into the bungalow.[17] Clara's husband, Pearl Morrill, attained a clerk and stenographer position in the legislature.[18] The two men spent the legislative sessions in Olympia. Olive's husband, Captain D'Arcy, was often away from home piloting boats in the islands, particularly during the fishing season.[19]

Selling the Constance

After moving to Friday Harbor from Deer Lodge, Peter sold the *Constance* for $2,300, which according to some was an amount far less than what he had paid for the yacht.[20] Months later, the Seattle buyer,

Mr. Pontius, found fault with the purchase, claiming the launch was in ill repair. He complained to Peter Kirk and they renegotiated the sale, agreeing Kirk would refund a portion of the amount tendered to the Seattle buyer. However, Kirk delayed Pontius' refund, further inciting him over the apparent unfairness of Kirk's treatment. Pontius issued more complaints:

> Now I ask you again do you think it is fair to delay the sale of a boat that I purchased in good faith from you. A boat that was to be delivered once in good condition, but was not. I asked you to take the boat back & refund my money but this, it seems, you did not want to do. I then agreed to except $500.00 & call it square, now you ask me to wait two or three months for my money, I can't understand the fairness in this…a man in your position in the business world must surely have $500.00, or if not, can readily raise it to liquidate an honest and just claim. I did not ask you to wait one moment after you delivered the boat for your money and I am surely entitled to the same treatment at your hands.[21]

Kirk further disgruntled Pontius when a promised check failed to appear. In December, he wrote with a more honeyed approach:

> Your letter of Nov 27/14, in which you state you will send in a check in a few days, was received by me about a month ago. I have not, as yet, received the check. I should have answered your letter before, but kept postponing the matter thinking the check would arrive, and I could acknowledge receipt of both at the same time. It just occurred to me that perhaps you were waiting for a reply from me before mailing the check, hence this letter. Wishing you & yours a happy New Year and awaiting your reply.[22]

Peter had agreed in their first exchange of letters that he would refund the money by January 15, 1915.[23] Apparently, he meant to keep his word.

Loss of an old friend

Walter Winston Williams may have been Peter's best friend. They were associated as early as 1874 when they both sang bass for the Workington Glee Society.[24] It is not known when he first joined one of Peter's enterprises, but it may have been in those early years. All told, Williams remained a trusted business associate for many decades. Documents concerning the Kirkland startup usually named Kirk as a director or executive, closely followed by W. W. Williams, who often signed as secretary, treasurer, or both.

Even after the mill failure, Kirk and Williams remained close, professionally and in friendship. At one point, Williams wrote concerning some business but added a personal note asking, "When are you coming down? Business is very dull and not promising. Politics at the bottom [of it] no doubt."[25] Curiously, when Peter wrote to Walter, he addressed him as *Mr. Williams*. One can imagine the lively discussions between these two intelligent men when they called on one another. When they exhausted the topics of the day, music graced the hall, both men being gifted and adept.

Music filled Williams' life even more than Peter Kirk's. A family friend noted, "The Williamses, the Kirks and the Rosses [Walter's daughter, Freda's family] were all musical (Lannie—Lancelot Ross, for example, was the star of *Show Boat*) and in an earlier day the Williams home in Seattle was headquarters for Sir Harry Lauder when he played Seattle. And what music would be made (with bagpipes, too) after performances!"[26]

Surely, grief overwhelmed Kirk when he learned of Williams' death of a heart attack in March 1915 at his Seattle home. He may have taken solace in knowing Williams had enjoyed a Welsh concert in downtown Seattle the same evening he passed.[27] Williams, himself a Welshman, left a widow and eight children. Florrie Kirk Dixon wrote to her father expressing the concern they all must have felt, "Clara tells me in her letter that you have lost your old friend Mr. Williams, you would be sorry it would be a great shock to Mrs. Williams, being so sudden & an invalid herself."[28]

The Great War erupts

Florrie's letter went on with more sad news as she wrote about her family's experience in war-ravaged England. The First World War had erupted the summer Peter built his Friday Harbor bungalow. Surely, he was terrified for his daughter and the rest of his family living in England after reading her letter:

> Everything here is very bad owing to the war. One has to be very careful, as we don't know how long it may last, so we don't want to spend any more money than necessary. Everything is getting very dear & scarce, but still we have a lot to be thankful for, as if it had not been for our grand navy, I am afraid my land would soon have been starved out. I don't like the towns darkened, I was frightened the last time in Manchester; the place is so dark there is danger of getting run over. It is necessary to darken all places now, on account of Zeppelins flying over & dropping bombs. The war is dreadful; you will be interested to read all about it in our papers.[29]

"[Maurice] talks very seriously about the war, & has learned so much geography," Florrie added. "One day he said to me, 'Mother I hope when the next war comes I will be too old to fight.' Poor boy he has heard of so many of the horrors of it. Then he said they can't take my Dad to fight—any way as he is too delicate, & then Lucile said, 'that is one consolation in having a delicate father.' This war is too terrible is it not?"[30]

Opening of the Fribor

Despite the grim war news, Peter facilitated some levity by granting newlyweds Vivian and Alfred Middleton a loan in 1915 to build the Fribor Theater. Since the fall of 1912, Alfred had been proprietor of the Star Theater.[31] Family myths advanced the notion Alfred needed a piano player to lend emotional impact to his silent movies.[32] Whether he hired Vivian Bell for the job is unknown, but she did play at the Star Theater after their marriage.

With the seed money from Peter, the Middletons bought property on Spring Street and built a new theater, grand in scale and elegance compared to the Star Theater. They called it the Fribor Theater, taking the first and last syllables of Friday Harbor to form the name. They completed construction by the end of the summer. Peter's taste for high quality and luxury may have influenced the design and decor of the theater. It had new opera chairs of the latest design, state of the art technology for the projector, and a dual-purpose stage for 'photoplays,' large enough for live presentations.[33]

Peter most assuredly attended the grand opening on October 7, 1915, with the rest of the family. The Caprons may have chauffeured him in their automobile, all dressed to the nines for the celebration. They probably enjoyed "House of a Thousand Candles" in the special 35-cent box seats, while hundreds of fellow islanders attended the opening with 20-cent general admission tickets.[34]

Twenty-four—The Final Battle

In early 1916, Old Man Winter proved particularly testy in the Pacific Northwest, breathing a crisp northeast wind over the snow-packed Cascade Range, and causing lakes to freeze in the Puget Sound area.[1] In the midst of the cold snap, mountainous waves roiled the waters around the San Juan Islands. In January, record-breaking snowfalls pummeled the area. In the first half of February, the area received more snow that lasted longer than any other snowfall ever recorded in the previous twenty-five years. Rarer still in the temperate Pacific Northwest, where snows usually melt in a day or two, three feet of snow remained on the ground for weeks, lingering in shady places into March.[2]

Dubbed 'The Mother of All Storms,' the 1916 blizzard wreaked havoc in its path.[3] The great quantity of wet, heavy snow collapsed roofs. The island's milkman had to use a sled on the main roads, carrying a big metal milk can on a saddled horse to deliver to folks living along the smaller tracks.[4] The tempest offered no sympathy even for the lambs. Sheep ranchers, undoubtedly including Peter Kirk's Deer Lodge operation, experienced considerable loss to their flocks.

The bad weather caused other disruptions. The theater closed, ironically delaying the showing of "The Diamond of the Sky."[5] Stormy seas prevented the mail boat from its rounds to Bellingham. Fierce winds caused the cancellation of school. However, the children stayed busy indoctrinating themselves into Old Man Winter's game. They rallied on Friday Harbor's main avenue, Spring Street, and threw snowballs at the already miserable pedestrians.

Old Man Winter hurled a final icy spear by facilitating the spread of influenza, which confined many Friday Harbor residents to their homes,

Peter Kirk among them.[6] The comfort of his new home could not heal his aging body, nor could the proximity of his daughters ward off the severe effects of the weather. Peter had been ill since Christmas with several extended bouts of bronchitis and flu.[7] His ill health persisted for months.

Peter's bold, decisive script remained legible, but his hand was shaky. In his last weeks, others, presumably family members, responded to his incoming mail. His mind remained sharp and he kept abreast of new ideas with a subscription to the *Mentor Magazine*, a publication that described itself as intent on helping readers "to acquire useful knowledge…in art, literature, science, history, nature and travel."[8]

Kirk also continued his business endeavors. In early May, a man selling stock in Hyde Ship Brake Company wished him well in his recovery from bronchitis but quickly got to the point: "You seemed to think that it is a bigotry for you to pay in full."[9] The man offered a final price of 100 shares at 75 cents each if Kirk bought before May 6. After that date, the broker guaranteed the shares would be worth $1.00 each. A deal was struck.

The freshness of spring and warm hopes of the San Juan summer failed to rekindle Peter's health. His breathing remained strained as it passed over bluish lips caused by his compromised circulation. Chest pains and palpitations may have been more frequent. Applying a stethoscope to his heart and hearing the labored beats amid the sound of backwashing, like a modern washing machine, the doctors knew the diagnosis immediately: a leaky mitral heart valve.[10] The symptoms were probably evident for years. This time, Peter's family expressed fear he might not recover.

Another spell of cool weather with wind and rain planted itself over San Juan Island in early May.[11] Undeterred by the weather, the 76-year-old patriarch was out of bed for a few days, but then his heart finally failed. On a cloudy and blustery day, Peter Kirk passed away mid-morning on May 4, 1916.[12]

The following Saturday, the same dreary weather beset the Episcopalian services held at the family residence.[13] Peter's body had been prepared for an open casket viewing held (according to family lore) at

Peter's Park Street bungalow. Afterward, the mortician's fine new hearse conveyed Peter's casket amid heavy rain and sorrow to Valley Cemetery.[14] A somber procession of black horse-drawn buggies and early model automobiles followed, carrying many friends and family to the Kirk family plot overlooking a quiet valley of farms. Forested hills and small pockets of fir trees, maple, alder, oak, and cedar enclosed the valley. Wrapped in a grey blanket of grief, his devoted family buried Peter beside his wife Mary Ann.

"The loss of so good a man is indeed great to both his immediate family and those closely associated with him, and I myself am feeling the loss very keenly," responded a family member (possibly Dr. Victor Capron) to an associate's condolences. "After having been associated with him so closely and knowing him so well, I doubt very much if I could feel the loss greater if he had been my own father. It is my fondest hope that I may be able to develop some of his good qualities in the years to come, and at his age have as many friends and so few enemies."[15]

Conclusion

Peter Kirk's inventive mind went quiet, but its influences did not. Throughout his life, his intellect allowed him to look at problems from different angles. He did not have to accept the status quo—he found a new solution. His efforts were akin to the music he created at the piano or organ. His mind invented a new string of notes and his fingers followed. Likewise, with his businesses—he thought something, and his actions made it so.

He developed efficiency models and new products, shoring up his enterprises during times of recession. His early achievements and proclivity for quality paved the way for Moss Bay Iron & Steel, Ltd. of England to be one of the last steel mills operating in Workington, surviving well into the 20th century. As the world transitioned their machines from coal and steam to crude oil, he positioned himself on the cutting edge.

In the Pacific Northwest, Peter Kirk orchestrated a working relationship with competing railroads and mine owners. His perseverance in his plans to build a steel mill achieved results that benefitted two feuding towns: Seattle got the plant and a new suburb; Tacoma won the Pacific Investment Company's coal freighting business. Kirk's huge project ignited worldwide attention for Seattle. His steel mill venture launched development along the east shore of Lake Washington, including more transportation, industry, and a stable community.

Even though the steel mill never produced an ingot, Peter Kirk's peers continued to seek his expertise. Former British colleagues remembered his proficiency decades after his departure from Workington. One referred an executive of the US & Canada Steel Company to Peter Kirk when the firm hoped to develop a mill in the Seattle area in 1915. Kirk's knowledge of Washington's resources proved invaluable.[1] Investors interested in resurrecting the Irondale plant in the early part of the century commissioned Peter to investigate the ironworks, take an inventory of the machinery, evaluate its condition, and offer recommendations on making the plant operational. His report underscored his eye for detail; proclivity for efficiency; and extensive knowledge of a variety of machinery, operations, practices, and raw materials.[2] In a separate consultation months before his death, he had received inquiries from potential developers concerning the Denny iron ore quality and "the best way to treat it," a nod to the successful hotshortness solution he and his brothers devised for Workington's ore.[3]

When Burke and Farrar offered to buy out his interest in the town site tract in Kirkland, Kirk agreed he could use the money. "But I have no worry concerning the future of that property," he stated, affirming his belief in "the bright future he had always predicted for the entire east shore of Lake Washington."[4] Indeed, as early as 1889, one source noted Kirk was developing "a great business as a land agent."[5] In those early years, his efforts concentrated on building an industrial center, only some of it realized. Kirkland, with its unique location and design, was the womb in which Peter incubated his hope for the future. Over one hundred years later, Kirkland is a bustling town within a sprawling city. Once called a bedroom community to Seattle, its modern neighborhoods are stacked with trophy homes, its business district lined with quaint shops and gourmet restaurants.

Peter Kirk also knew success hinged on the opening of the Lake Washington Ship Canal. He watched its progress and knew of its proposed completion. Echoing his own thoughts, his daughter Florrie wrote to him, "Fanny says the canal is nearly complete now so the land is sure to increase in value."[6]

Even as he lay dying, Peter Kirk believed he "could leave his friends confident that his predictions concerning the country across Lake Washington would soon be fulfilled."[7] The Canal officially opened one year later.

The prize of overall success in America was won, but at a heavy cost. Ashamed he had disappointed his investors when the steel mill failed, Peter Kirk's pride prevented him from returning to his homeland in England. For that, he never again saw his sister, Ann, her children, or her husband, Charles Valentine, Peter's long time business associate. He did not see his brothers Henry and Thomas or their families again. It may have pained him more not seeing his daughter Florence, her husband Louis, or their two children whom he never met. Florrie penned her yearning a year before Peter died: "I wish I could see you, Lucile & Maurice don't know any of you. But they know you all well enough by name as I talk so much about you all!"[8]

Instead of returning to England, Kirk opted to live in a place reminiscent of his Derbyshire boyhood home, Chapel-en-le-Frith. Both places were islands of sorts, the first kept secluded by craggy mountains, the other by the sea. The pastoral landscape of grassy fields dotted with sheep surely burned in his memory, as did the smell of those fields after a rain washed over the temperate landscape.

Peter Kirk rests in a spot where, at sunset on a particular autumn day, the distant honking of a small flock of Canada geese breaks the valley silence as they rise on the warm westward currents. The sound fades as they collect themselves into a familiar V-shape formation and cross the open valley. Westminster chimes ring out each hour from the white chapel in the cemetery followed by a selection of pre-recorded songs. Pressing forward, the geese pass fifty feet above the Valley Cemetery, barely clearing the steeple. As they depart, a subtle breeze stirs the grass surrounding the Kirk family plot. Is it the beating of their wings or an errant waft of wind making its way from the Salish Sea? The last notes of the hymn "In the Garden" plays from the church spire's speaker as the geese fly with heavy, purposeful wings toward the ocean shore where Peter Kirk first landed in 1886, bringing his own strong determination and pioneering spirit.

"He accomplished a big thing," noted a former Kirkland resident, "though it was not the thing he intended. The best part of his work lives."[9]

What mattered were not the moneys gained and lost, nor the waxing and waning of Kirkland's industry. To Peter Kirk, "This is only a drop in a bucket to launch so rosy an undertaking."[10]

Appendix A–Peter Kirk Ancestors

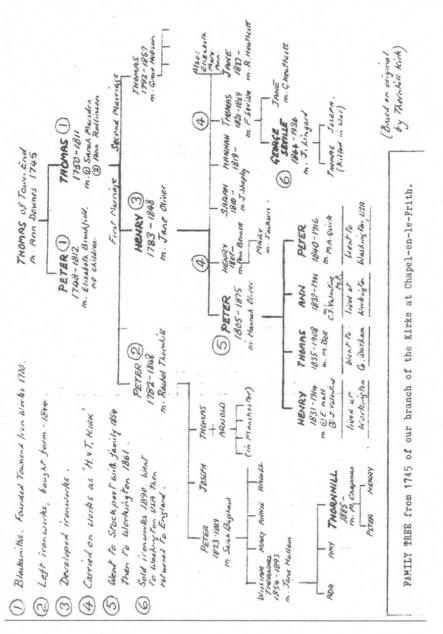

Figure 15 "Thomas Kirk of Town End" Family Chart

Appendix B—Kirk Children & Other Family Stories

The close ties developed between Peter and Mary Ann and their children remained throughout their lives. Florence always kept in touch with letters to her parents and siblings in America. Likewise, the American siblings stayed close through letters or proximity, their lives were interwoven. The Kirk siblings resided on San Juan Island during the 1940 census.[1] All the sisters lived together in Friday Harbor at Fanny's house, drawn together in their grief over multiple deaths. In only a few months, three men died: Pearl Morrill in September 1939, and both Ralph Charlton and Marie's husband, James Bell, in January 1940. Extended family revered Olive, Fanny, Clara, and Jessie as the "Aunties" and considered them the matriarchal figures of the family. They were renowned for their kindness, cookies, and other baked goods.

Figure 16 Aunts Fanny, Jessie & Olive, 1942
Photo by Vivian Middleton

Florence & Louis Dixon

Figure 17 Louis, Florence, Maurice & Lucile Dixon
Photo courtesy of Kirkland Heritage Society, circa 1908.

Life was difficult in England for Florrie and Louis Dixon's family. Louis worked hard despite many health issues. Florrie's letters to her American family often included details of Louis' health, directly affected by a stressful work environment and his strong work ethic. The pressure aged him prematurely. Florrie despaired of his health and their situation, "He has no energy and seems weak. His moustache is almost white and his hands so thin. He seems to be in a bad way…He cannot remember people's names…He has simply slaved all these years. And we have only taken from the business bare living expenses and done without things…I believe if Auntie had not given Louis these Swiss holidays he would have died long since."[2]

They endured the First World War only to have their lives broken up again with World War II also. They suffered through more bombings, rationing, fear, and hardship. Florrie's son, Maurice, and his family had their

London home destroyed in a German bombing raid that lasted throughout the night. Florrie wrote to her sister Fanny, "A bomb dropped in an upstairs room, and before anything could be done, the place was a raging furnace. Bombs were dropping all around them. Water was scarce, for the water system had been damaged. They saved a few things. A neighbor took them in until they found a place ten miles away in the country where they are boarding. Their home was destroyed, but as long as they are safe—nothing else matters. It was a night of horror, but they are not down-hearted."[3]

Despite the hardships, Louis and Florrie lived into their seventies. They celebrated their 50th wedding anniversary before Louis died in 1944; Florence followed in 1949.[4] After their deaths, their daughter, Florence Lucile, visited her Kirk relatives in Friday Harbor, getting to know them for the first time.

Olive & Frank D'Arcy

"Olive was an accomplished artist and craftswoman, as well as a musician," recalled Kirk descendant Christine Bergman.[5] "Olive designed and constructed a number of pieces of furniture in split bamboo and rush matting popular in the 1920's. She also enjoyed carving and embroidery. As an oil painter she did still-life and figurative work that had the charm of the Italian life she enjoyed on travels to Europe." Olive's musical talent had surfaced early in life. She sketched out songs on the letterhead of Kirkland's Moss Bay and Steel Company in the early years of that endeavor. In 1916, she published two songs: "Song of San Juan" and "In Dreamland."[6]

Frank D'Arcy was described as "one of the most popular and worthy young men of the state."[7] Born in Australia to a Nova Scotia mariner and his English wife, who farmed near LaConnor, Frank followed his father into the mariner trade.[8] "Frank was a captain of some of the local ferries and other boats in the area," recalled Kirk descendant Dan Morrill.[9]

Frank also skippered the *Calcite* after it returned to service in February 1910.[10] McMillin kept the tug and her crew busy. Captain D'Arcy hauled cedar log booms, water loads, and scows of other materials and supplies. He ferried McMillin to Rosario on business trips and pleasure excursions around Henry Island and Victoria. The *Calcite* took a crowd to Bellingham to hear Reverend Billy Sunday as the Earth passed through the tail of Halley's Comet.[11] Perhaps Olive was aboard.

Sometime after that, Frank and Olive began their romance. While away, Frank wrote many postcards to her. He once penned on the back of a white rose postcard addressed to Miss Olive Kirk of Roche Harbor, "From a marooned sailor."[12] Another reassured Olive, "We are still wind bound. But our chances are good we will get away in morning. All is well."[13]

Marriage preparations came at summer's end in 1911 for Olive and Frank. She ordered a new dress and coat from a Seattle dressmaker. The shop mistakenly shipped these items to the wrong address instead of Jessie's Ballard home, and she feared her wedding garments were lost. The dress shop finally located the parcel in the next block. A boy was quickly dispatched to retrieve it, and the shop promptly sent it to Olive.[14]

The couple exchanged vows in September in Bellingham before a Justice of the Peace.[15] The marriage was the second for Frank, 49, and a first for Olive, 41. The corresponding newspaper announcement described Olive as "one of the most charming, accomplished and popular young ladies of San Juan County...who draws about her a circle of friends the warp and woof of whose friendship will last as long as life."[16]

After a short wedding trip, Mr. and Mrs. D'Arcy returned to Deer Lodge where they resided for a time.[17] They shared the house with Olive's father and her brothers Peter Jr. and Arnold. Olive and Frank both had land at Griffin Bay where they operated a ranch.

A letter from her Nantucket friend in 1912 gave the first indication of a nervous condition from which Olive suffered. She wrote, "Oh, so sorry to hear of all the trouble and anxiety you have been experiencing!"[18] Later, Olive wrote to her father and described her suffering in detail, "I am very little better...I have almost had nervous prostration & have been frightened of nothing. Frank has had to change our plans because of my health & will not take me out to the farm for winter, as it is too lonely. So, he is going to have the Walrod house fixed up for a few months & he can ride over to the farm every day to his work. I am sorry he has to be away two nights just now. But I will get someone here to keep me company for I get so nervous when night comes."[19]

Frank's maritime work kept them on the move. They relocated to Anacortes when he accepted a position with the Coast Fish Company as master of their tug, and they returned to Friday Harbor after the fishing seasons.[20]

Beyond the yard and a small orchard where Peter built his Friday Harbor house, Olive and Frank built one of her own design.[21] They enjoyed traveling to St. Martin's Hot Springs in Skamania County for the treatment of Frank's rheumatism, sometimes staying for weeks at a time.[22] During the last ten years of his life, Frank mastered the *Fearless*, tending various fish canneries around the Salish Sea.[23]

Captain D'Arcy quite suddenly succumbed to death in January 1929 in Friday Harbor at age 66. The local paper reported he was "in his usual good health and less than an hour before his death was down town chatting with acquaintances. On his way home he stopped at Dr. Capron's office for the mail and proceeded to the Capron home where he passed away while visiting with members of the family."[24] The heart attack took him instantly and left the family in shock.

Olive continued to live near Fanny and visited the many family members in Friday Harbor. "If any of the family were up for some reason late at night, or even at 2 a.m.," remembered her niece, Barbara Dickinson, "Auntie 'O' would be sure to be out, mailing a letter or some such, and would drop in for a chat."[25]

After an extended illness involving heart problems, a heart attack finally took Hannah Oliver Kirk D'Arcy in September 1944 at the age of 74 years.[26] The family held Episcopalian services for her in Bellingham. Olive's cremated remains joined her husband Frank and his D'Arcy family in an Anacortes, Washington cemetery.

Marie & James Bell

Figure 18 James & Marie (Kirk) Bell family
1899, James holding Charlotte, Marie standing with Vivian, Clarence sitting on floor.
Photo courtesy of Kirkland Heritage Society.

Marie's musical legacy continued down the generations. Marie's daughter Vivian won a piano in a grocery store contest and gave lessons as early as 1913.[27] She played the piano for the silent movies she and her husband Alfred featured in their theatres, the Star and Fribor. Vivian, Alfred, and their older children all played in various local bands for dances on the island. She often wrote songs; as her youngest son well remembered during WWII she titled one tune "Knock the Hit out of Hitler."[28]

Marie and Jimmie's son, Clarence, possessed a beautiful voice and sang at family gatherings. Clarence's grandson had a talent for the pipe organ and received lessons. He learned quickly, and the instructor soon had to inform his parents he had exceeded the instructor's abilities.[29]

"Mother loved to sing," recalled Barbara Dickinson of Charlotte, the youngest Bell child. "Singing was the way we passed the time in the long drives from Montana to Seattle and Friday Harbor. The love of music was always there in the family and evident in the next generation, as I remember vacation times on the Island with the adults congregating around the piano while the kids were put to bed—oh, I remember trying to get warm under the heavy homemade quilts. Mother would be leading the singing, Aunt Vivian on the piano, and Uncle Alfie with his sax. They would sing the night away until time to catch the early morning ferry."[30]

Marie's unmarked grave

For almost eighty years, Marie Kirk Bell's grave in the Kirkland Cemetery remained unmarked, the town founder's daughter, who died so young, nearly forgotten. But one local historian remembered. Dave Cantrill conducted walking tours in the cemetery and told local history stories of the founding families. He always stopped by the empty space where Marie rested.

One of Marie's grandsons, Morris Middleton, was interested in his family's history. When he discovered his grandmother's grave remained unmarked, he hatched a plan to provide a headstone for her. He enlisted the aid of his brother, Gordon, his cousin Joan (Bell) Smith, and possibly other cousins to put a marker on her grave.[31]

On a typical walking tour in the summer of 1981, Cantrill was pleased to discover a blue pearl headstone marked Marie's grave.[32] He was unaware of the Middleton effort. In 2003, as suddenly as it had appeared, it disappeared.[33] A marred swath of grass and a depression were all that remained, leaving Cantrill incredulous as to why someone would steal her headstone. Years later, he learned the truth. Thinking Marie should rest with her loved ones in the Kirk family plot on San Juan Island, Morris Middleton attempted to exhume her remains, recalled his daughter MaryJo Mazick. Unable to locate a coffin, Morris instead took some dirt and her stone. Before placing it in the family plot on San Juan Island, he added details of her husband, James Bell, to the headstone.[34]

After Marie's death, James Bell had continued as an active businessman in Kirkland. He was one of the charter members of the Kirkland Commercial Club (KCC), begun in the spring of 1907.[35] The KCC encouraged development of Lake Washington's eastside business community. Later, Jimmie wore a multitude of hats as a Notary Public, fire insurance salesman, and realtor.[36] When he moved to North Bend, he managed the town's telephone utility and continued to own the Lake Washington Telephone Company for several more years.[37] After living in North Bend for some time, he moved around the Seattle area, working in real estate.

Jimmie Bell died in 1940, and his remains were cremated.[38] Vivian tucked away her father's ashes in the Middleton attic, where the urn collected dust and became fodder for ghost stories. Her son Gordon remembered playing with a box that rattled in the attic. He would take his friends up there to play and shake the box at his friend. "What's that?" a friend would ask. "My grandfather," Gordon replied. "What's rattling in there?" asked the friend. "His teeth!" Gordon mischievously exclaimed.[39] Vivian later spread her father's ashes in a corner of her garden under a rose bush.

Fanny & Victor Capron

Fanny and Vic Capron had two children: Marjorie, born in 1903, and Victor Jr., born in 1908.[40] Fanny's aunt Emily Quirk wrote in a letter to Mary Ann, "How interesting little Marjorie seems in her ways, & how she can imitate her father."[41] Marjorie's granddaughter, Christine Bergman, remembered her Capron relatives: "Both [Marjorie and Vic Jr.] were very proper, calm and reserved but had a wonderful dry sense of humor. They loved to laugh…Both were musicians. Marjorie played the piano and sang; Vic played the saxophone. They performed for the local dances with a small band."[42]

Victor Capron facilitated many improvements to Friday Harbor, including a city water piping system.[43] Fanny's involvement in civic and church organizations throughout her life complemented her husband's career in politics. Fanny was a charter member of the Women's Study Club in Friday Harbor. She and her husband also helped launch the Eastern Star Lodge when it organized in 1911.[44]

Figure 19 Capron family with Shetland ponies
Photo courtesy of Kirkland Heritage Society. Vivian & Charlotte Bell with saddled ponies, Dr. Capron and possibly James Bell on stairs, Fanny Kirk Capron and Marjorie with unsaddled pony, unknown lady at top of stairs, possibly Clara Kirk.

On their expansive acreage near Cady Mountain, Fanny and Victor raised award-winning Shetland ponies for many years. One shipment of prized stock was big news in town: "...half the children in town have been to see the new baby Shetland colt...It is a beauty, and so tiny as to almost be carried in the arms of a child."[45]

Fanny's niece, Charlotte Bell Westerman (referred to as Tottie) remembered children riding the ponies. Her daughter Barbara recalled the stories told to her by her mother. "They were so tame they would follow anyone anywhere, just like little dogs. [They] even had to be discouraged from going in the house. Tottie remembered 'Merry Legs' getting frisky, kicking up her heels, and luckily, just missing Tottie's head in the kick as she was standing in a depression on the ground."[46]

Dr. Capron's career included stints as city council member and mayor, county health officer, and state representative.[47] While in the legislature, he introduced a bill to funnel San Juan County's share of vehicle fuel taxes to maintain the islands' roads. The county had no federal or state roads that benefited from the fuel taxes residents paid, nor did they have direct access to Olympia, he argued. The Capron Act passed in 1919, and later those funds transferred to the Washington State Ferry system, which continues to benefit island residents to this day.

Vic Capron died in 1934, while Fanny remained in their Blair Street home for two more decades, passing away in 1956.[48]

The capers of Doc Capron

Victor James Capron, a native of New York, moved to San Juan Island with his first wife after they had lived in Hawaii for several years.[49] There, he had been a government physician and served as resident physician on a sugar plantation.[50]

Being one of the only doctors in the San Juan Islands made Capron a well-known man, but his exploits off-duty also contributed to his notoriety. Before Fanny entered the picture, he seemed a bit accident-prone, his good nature on display as the county newspaper enumerated many mishaps with his fine gray horse, Murphy.[51]

The brake was often the culprit in these tales. After Capron and a friend capsized his boat off Henry Island in the summer of 1899, he received yet more attention for an incident on the road. "Dr. Capron met with another mishap with his buggy on the road to Friday Harbor," the local paper reported. "His 'brake' capsized, somewhat in the manner that his boat did the previous week and he was dragged along the road by his horse, 'Murphy,' for some distance in a rather ungraceful way. The cart was a little disfigured, but not so much so as when it upset with the Stuart Island election returns. It is reported that it can be purchased now at less than cost."[52]

At one point, Doc Capron went missing. Again, the local paper added a little side story at his expense: "Lost, strayed, or stolen, while trying to find the old Cady mountain road last Friday between the hours of four and seven p.m.—one doctor, mounted on a gray horse called Murphy. The finder, of either the doctor or Murphy, will be suitably rewarded. Later— The doctor viewed the landscape o'er from many hill-tops and finally found his way on foot to Isaac Sandwith's, and the next morning Joe went out and brought Murphy safe into Camp."[53]

After all the mishaps with Murphy in his younger days, it is no wonder Capron jumped at alternate modes of transportation. He bought a nice launch with 3-horsepower Palmer gas-powered engine that reportedly got him from Roche Harbor to Friday Harbor in only an hour and 40 minutes.[54] Later, he was one of the first on the island to own a motorcycle and an automobile.

But even the launch failed him at times. Peter Kirk's *Constance* came in handy when Victor Capron's own launch malfunctioned in the dreary month of February. Dr. Capron had gone to Waldron Island on business. On his way home in the evening, his engine quit near Limestone Point. Unable to restart it, he drifted back to Waldron in heavy rain and wind. In his new boat, Peter Kirk retrieved him a couple days later.[55]

Peter Jr. & Cora (Scribner) Kirk

Peter Kirk Jr. grew into a tall, handsome man of medium build. His brown wavy hair made his gray eyes even more striking.[56] Peter Jr. suffered from asthma and often traveled to drier climes for relief.[57] He received his education in Los Angeles, California.[58] Described as a very striking woman, Cora Y. Scribner, born in 1886 in Michigan, was the oldest child of eleven born to longtime local residents Edward and Alice Scribner.[59] The boat-building family moved to San Juan Island in the early 1890s with Edward's parents and siblings. "Cora lived in a small log cabin her father built, where six more children were born," shared Scribner cousin, Margie Harn. "The community got together and helped add a wing to the cabin. The night they finished, they had quite a party with fiddling and dancing late into the night. A good time was had by all and the children went to bed in the loft of the main cabin and listened until they fell asleep."[60]

Early on, Cora possessed a helping nature for children.[61] As an adult, she became a schoolteacher, working in various San Juan Island and upper-sound communities. She also harbored a reputation for being a "feisty lady who attended the Seattle World's Fair after a three-day buggy ride when she was only [23] years old," according to Harn.[62]

Peter Jr. and Cora Kirk celebrated the birth of their first child, Peter Warren, in 1918 at Deer Lodge. They sold the Mitchell Bay estate soon after to Theodore Larsen and moved to Kirkland. After their father's death, the family also sold the old family home Fir Grove. The new owners tore it down. Peter Jr. retained three Kirkland lots and built a modern new residence, where their second child, Clara Alice, was born in 1922.[63] Later, they moved to Alderwood Manor, where they had a poultry farm.[64] By 1940, Peter Jr. and Cora had rejoined their families on San Juan Island. He farmed and cut timber close to his sister Clara and Pearl Morrill's farm.[65]

During the WWII years, tragedy struck Peter and Cora's family when their son, Sergeant Peter Warren Kirk, was taken prisoner on April 9, 1942, by Japanese troops in Luzon, Philippines. Warren (as family members called him) wrote a book recounting his ordeal called *Diary of a Bataan Prisoner*. Of reaching the POW camp, he wrote:

> Our first glimpse of the prison camp was from a slight rise in the road, about a mile away, and it surely was one bleak and desolate, dismal, and terrible looking place. We could see high guard-towers along barbed-wire fences and scores and scores of tumbled-down buildings of bamboo with grass roofs. The entire camp looked to be overgrown with long dry grass. So, it was around seven or seven-thirty in the evening that we finally stumbled up to the gates of our prison camp. And I remember thinking at that time, that I was entering a prisoner-of-war camp on my sister's birthday, April 17th (1942).[66]

Warren's medic training helped him survive the horrific Bataan Death March and three years as a POW. American forces liberated the prisoners in 1945. He returned home and received many medals. Warren continued his military career with the Air Force through 1953.

After living for a time in Friday Harbor, Peter and Cora homesteaded in Wenatchee. Peter Jr. died there in September 1951 after surgery and a critical illness lasting two weeks.[67] After losing her husband, Cora moved to Bellingham and lived with her daughter, Alice, later moving to Anacortes near her son Warren. She died in February 1987, at age 100.[68]

Clara & Pearl Morrill

Figure 20 Clara & Fannie Morrill
Circa 1914, photo courtesy of Kirkland Heritage Society.

While eight-year-old Clara Kirk was traveling across Canada to her new home on the Pacific seaboard, her future husband, Pearl Calvin Morrill, was born on the southwestern edge of Nova Scotia in the village of Brooklynn in Yarmouth County.[69] As with many Nova Scotia families, the Morrills depended on the sea for their livelihood. Pearl's father supported the family as a master mariner.

Family lore indicated Pearl and his brothers did not want to follow their father in the shipping business.[70] They moved to Michigan and went into office services such as bookkeeping and typing. Pearl moved further west and worked as a bookkeeper in Baker City, Oregon.[71] Early in 1908, he accepted a job in Roche Harbor as personal secretary of John McMillin, who owned Roche Harbor Lime Company. Pearl befriended the Kirk siblings and occasionally traveled to Victoria with Clara and her brothers during the summer of 1908.[72]

After working for the lime company for nearly a year, Pearl Morrill resigned as stenographer and accepted a similar job in Montana.[73] In 1910, he returned to Ann Arbor, Michigan, and worked with his brother in their typewriting firm.[74] By August, he had filed for a homestead in Coronation, Alberta, from his residence in Calgary.[75]

Pearl soon returned to San Juan Island. Whatever courtship happened between Pearl and Clara in 1908, or by post in the ensuing years, soon came to fruition. In February 1911, Clara, aged 32, and Pearl, 23, married.[76] A decidedly attractive woman, Clara must have been stunning in her pale blue satin wedding gown. Clara's sister Jessie decorated her Ballard home with spring flowers for the evening ceremony.[77]

The Morrill newlyweds took their honeymoon in Victoria and Vancouver then returned to Deer Lodge after a few weeks.[78] Pearl and Clara spent their first winter in Seattle, near Leschi Park, with Pearl taking "his old job with the CPR," according to Clara in a letter to Olive.[79] The couple had a phone, enabling frequent contact with Jessie and Ralph and the rest of the family. They sometimes made the trip to Ballard to spend the day, often joined by their father and other family members.

Family described Clara as having a personality of gold but also strong in perseverance and resilience. Pearl and Clara enjoyed a happy marriage full of laughter and dedication to each other. One family story revealed Pearl's devotion to the Republican Party; as a family joke, Clara would sometimes tell him to calm down or she would vote democratic. According to descendants, Clara and Pearl loved to travel together.[80] Having honeymooned in Vancouver, BC, they returned months later for the coronation celebration of King George V.[81]

After living in Seattle for a year following their wedding, Clara and Pearl had traveled to Alberta to develop Pearl's homestead. Coronation, Alberta sat on the prairie due east of Red Deer, halfway between Calgary and Edmonton. The Canadian government encouraged people to move there by offering homesteads. Pearl used his Canadian birthright to obtain the land.

He made no changes to the land the first year he owned it. After he and Clara moved onto the property in 1911, he cleared 20 acres. The following year, they planted the field and cleared another 55 acres; they also acquired fourteen cattle. The third year, he cropped all 75 acres. Having started with seven horses the first year, he built his herd to twelve by 1913. At one point, he listed a house with a well, a large stone building (probably a barn), and a smaller machine shed as improvements to the property.[82]

Pearl and Clara occasionally traveled to San Juan Island to visit family. After delivering their first child, Francis Constance, in Friday Harbor, Clara moved into the Rethlefsen cottage across from the courthouse while Pearl spent a lot of time in Coronation "holding down the homestead."[83] During the most severe winter months on the Canadian prairie, he likely got away to the coast whenever he could leave the farm. Over the years, he added a three-mile-long fence, a granary, and a straw pig house to the property. Completing the five-year Canadian homesteading requirements, he finally received title to the land in 1914.[84] Pearl and Clara sold the homestead soon thereafter and returned to San Juan Island.

Pearl took a stenographer's position at the state legislature in Olympia in 1915.[85] When absent, Clara and daughter Fannie moved in with her father. The following spring, Clara and Pearl bought two acres of land from Vic and Fanny Capron, adjoining their Blair Avenue property. Pearl wanted to raise chickens on an extensive scale.[86] He eventually bought 144 acres near Trout Lake and engaged in farming as their neighbors did.[87] Pearl and Clara had two more children: Lillian Kirk Morrill in 1917 and Calvin Claire Morrill in 1921.[88]

Pearl enjoyed fishing and hunting, and he often joined locals, including Jack Geoghegan and Edgar Coffelt, for these excursions. On one fishing expedition, spanning several days at Cascade Lake, the men stockpiled over 100 fish between them.[89] In the fall, Pearl joined some of these same men on a hunting party "to the wilds of Orcas Island," where he and most of his companions got their deer.[90] Another Orcas fishing trip with Virgil Frits became quite notorious for other reasons. Dan Morrill related the story told to him by Frits. "Arriving after dark, they started a fire and set up camp with the sleeping bags in the nice dry tent. They finally got to bed in the wee hours. Then all **** broke loose with screaming, yelling, and rushing to get out of the tent. They discovered they had put their tent in the middle of an ant hill and the ants didn't like it at all. Virgil said it was a long two-day fishing trip, sleeping by the fire, and trying to shake all the ants out before they returned home."[91]

Morrill descendants remembered Clara "as being a beautiful piano player and avid music lover. Her singing around the house and at church was fondly remembered by her children and the community. She was a good cook who enjoyed making scones and pastries."[92] Dan Morrill related stories of his Grandma Clara as "a hell of a cook," adding that her bake sale items were a big hit. Dan spoke of stories that painted his Grandpa Pearl as a jokester who enjoyed pulling pranks on people.[93]

Pearl and Clara had a good life on San Juan Island near their many relatives. After Pearl died in 1939, Clara and her young son Calvin moved in with Fanny, and she rented out the farm to Wallace Botsford.[94] Later, she moved to Seattle to live with her daughter Lillian. She died there in August 1946 following an operation for the cancer she had suffered for some time.[95]

Jessie & Ralph Charlton

By the end of summer of 1909, Jessie Kirk had made several trips to Seattle, including one to the AYP Expo.[96] Later in the fall, wearing a hat with a veil fashioned by a local milliner, Jessie and her sister Olive left for

Seattle in the morning of November 16. Jessie, 29, and Ralph Charlton, 43, married later that day, a first for both.[97]

Ralph emigrated from Ontario in 1888, and first appeared in the Seattle area in 1891, living in Ballard with his brother and working as a shingle maker.[98] He continued in various jobs at the shingle mill for many years before changing careers to fishing and piloting a tug.[99] Ralph found his way to the San Juan Islands and mastered the tug *Rescue* for the Friday Harbor Packing Company during the fishing seasons.[100]

When the Charlton machine shop in Ballard was doing well, Jessie wrote to her father, "Ralph is doing fine with the shop. He is so busy he works most of Sundays & does our wood & launch work in the evening…. He has been working hard to get our little launch finished & he was waiting to tell you how it ran…I must try & get him to stop the evening work or he will get sick."[101] Ralph's work included off-season repair work to the fishing fleet.

Other times, life was neither easy nor lucrative for the couple. Jessie's worry about Ralph working himself sick materialized. At age 46, he might have any number of maladies. Their daughter, Ethel Mary, born in 1912, also had some health issues, evident in a 1914 letter from Florrie to their father: "I am sorry Jessie seems to have got such a delicate husband too. I hope things are better now again. Poor Jessie and her little baby girl as well. Fanny says she is not very strong either. Jessie will have her hands full."[102] Ethel remained an only child for over five years until her brother Edward Arnold joined the family in 1917.

Writing to his father-in-law, Ralph explained how the fluidity of the market affected their lives: "I have tried to collect some debts but cannot. When I was sick, there was work here now I am well there is nothing to do. I was crazy when I sold the *Rescue*." A few days later, he writes again, "This is the last of the rush of fishermen work and there is no other work this year. I have not seen it so slack since I started."[103]

The situation failed to improve for the young Charlton family. They took out an $850 loan with Peter in 1915.[104] Days later, Jessie wrote to her father about an injury to Ralph's hand: "Ralph was going to write to you some time ago, but his hand is so bad he really can't. Ralph was disappointed I did not write to you sooner to tell you what we had decided to do with the shop machinery. Ralph won't work in the shop & there is no work even if he could & it is getting spoiled standing idle & we cannot collect any of his bills so today he has arranged to sell it. I am afraid we won't get much out of it. Ralph is hoping he will be able to get a trolling boat. We will transfer your mortgage on either the boat or the tide lot just as you like."[105]

After selling the machine shop, Ralph and Jessie moved, but stayed in Ballard.[106] Ralph continued working as a machinist, master mariner, and eventually a mechanic at a shipyard.[107] About 1920, the Charlton family traveled the full length of the Pacific coast to settle in San Diego, California. Ralph went to work as an auto operator for Peerless Lundy Co. He held several jobs over the years, including delivery of laundry, soft drinks, and cigars.[108] By 1930, Ralph, Jessie, and their children, Ethyl and Edward, moved to Tuolumne County, California, where Ralph worked as a teamster at a lumber mill.[109] There, the family remained until Ralph died in January 1940.[110] Following his death, Jessie moved to Fanny's house in Friday Harbor and lived there for many years.[111]

Family remembered Jessie as being one of the favorite aunts. Her cookie baking skills were highly acclaimed. Grandnephew Gordon Middleton remembered delivering groceries from Middleton's Market to "the aunties" as a teenager.[112] Delicious treats always rewarded his effort. Though Jessie generally had a happy and loving disposition, on occasion her patience was tested. According to Clara's grandson, Dan Morrill, his father, Calvin, at times overstayed his welcome when visiting. Aunt Jessie would say, "I think it is time for you to go, Calvin!"[113]

Jessie remained in Friday Harbor after all her siblings died. Sometime after Fanny and Arnold's deaths in 1956, she moved to California. At first, she lived on the outskirts of Santa Cruz in Soquel.[114] From her home in the mountains, she wrote long and detailed letters about her life.[115] In upbeat tones, she spoke lovingly of how Ethel helped her or took her to the doctor appointments and other daily activities. At the age of 84, Jessie Kirk Charlton died in February 1965, the last of the Kirk immigrants.[116]

Arnold Kirk

Like his older brother Peter Jr., Arnold was a lanky six-foot tall man of slight build, with the same brown hair and gray eyes.[117] Like his father's, Arnold's wavy locks went completely gray before he turned sixty.

Newspaper gossip rarely noted the youngest child of Peter and Mary Ann without mention of an older sibling or brother-in-law. Arnold often stayed with family. He lived in Ballard for a year, possibly working with Ralph Charlton at the machine shop.[118] Most often, he tagged along with Peter Jr. At times, they went into business together. They invested in the Friday Harbor Lumber & Manufacturing Company in 1907, only to have it go into foreclosure a few months later due to insufficient investments.[119] Arnold also helped Peter Jr. with the sheep ranch at Mitchell Bay when their father moved to Friday Harbor. In response to Peter's marriage to Cora, Florrie asked their father, "Will Arnold live with them when he is on shore?"[120]

Arnold remained a bachelor throughout his life, moving about in search of his place in the world. The 1920 census shows him working in San Diego as a marine engineer.[121] By 1930, he was performing general farm work in Ferndale, Washington, where he operated his own chicken ranch throughout the decade.[122] By 1940, Arnold had returned to San Juan Island and was working with Peter Jr. on his farm, cutting cordwood.[123] In 1942, he resided at Roche Harbor, where he worked for Roche Harbor Lime and Cement Company.[124] The following year he hired on at Boeing Aeronautical Corporation, where he worked as an engineer and a boiler operator.[125]

Diagnosed with stomach cancer in September 1952, Arnold continued to work at Boeing until the illness forced him to retire in 1955.[126] He passed away in May 1956, and the family buried him in the Kirk family plot on San Juan Island.

Figure 21 Peter Jr. & Arnold Kirk, 1942
Photo by Vivian Middleton

The Demise of Bankfield

Like many big residences, Bankfield served as a War Department military hospital for the wounded during World War I. Following the Great War, the class system in England was eroding. The Iredale family, who had acquired the mansion after Kirk defaulted on the mortgage, may have considered it a burden to employ added servants to maintain their property and lifestyle.

In 1944, the Borough Council bought Bankfield, then leased it to the National Coal Board, which used one side of the mansion for its offices. In following years, the property bounced back and forth between local and county councils. In the late 1960s, civic leaders discussed using the mansion as a town hall. Bankfield served as a temporary school when one of the local schools burned. One student described it as "bloody freezing, it was."[1] Another remembered having morning assemblies on the two massive staircases in front of huge windows.

Like many old buildings after WWII, Bankfield mansion fell into disrepair. Public facilities were allocated insufficient funds to fix damages, let alone perform upkeep. After all the bombings, priority went to repairing the nation's infrastructure and rebuilding private homes and businesses. Going forward, charitable organizations lacked the resources to save many buildings, no matter the historical or esthetic quality. Even as the city registered Bankfield as a historical building in 1977, it fell into ruin. As the local council put out bids for development, they simultaneously sought permission for demolition.[2]

Bankfield's usefulness did not escape the imaginations of the local Workington youngsters, however. Remembered by locals as "The Mansion," it became a favorite haunt for adventure, "sneaking ciggies" and "ratcheting around."[3] Dares were made to see who could go up the stairs and risk the haunts of the dilapidated old house. One brazen young man admitted spending his lesson time on the roof collecting lead to make fishing weights.[4] The kids climbed the trees and raced bikes down the great expanse of playing fields and the adjoining hill.

Another adventurer remembered, "There's a tree with a rotten branch sticking up vertically in the shape of a human foot and lower leg. As kids, we used to convince ourselves the foot would sometimes point one way, then sometimes another. On darkening late summer nights, with bats whizzing about our heads, we'd sit there watching it to see if we could catch it turning!"[5]

"Hide and seek was not for the faint hearted," volunteered another local, "Especially if you were seeking."[6]

Bankfield was spooky and unsafe. The elements and vandals took their toll. Graffiti defaced the outer walls, and boarded-up windows were broken in. The collapsing roof showed only crossbeams in places. The reinforced concrete Peter Kirk used to build the mansion became its demise.

In the wet environment, the iron tailings rusted, swelled, and disintegrated over time. About 1980, officials finally decided to tear Bankfield down, sparing only the servant's quarters and the carriage house. It would take a month to raze the mansion. Spectators to the event engaged in a lively Facebook discussion in 2013:

"It was so strongly constructed that explosives had to be used," remembered one witness.[7]

"This is very near the end! The left side of the main building was knocked down which has left the front tower standing alone," responded another.[8]

Figure 22 Bankfield, about 1980
Photo by Russell W. Barnes, *Flickr*.[9]

"The police and fire service closed all the roads and some bright spark thought 'we will blow it up.' There was a bit of a bang and it never moved so they had to get the big lads in to knock it down," added another.[10]

"I was one of the demolition team. It was only the front tower (on the left of the main pic) we blew up! It jumped up in the air & came back down but did not fall over! It must have been 20 mins later as the bombers (explosives experts) were assessing the situation that it started to fall down. This footage was live on border news of all of us running away as it fell behind us!" reported a local.[11]

Peter Kirk's Siblings

Peter was not the only Kirk with an intelligent mind. His brothers Henry and Thomas were brilliant as well. Peter, Henry, and Charles Valentine joined the Iron and Steel Institute, but Henry, a charter member of the elite institution, also submitted papers and lectured on trends and subjects pertinent to the group.[12] Henry was said to have "made a special study of the puddling process, in connection with which he was regarded as an expert." He wrote two papers about the process and ordinary rotary furnaces. He was also acclaimed for "successful experiments in the puddling of molten iron direct from the blast furnace, and effected considerable improvements in puddling and reheating furnaces and in rolling mills and the design of rolls."[13] However, neither brother seems to have registered any patents.

Manufacturers of similar products, the Kirk brothers might have retired to the smoking room after family dinners to debate the nuances of the industry, bemoan current mill problems, and exchange ideas on new trends. In at least one case, the Carlton Iron Company (the iron works later managed by Thomas) utilized Peter's patent for rolling mills.[14] The various Kirk enterprises likely shared other patents and ideas.

Henry Kirk

Figure 23 Henry Kirk
Circa 1895[15]

It was said Henry Kirk "threw himself whole-heartedly into the business, and acquired first-hand knowledge of the subsidiary operations, being an expert roller, furnaceman, and shingler. On one occasion, when the shinglers went out on strike, he served at the hammer and shingled the first round, a form of competition, which led to the collapse of the strike."[16]

Writing of his great uncle's keen business sense after Kirk Brothers disbanded, Geoffrey Peter Kirk said, "Henry Kirk was the company, and although well served by his managers, he had no partners or associates of comparable status. It was indeed remarkable that one man had for so long been able to run such a diverse and complex business, for which expert knowledge was required in many technologies."[17] Henry sold Kirk Brothers Ltd. in 1908.

Henry seemed to take after their father in his public service. He also seemed to be more gregarious than his brothers. He held temperance meetings in the fitting shop at the works at New Yard.[18] On the ironwork's grounds, he established a Sunday school, which was expanded to a working man's club for entertainment and to socialize.[19] Henry's idea for this club was that it be not just for the worker class but for everyone, so they could mix and exchange ideas. He believed "the great want of English society was not goodwill, or kindness, or preaching, or lecturing, but it was sympathy between class and class—each class working heartily with the other for the common good."[20] The Marsh Side Club was reported to have "a fairly good library and hot baths, down to bowls, cards, and dominoes… It was intended to compete with the pub, but as the pub's attraction is the convenience afforded of getting drunk, a temperance house stands no chance as a rival, and it accordingly failed."[21]

He also felt music was important to his laborers. Addressing the Eisteddfod in 1900, as he and Charles Valentine had in 1875, he said, "The Eisteddfod had been very useful to the community, as well as a pleasure to those attending it. It had encouraged a love for music, and as an employer of labour I would much rather have a man who spent his nights studying music, than a man who spent his nights in someplace that would make him unfit for work for the rest of the week."[22]

Henry's marriage to Emma Hall produced seven children; all but one lived to adulthood. After Emma's death in 1893, he married his brother-in-law's sister, Jane Elizabeth Valentine. They were active in the community, putting on fundraising bazaars to help the less fortunate and hosting teas for the working man's club and Sunday school.[23] Jane preceded him in death by three years.

Like his brother Peter, Henry may have had a heart condition. Writing to Peter, he said, "I saw my doctor a few days ago & asked him if it would be safe for me to go & stay at Mockerkin with Emily & Tom, 500 ft. above sea level. He said decidedly, No! I must avoid all high & all hilly places. I have been more or less troubled with the heart the last 7 ½ years & high & hilly places are considered bad for it."[24] Henry was in good shape, however, and attributed his condition to the methods in the health and healing articles in a magazine he subscribed to called *Unity*. He sent a subscription to Peter. The advice from the magazine may well have helped his health; Henry lived to be 84 years old.

Thomas Kirk

Figure 24 Thomas Kirk
Photo courtesy of Robert Kirk. Used with permission.

When a depression in the iron market hit in 1874, Thomas left Kirk Brothers and moved across England to Stockton in the county of Durham. There he managed two ironworks with his sons, the Carlton Ironworks Company and the Seaton Carew Iron Co. Ltd.[25] He was quite successful, taking advantage of all the intellectual collateral of his experience and his family's as well as the cheaper raw material costs in that part of England. Thomas was described as "well known and highly respected in the iron trade as a businessman of the strictest integrity."[26]

He leaned to the conservative side of politics but took no active part. "In local affairs, however," noted a local paper, "he took the keenest interest."[27] He held an official position in connection with the parish for twenty years. He was congratulated for "his untiring work, wise counsel, and generous support" on behalf of the Church of England chapel he attended, but also offered his home for meetings of the Primitive Methodists before they built their place of worship.[28] He served on the school board in Stockton.[29] He also sponsored an ambulance class for his workers to become qualified in rendering first aid.[30] When a worker who lost his life in Thomas' ironworks, leaving the man's children orphans, the company "very sincerely sympathized with the children of the deceased and intended to alleviate the sorrow of those children by providing a house for them, and by making them some allowance or giving them such employment as could be found for them."[31]

Thomas died before his brothers in 1908. He and Mary (nee Bell) had eleven children. All survived to adulthood save one son who died as a child and another who died the same year as his father.

Ann (Kirk) Valentine

One can imagine that Ann was just as intellectually gifted as her brothers. She seemed to have similar energy as well and was highly active in her community. She organized bazaars to raise money for various causes and was a principal stallholder at many of them, including one that benefited the Conservative Working Men's Club. She contributed 1,000 toys "of that unique kind to be found in the London streets, and which, are marvels as showing what can be produced for one penny."[32] She held high office in the Primrose League in Workington as well. Toward the league's purpose, which was to further the Conservative cause, it hosted an annual tea; one was organized for 1,000 people.[33] In any given year, the group would hold dances, social meetings, a members' tea, and an anniversary tea, each attended by hundreds of people.[34]

Ann was active in the Workington Volunteer Lifeboat Brigade and served as president for the Lifeboat House. She helped organize bazaars benefiting that institution as well. At one, she offered paintings and drawings for sale, though whether she was the artist is unknown.[35] In addition, she helped organize a tea for St. John's Temperance Society.[36]

Ann and Charles lived at Bankfield until at least 1894.[37] She resigned from the Primrose League in 1899, having served the institution since its inception in 1886, many times holding the office of Dame President.[38]

Ann seemed to embody the same civic mindedness as her husband, Charles James Valentine. A local paper lauded his efforts in 1890 stating, "If ever there was a willing and useful public man in a town, Workington has had such a one in Mr. C. J. Valentine. In season and out of season he has been ever willing and eager to help everything, and to take his full share in all local affairs."[39] He was the first member of Parliament for the Cockermouth Division in 1885. It was said his beautifully worded and polished speeches gave him the upset win over the Liberal favorite.[40]

Besides his partnership with the Kirk enterprises, he was director of the Cleator and Workington Junction railway, which was built to serve the Moss Bay iron works. He was instrumental in starting a glee society in Workington, considered the "most unmusical town in the country" prior to his efforts.[41] The glee society often had between thirty and forty voices, which Charles conducted. Before joining Kirk Brothers Iron, Valentine considered teaching music as his profession.[42] Valentine was highly regarded amongst the citizens, and they showed their gratitude with a marble bust placed at the library.[43]

Figure 25 Charles Valentine
Portrayal as he entered the House of Commons, 1886[44]

Upon returning from a tour of America that lasted nearly a year (partially helping Peter Kirk in Washington with the steel works venture), Charles gave an account of his travels at a meeting of the Primrose Club. He had traveled nearly 17,000 miles. A Workington reporter summarized Charles' lecture:

> He said it was very pleasant to him to be back again after so long a journey by sea and land. He was a bad sailor and would never go to sea for pleasure, and if on arriving at Liverpool recently, he had found a telegram asking him to go back again, he should have started out with very mixed feelings. Through nearly the whole of his journeying he was fortunate in having one of the best travelling companions he ever met with, a man who could talk well on everything, knew everybody and every place nearly, and was a host in himself on almost every subject.

> Mr. Valentine said he was 17 nights on shipboard, seven in a paper house, and two in a log hut. He slept well in the log hut, but in the paper house he thought the hair was going to be blown off his head it was so draughty.

> He was a week in the mountains of Kentucky, where they had 10 or 12 kinds of food every day, but so badly cooked that not much

of it was eatable. They boiled the tea, and when he asked for water, he vowed after once tasting it to have no more, for it was more like petroleum than anything else. When they complained to the waiter of anything, and asked him to get them something different, he had the stereotyped answer, 'Ken't do it.' The people there raised pigs, grew Indian Corn, hunted game, and shot at each other as a variation.

The state of society in some of the Southern States was not all that could be desired. In Western Virginia, South Eastern Kentucky, and Eastern Tennessee people were shooting each other freely, and it was next to impossible to get any jury to bring in a verdict of guilty. This shooting and killing of each other might go on for a long time, and people who had killed as many as six persons went about boasting of the fact. Arms were carried freely, and it was no uncommon thing for one man to shoot another, and often when a person was tried for murder his friends would appear in court armed in order to take revenge on the jury if they convicted the murderer.

There had been a man shot on each Sunday for the four weeks just before Valentine's visit. In a court the judge would sit with revolver on each side, the courtroom would be packed with men with long Kentucky rifles, and it was a bold jury who would say 'Guilty.' If a man threatened to shoot at another, even if he made no attempt to do it, the other could shoot him dead, and the law held him blameless. The very day before he and his friend arrived at one place a meeting had been held by some parties who knew his friend was coming, and they had arranged to shoot him and two others, however it didn't come off as they got to know of the arrangement in time.

On the whole he found the American people very kind and with a good feeling towards the old country, and more kindly than they were when he was there two or three years ago. In Canada, he found an exceedingly loyal and kindly feeling. In fact, the Canadians were more English than the English themselves.[45]

In their later years, Ann and Charles moved to London. Born within months of each other in 1837, their deaths in 1900 mirrored the same.[46]

Notes

Preface

1. Hunt, Thomas Francis, "Kirkland City's Founder Passes Firm in His Faith," *Seattle Post-Intelligencer* (Seattle, WA), May 9, 1916, Peter Kirk Collection, Kirkland Heritage Society, Kirkland, Washington.
2. Kirk pocket notebook, Peter Kirk Collection, Kirkland Heritage Society, Kirkland, Washington. And: Kirk pocket notebooks, Accession No. 0049, Box No. 2, Folder: Notebooks, Peter Kirk Papers, University of Washington Libraries, Special Collections, Seattle, Washington.
3. "A Talk with Mr. Jeffs," *Seattle Daily Post-Intelligencer* (Seattle, WA), March 22, 1887, p. 3, c. 2.
4. Correspondence from Florence Dixon to Peter Kirk, March 31, 1914, Accession No. 0049, Box No. 2, Folder: General Correspondence, Peter Kirk Papers, University of Washington Libraries, Special Collections, Seattle, Washington.
5. "Hotel Arrivals," *Seattle Post-Intelligencer* (Seattle, WA), May 26, 1894. And: "Delinquent Taxpayers," *Seattle Post-Intelligencer* (Seattle, WA), May 16, 1894.
6. "What People Say. A transient record of private opinions publicly expressed," *Yakima Herald* (Yakima, WA), November 23, 1899, p. 10, c. 1.
7. Letter from Arthur Dixon to Peter Kirk concerning Mary Ann Kirk's estate in England, September 14, 1909, p. 3, Peter Kirk Collection, Mary (Quirk) Kirk Estate, Kirkland Heritage Society, Kirkland, Washington.
8. Bunting, *Parish Magazine*, part VII, 1906, "Some 17th Century Quakers," Derbyshire Record Office, D6771/9/3, Matlock, Derbyshire, England.
9. *St. Thomas Beckett of Chapel-en-le-Frith Book of Memorial Inscriptions*, Derbyshire Ancestral Research Group, Derbyshire Record Office, Matlock, Derbyshire, England.

Introduction

1. Hunt, Thomas Francis, "Kirkland City's Founder," May 9, 1916. Hunt added that William Anderson, another of Kirk's engineers accompanied them on the trip, but I have found no evidence in ship lists or Kellett's sparse journal notes that spoke of him on the first trip. He may have come over on a subsequent trip. He came over with Kirk's family in 1887.
2. "New York, Passenger and Crew Lists (including Castle Garden and Ellis Island), 1820-1957," digital image s.v "Peter. Kirk" Date, 1886, Aug, 23, Umbria, *Ancestry.com*.

3.　Correspondence from Jean Kellett Kaye to Arline Stokes detailing history of Kirkland, n.d., Arline Stokes Andre Collection, Correspondence Folder, Kirkland Heritage Society, Kirkland, Washington.

4.　"The Iron Mines," *Seattle Daily Post-Intelligencer* (Seattle, WA), July 27, 1887, p. 3, c. 2.

5.　"…Interesting Scrap of History," *Seattle Post-Intelligencer* (Seattle, WA), August 12, 1888, p. 5.

6.　Jean Kellett Kaye to Arline Stokes, no date.

7.　Ibid.

8.　Hunt, Thomas Francis, "Kirkland City's Founder," May 9, 1916.

9.　Jean Kellett Kaye to Arline Stokes, no date.

10.　"Workington," *Cumbria County History Trust*, Lancaster University, Cumberland and Westmorland Antiquarian and Archaeological Society, https://www.cumbriacountyhistory.org.uk/township/workington (accessed May 18, 2020). 1891 population of Workington.

11.　Ruffner, William Henry, *A Report on Washington Territory* (New York: Seattle, Lake Shore, and Eastern Railroad, 1889), 171.

12.　Ruffner, *Report on Washington*, 26.

13.　Peter Kirk, birth certificate, 15 Feb. 1840, no. 98, General Register Office, Chapel-en-le-Frith, Derbyshire, England.

14.　"Derbyshire, England, Church of England Marriages and Banns, 1754-1932" digital image s.v. "Peter Kirk & Hannah Oliver," 7 Jun 1830, Chapel-en-le-Frith (1754-1892), *Ancestry.com*.

Chapter 1

1.　"Chaloners," *High Peak Reporter*, October 18, 1943, Derbyshire Record Office, D6771/9/6/11, Matlock, Derbyshire, England.

2.　Kirke, Henry, "The King's Forest of the High Peak," *The Reliquary Quarterly, Vol. VIII*, (London: Bemrosi & Sons, 1867-8), 33-44.

3.　Ibid.

4.　*St. Thomas Beckett of Chapel-en-le-Frith Book of Memorial Inscriptions*, Derbyshire Ancestral Research Group, Derbyshire Record Office, Matlock, Derbyshire, England.

5.　"England, Select Births and Christenings, 1538-1975," Index s.v. "Thomas Kyrk" (baptized 19 Oct 1750), Chapel-en-le-Frith, Derbyshire, *Ancestry.com*. And: "Derbyshire, England, Church of England Baptisms, Marriages and Burials, 1538-1812," digital image s.v. "Peter Kirk" (baptized 7 Aug 1748), Chapel-en-le-Frith, (1620-1782), *Ancestry.com*.

6. Kirk, Thornhill, "Notes on the Kirk Family of Town End, Chapel-en-le-Frith," 1935, D6771-1-10-6_00001-7, Genealogical research papers relating to the Kirk family of Chapel-en-le-Frith, Derbyshire Record Office, Matlock, Derbyshire, England.

7. "Derbyshire, England, Church of England Marriages and Banns, 1754-1932," digital image, Chapel-en-le-Frith (1754-1892), *Ancestry.com*. s.v. "Thomas Kirk & Sarah Marsden" (married 15 May 1781); s.v. "Peter Kirk & Elizabeth Brushfield" (married 16 May 1783; s.v. "Thomas Kirk, Junr Wid^r & Ann Rollinson" (married 9 Dec 1787).

8. Burchill, Shirley, "Two Centuries of Revolutionary Change," Open Door Web Site, http://www.saburchill.com/history/chapters/IR/036.html (accessed 2/22/2019).

9. Kirk, Geoffrey Peter, *The Kirk Family and Their Industrial Background of Iron and Steel* (Geoffrey Peter Kirk, 1973), 7.

10. "Copy lease for 42 years by Robert Needham, yeoman of Perryfoot, Peak Forest to Peter Kirk, blacksmith of Townend, Chapel-en-le-Frith," D2575/E/1, Needham family of Peak Forest, Derbyshire Record Office, Matlock, Derbyshire, England.

11. Kirk, Peter, Last will and testament, 1812, P/C/11, Prerogative Court of Lichfield, Lichfield Record Office, Lichfield, Staffordshire, England.

12. "Derbyshire, England, Church of England Marriages and Banns, 1528-1812," digital image s.v. "Thomas Kirk" (buried 14 Dec 1811), Chapel-en-le-Frith (1746-1812), *Ancestry.com*. And: "Derbyshire, England, Church of England Marriages and Banns, 1528-1812," digital image s.v. "Peter Kirk" (buried 21 Apr 1812), Chapel-en-le-Frith (1746-1812), *Ancestry.com*.

13. Derbyshire, England, Church of England Baptisms, marriages, and Burials, 1538-1812, Chapel-en-le-Frith, 1746-1812, *Ancestry.com*. Author combed through parish records for second half of 18th century.

14. "Derbyshire, England, Church of England Baptisms, 1813-1916," Chapel-en-le-Frith, England, 1813-1874, *Ancestry.com*. And: "Derbyshire, England, Church of England Marriages and Banns, 1754-1932," digital image s.v. "Henry Kirk and Jane Oliver" (marriage 2 Dec 1804), Chapel-en-le-Frith, 1754-1892, Digital image, *Ancestry.com*. Also, same record: "Peter Kirk and Rachel Thornhill" (marriage 22 Jul 1822).

15. "UK, City and County Directories, 1766-1946," Henry Kirk and Peter Kirk, 1829 Glover's Directory, Bowden's Edge of Chapel-en-le-Frith, Derbyshire, England, digital image, *Ancestry.com*.

16. "UK, Midlands and Various UK Trade Directories, 1770-1941," Henry Kirk, 1828 Pigot's Directory of Derbyshire, digital image, *Ancestry.com*.

17. "Lease for 42 years by Robert Needham, gentleman of Perryfoot to Henry Kirk, ironmaster of Townend, Chapel-en-le-Frith," September 1, 1837, Derbyshire Record Office, D2575/T/49, Matlock, Derbyshire, England.

18. "Chaloners," *High Peak Reporter*, October 18, 1943.

19. "1841 England Census," digital image s.v. "Peter Kirk" and "Henry Kirk" (Townend, Bowden Edge), Derbyshire, Chapel-en-le-Frith, District 13. *Ancestry.com.*

20. "Peter Kirk's notebook," Derbyshire Record Office, D6771 1 1 10_00001, Matlock, Derbyshire, England. The owner of the notebook is Peter Kirk, born in 1823, son of Peter Kirk the Younger. He is cousin (once removed) to Peter Kirk (born in 1840) who later moves to America.

21. Kirk, Thornhill, "Notes on the Kirk Family," D6771-1-10-6_00003, Derbyshire Record Office. As told to him by his grandfather's brother, Thomas.

22. *Derby Mercury* (Derby, Derbyshire, England), August 24, 1842, p. 3.

23. Ibid.

24. "1841 England Census," digital image s.v. "Henry Kirk" and "Thomas Kirk" (Townend, Bowden Edge), Derbyshire, Chapel-en-le-Frith, District 13. *Ancestry. com.* Henry and his adult sons, Peter and Henry, were listed as iron founders, while half-brother Thomas and his son Samuel were forgeman.

25. "Obituary. Henry Kirk," *The Journal of the Iron and Steel Institute,* Volume 90, The Institute: 1914, 254.

26. "UK, Midlands and Various UK Trade Directories, 1770-1941," digital image "Chapel-en-le-Frith" (1828 Pigot's Directory of Derbyshire), *Ancestry.com.*

27. "1851 England Census," digital images s.v. "Peter Kirk," "Henry Kirk," "Thomas Kirk" (Town End), Derbyshire, Chapel-en-le-Frith, 5a. *Ancestry.com.*

28. "1841 England Census," digital image s.v. "Peter Kirk" (Bowden Edge), Derbyshire, Chapel-en-le-Frith, District 13, *Ancestry.com.*

29. "England & Wales, Non-Conformist and Non-Parochial Registers, 1567-1970," digital image s.v. "Hannah Oliver" (baptized 7 July 1804), RG4 Registers of Births, Marriages and Deaths, Derbyshire, Independent, Piece 0496: Chinley (Independent), 1682-1714, *Ancestry.com.* And: "Derbyshire, England, Select Church of England Parish Registers, 1538-1910," index s.v. "Hannah Oliver" (baptism), Mellor, Derbyshire, England, *Ancestry.com.*

30. Hannah Kirk, death certificate, 4 Apr 1841, no. 125, General Register Office, Chapel-en-le-Frith, Derbyshire, England.

31. *Derbyshire Advertiser and Journal* (Derby, Derbyshire, England), April 11, 1846, p. 3, c. 2.

32. *Glossop-Dale Chronicle and North Derbyshire Reporter* (Glossop, Derbyshire, England), January 1, 1870, p. 3, c. 4.

33. "Chapel-en-le-Frith. Band of Hope Meeting," *Derbyshire Times and Chesterfield Herald* (Chesterfield, Derbyshire, England), May 8, 1869.

34. *Glossop-Dale Chronicle and North Derbyshire Reporter* (Glossop, Derbyshire, England), January 8, 1870, p. 3, c. 4.

35. "Mr. Henry Kirk on the Union of Employers and Men," *Workington Star and Harrington Guardian* (Workington, Cumberland, England), February 15, 1901, p. 5, c. 4-5.

36. Ibid.

37. *Official Catalogue of the Great Exhibition of the Works of Industry of All Nations, 1851* (London, Spicer Brothers, 1851), Hathi Trust Digital Library, https://babel. hathitrust.org/cgi/pt?id=mdp.39015009221915;view=1up;seq=191 (accessed March 30, 2020).

38. Ibid.

39. Lampert, Maria, Information Expert: Intellectual Property and IP Centre at the British Library, email message to author, March 13, 2019.

40. "Partnerships Dissolved," *Morning Chronicle* (London, England), February 2, 1853, p. 2, c. 5.

41. Thomas Kirk, death certificate, 9 Jul 1869, no. 481, General Register Office, Chapel-en-le-Frith, Derbyshire, England. And: Henry Kirk, death certificate, 18 Nov 1859, no. 435, General Register Office, Chapel-en-le-Frith, Derbyshire, England.

42. Peter Kirk, death certificate, 17 Sep 1875, no. 454, General Register Office, Cockermouth, Cumberland, England.

43. *The Journal of the Iron and Steel Institute*, "Obituary. Henry Kirk," 254. The Star Ironworks was located on Newbridge Lane.

44. Wikipedia, s.v. "Stockport," last modified May 8, 2020, https://en.wikipedia.org/ wiki/Stockport. Description by Friedrich Engles in 1844.

45. *Birmingham Journal* (Birmingham, England), May 22, 1858; p. 4, c. 3. Set up by the "Trustees of Henry Kirk" and partnered with Frederick Charles Perry. Dissolved February 23, 1858.

Chapter 2

1. *Carlisle Patriot* (Carlisle, Cumberland, England), March 9, 1861, p. 3, c. 2. Also, series of advertisements: *Carlisle Journal* (Carlisle, Cumberland, England), August 2, 1861-July 1862.

2. "Mr. Henry Kirk on the Union of Employers and Men," 5.

3. *Cumberland Pacquet, and Ware's Whitehaven Advertiser* (Whitehaven, Cumberland England), March 12, 1861, p. 6, c. 6.

4. Lancaster, J. Y. and Wattleworth, D. R. *The Iron and Steel Industry of West Cumberland, An Historical Survey* (Workington, Cumbria: CN Print Ltd., 1977), 101.

5. "Mr. Henry Kirk on the Union of Employers and Men," 5.

6. *The Journal of the Iron and Steel Institute*, "Obituary. Henry Kirk," 254.

7. *Carlisle Journal* (Carlisle, Cumberland, England), August 2, 1861.

8. "The Manufactured Iron Trade in West Cumberland," *West Cumberland Times* (Workington, Cumberland, England), February 26, 1881, p. 4, c. 3. Extensive history of Kirk Bros. in Workington.

9. Ibid.

10. "Mr. Valentine, M.P.," *Maryport and Workington Advertiser* (Maryport, Cumberland, England), June 11, 1886, p. 5, c. 3. Biography of Charles Valentine when he became M.P.

11. *Carlisle Journal* (Carlisle, Cumberland, England), November 13, 1863.

12. James Quirk and Hannah Gibson, marriage certificate, 13 Jan 1838, no. 16, General Register Office, Cockermouth, Cumberland, England.

13. "Painfully Sudden Deaths at Workington," unknown newspaper, June 30, 1893, Peter Kirk Collection, Assorted Newspapers, Kirkland Heritage Society, Kirkland, Washington. Also: *Maryport Advertiser* (Maryport, Cumberland, England), June 24, 1893, p. 5, c. 2.

14. *Cumberland Pacquet, and Ware's Whitehaven Advertiser* (Whitehaven, Cumberland, England), March 30, 1847, p. 1, c. 3.

15. James Quirk, death certificate, 11 Nov 1858, no. 364, General Register Office, Cockermouth, Cumberland, England.

16. "1861 England Census," digital image s.v. "Hannah Quirk," Cumberland, Workington, District 12, *Ancestry.com*.

17. Lancaster and Wattleworth, *Iron and Steel Industry*, p. 66. Mary Gibson signed with Peter Kirk, C. J. Valentine, Peter Gibson Quirk, and others for lease of site for building blast furnace and works at Moss Bay. Also: "Lease of site for building blast furnace and works at Moss Bay, Workington," July 24, 1872, DCU/11/1/8/1, Curwen Family of Workington Hall, Cumbria County Council, Cumbria Archive Service Catalogue, Carlisle, Cumberland, England.

18. *Cumberland Pacquet, and Ware's Whitehaven Advertiser* (Whitehaven, Cumberland, England), October 26, 1852, p. 2, c. 5.

19. "Rolled wrought scrap bar iron," *Carlisle Journal* (Carlisle, Cumberland, England) August 2, 1861.

20. "Marriages," *Carlisle Journal* (Carlisle, Cumberland, England), August 22, 1862, p. 8, c. 5.

21. "Marriages," *Carlisle Journal* (Carlisle, Cumberland, England), September 15, 1865, p. 5, c. 6.

22. Peter Kirk & Mary Ann Quirk, marriage certificate, 7 Sep 1865, no. 250, General Register Office, Cockermouth, Cumberland, England.

23. Cunningham, Helen, email message to author, December 22, 2016.

24. Thomas Kirk & Mary Bell, marriage certificate, 10 May 1859, no. 34, General Register Office, Stockport, Chester, England. And: Henry Kirk & Emma Hall, marriage certificate, 21 Feb. 1861, no. 395, General Register Office, Stockport, Chester, England. And: Ann Kirk & Charles James Valentine, marriage certificate, 14 Mar 1861, no. 407, General Register Office, Stockport, Chester, England.

25. *Cumberland Pacquet, and Ware's Whitehaven Advertiser* (Whitehaven, Cumberland, England), November 10, 1863, p. 4, c. 3.

26. "1861 England Census," digital image s.v. "Henry Kirk," Cumberland, Workington, ALL, District 19, *Ancestry.com*.

27. *Cumberland Pacquet, and Ware's Whitehaven Advertiser* (Whitehaven, Cumberland, England), November 10, 1863, p. 4, c. 3.

28. Frank Kirk, birth certificate, 6 Nov. 1866, no. 116, General Register Office, Cockermouth, Cumberland, England.

29. Birth certificates, General Registry Office, Cockermouth, Cumberland, England: Florence, 28 Nov 1868, no. 84; Hannah Oliver, 16 July 1870, no. 424; Mary Gibson, 2 Oct 1872, Fanny Valentine, 29 Aug. 1874, no. 15; Peter Jr., 14 Dec 1876, no. 110; Clara Constance, 29 Oct 1878, no. 11; Jessie, 1 Dec 1880, no. 117; Arnold, 28 Oct 1883, no. 409.

Chapter 3

1. Kirk, Peter, 'Rolling Metals, GB2895,' England, 1866.

2. Ibid.

3. Kirk, Peter, 'Rolling Mills, GB3459,' England, 1872.

4. Kirk, Peter, 'Rolling Iron and Steel, GB470,' England, 1876.

5. Kirk, Peter, 'Rolling Mills for the Manufacture of Iron and Steel, GB637,' England, 1881. Provisional specifications to #470.

6. Kirk, Peter, 'Rolling Mills Used in the Manufacture of Metals, GB913,' England, 1882. Provisional specifications to #470 & #637.

7. Kirk, Peter, "Puddling Furnaces, &c., GB1668," England, 1869.

8. Kirk, Peter, 'Furnaces &c., GB885,' England, 1875. And: "Improvements in Puddling and Heating Furnaces and in the Fire-Grates of such Furnaces, and in the method of Supplying the same with Fuel."

9. Ibid.

10. Kirk, Peter, 'Stoves or Fire-Grates, GB1782,' England, 1873.

11. Lancaster & Wattleworth, *Iron and Steel Industry*, 99.

12. "Indenture relating to the Workington Iron Co. Ltd," December 24, 1879, YBSC/3/1/4, Carlisle Archive Centre. Carlisle, Cumbria, England. And: "Correspondence and share certificates from Secretary of Workington Hematite Iron & Steel Works to Peter Kirk," January 29, 1880, Peter Kirk Collection, Kirkland Heritage Society, Kirkland, Washington.

13. Lancaster & Wattleworth, *Iron and Steel Industry*, 135-7.

14. Ibid., 99.

15. "Indenture relating to the Workington Iron Co. Ltd," December 24, 1879. And: "Correspondence and share certificates to Peter Kirk," January 29, 1880.

16. "The Moss Bay Iron and Steel Company's Works," *English Lakes Visitor and Keswick Guardian* (Keswick, Cumberland, England), November 20, 1886, p. 5, c. 2-3.

17. Kirk, Peter, "Irondale Report," February 7, 1903, p. 3, Peter Kirk Collection, Misc. Folder, Kirkland Heritage Society, Kirkland, Washington.

18. Unless otherwise noted, the information about Kirk's Moss Bay plant is taken from the following article: "The Moss Bay Iron and Steel Company's Works," *English Lakes Visitor and Keswick Guardian* (Keswick, Cumberland, England), November 20, 1886, p. 5, c. 2-3. Reprinted from *The Engineer*. In depth article covering plant layout, production practices, and history.

19. Kirk, Peter, 'Rolling Mills Used in the Manufacture of Metals, GB913,' England, 1882. Provisional specifications to #470 & #637.

20. Kirk, Peter, 'Improvements in Ovens or Furnaces for Heating Ingots and Blooms or for Maintaining the Heat thereof, GB15497,' England, 1884.

21. Ibid.

Chapter 4

1. "The Iron and Steel Institute," *Soulby's Ulverston Advertiser and General Intelligencer* (Ulverston, Lancashire, England), September 17, 1874, p. 6, c. 6.

2. "The Grand Jury," *Cumberland Pacquet, and Ware's Whitehaven Advertiser* (Whitehaven, Cumberland, England), October 27, 1874, p. 4, c. 1.

3. "Election of Churchwardens," *Carlisle Express and Examiner* (Carlisle, Cumberland, England), April 27, 1878, p. 6, c. 5.

4. "Wesleyans' Sale of Work at Workington," *West Cumberland Times* (Workington, Cumberland, England), December 17, 1904, p. 3, c. 8.

5. "The Ceremony of Opening the Dock," *West Cumberland Times* (Workington, Cumberland, England), May 28, 1884, p. 3, c. 4.

6. "Performance of 'The Creation' at Workington," *Carlisle Journal* (Carlisle, Cumberland, England), November 7, 1882, p. 2, c. 5.

7. "Workington Coal Charity Concert," *West Cumberland Times* (Workington, Cumberland, England), December 26, 1874, p. 5, c. 4.

8. Barnes, Russell, "Old Workington Facebook Group," August 19, 2016, https://www.facebook.com/groups/103710749754449/?post_id=383999898392198 (accessed May 31, 2020). Barnes referenced: Byers, Richard L. M. *History of Workington (1866-1955): An Illustrated History* (Richard Byers, 2002).

9. "Sale by Auction," *West Cumberland Times* (Workington, Cumberland, England), June 18, 1887, p. 1, c. 8. Kirk hired John Jenkinson to auction the family's furnishings before their move to America. This chapter describes the rooms and items detailed in his auction catalogue.

10. "1911 England Census," digital image s.v. "Frederick Iredale," district 11, Workington, Cumberland, district 11, *Ancestry.com*. Iredale acquired Bankfield later. The 1911 census listed how many rooms a house had.
    I surveyed the homes surrounding Bankfield to get a comparison of the homes around it.

11. "Sales by Auction at Bankfield," 1.

12. Correspondence from Florrie Dixon to unknown recipient, Fall 1905, Peter Kirk Collection, Florence Kirk Dixon Folder, Kirkland Heritage Society, Kirkland, Washington.

13. "Peter Kirk, Sr., Summoned by the Hand of Death," *Friday Harbor Journal* (Friday Harbor, WA), May 11, 1916, p. 1, c. 2. San Juan Historical Museum Archives.

14. "Sales by Auction at Bankfield," 1.

15. Kirk, Peter, 'Stoves or Fire-Grates, GB1782,' England, 1873. For use in dwelling houses and other buildings.

16. "Sales by Auction at Bankfield," 1.

17. Ibid.

18. Ibid.

19. Todhunter, Elly, email concerning Bankfield, September 3, 2020. Elly is a representative of Workington's Helena Thompson Museum.

20. "Sales by Auction at Bankfield," 1.

21. "Carriage Accident at Workington," *Carlisle Journal* (Carlisle, Cumberland, England), August 7, 1883, p. 2, c. 6.

22. "Sales by Auction at Bankfield," 1.

23. Ely, Arline. *Our Foundering Fathers* (Kirkland, Washington: Kirkland Public Library, 1975), 40.

24. Kirk, Geoffrey Peter, *The Kirk Family Industrial Background*, 24.

25. "Singular Defence to A Charge of Theft," *Carlisle Patriot* (Carlisle, Cumberland, England), August 16, 1889, p. 3, c. 6.

Chapter 5

1. "1871 England Census," digital image s.v. "Peter Kirk," Cumberland, Workington, Seaton, All, 1, *Ancestry.com*. And: "1871 England Census," digital image s.v. "Mary Ann Kirk," Cumberland, Workington, All, 12, *Ancestry.com*.

2. Duncan, C. J., Duncan, S. R., and Scott, S., "The dynamics of scarlet fever epidemics in England and Wales in the 19th century," Epidemiology & Infection, National Center for Biotechnology Information, US National Library of Medicine, https://www.ncbi.nlm.nih.gov/pmc/articles/PMC2271647/ (accessed January 2, 2021).

3. Frank Kirk, death certificate, 18 July 1874, no. 42, General Register Office, Cockermouth, Cumberland, England.

4. Fanny Valentine, birth certificate, 29 Aug. 1874, no. 15, General Register Office, Cockermouth, Cumberland, England.

5. "Boiler Explosion at Workington," *West Cumberland Times* (Workington, Cumberland, England), September 5, 1875.

6. Kirk, Peter, "Irondale Report," 2.

7. "Mr. Henry Kirk on the Union of Employers and Men," 5.

8. "Alarming Fires at Workington," *West Cumberland Times* (Workington, Cumberland, England), April 30, 1884. Also: "Fire at the Moss Bay Works."

9. "The Moss Bay Iron and Steel Company's Works," 5.

10. Kirk, Peter, 'Reversible Girder Rail,' England, 1884. Also: 'Manufactured Combined Chair & Sleeper,' #15,396, England, November 22, 1884; 'Furnace For Heating Ingots,' #15,407, England, November 25, 1884.

11. *Carlisle Express and Examiner* (Carlisle, Cumberland, England), March 12, 1881; p. 8, c. 1. The marriage relationships included: Peter's sister, Ann married Charles James Valentine; Peter married Peter Gibson Quirk's sister, Mary Ann; and Joseph Ellis (1851-1920) married Sarah Martha Valentine, sister of Charles James Valentine. Ellis remained a director for the England Moss Bay ironworks for many years.

12. Ibid.

13. "The Manufactured Iron Trade in West Cumberland," *West Cumberland Times* (Workington, Cumberland, England), February 26, 1881, p. 4, c. 3.

14. *Carlisle Express and Examiner* (Carlisle, Cumberland, England), March 19, 1881; p. 1, c. 2.

15. Lancaster & Wattleworth, *Iron and Steel Industry*, 67. Conversion to present USA dollars equals $127,000. Peter also had income from dividends from the company or other investments.

16. "Deed of Mortgage of properties owned by Peter Kirk," July 6, 1881, YDX 473/1/3/11, Carlisle Archive Centre. Carlisle, Cumbria, England.

17. *West Cumberland Times* (Workington, Cumberland, England), February 4, 1882, p. 4.

18. Ibid.

19. *West Cumberland Times* (Workington, Cumberland, England), March 24, 1883, p. 5.

20. Lancaster & Wattleworth, *Iron and Steel Industry*, 67.

21. *West Cumberland Times*, March 24, 1883.

22. Bulmer, T. & Co. *History, Topography and Directory of West Cumberland* (Cumberland: T. Snape & Co., 1883), 304-5.

23. Kirk, Geoffrey Peter, *The Kirk Family Industrial Background*, 19.

24. *Carlisle Journal* (Carlisle, Cumberland, England), February 22, 1881, p. 2, c. 4.

25. Bulmer, *History of West Cumberland*, 304-5.

26. Lancaster & Wattleworth, *Iron and Steel Industry*, 68-9.

27. Ibid.

28. "Moss Bay Hematite Iron & Steel Company, Limited Workington. Director's Report, Balance Sheet, and Auditors' Report for the year ending, 31st December 1884, Workington," March 7, 1885, YBSC/6/2/1, Carlisle Archive Centre, Carlisle, Cumbria, England.

29. "New Steel Industry," *West Cumberland Times* (Workington, Cumberland, England), January 17, 1885.

30. "Steel Works," *West Cumberland Times* (Workington, Cumberland, England), January 24, 1885, p. 5.

31. *Carlisle Journal* (Carlisle, Cumberland, England), January 20, 1885, p. 4, c. 5. Concerning 1884 patent for Manufactured Combined Chair/Sleeper, #15,396.

32. "Moss Bay Hematite Iron and Steel Company, Limited," *West Cumberland Times* (Workington, Cumberland, England), March 28, 1885, p. 5.

33. Kirk, Peter, 'Improvements in Tram Rails and in the Manufacture thereof, GB10036,' England, 1884.

34. Kirk, Peter, 'Improvements in and in the Manufacture of Combined Chairs and Sleepers, GB15396,' England, 1884. Also patented in United States of America, Patent no. 325,094.

35. *West Cumberland Times* (Workington, Cumberland, England), February 6, 1886, p. 5, c. 4.

36. Kirk, Peter, 'Improvements in the Permanent Way of Railways, GB2024,' England, 1886. Kirk uses patent 15396 of 1884 and 785 of 1885.

37. Kirk, Peter, 'Improvements in Combined Metallic Chairs and Sleepers for Railways, GB785,' England, 1885.

38. Kirk, Peter, 'Improvements in and in the Manufacture of Combined Chairs and Sleepers, GB15396,' England, 1884.

39. Kirk, Peter, 'Improvements in the Permanent Way of Rail, GB4600,' England, 1886.

40. "The Moss Bay Iron and Steel Company's Works," 5.

41. "Peter Kirk, Sr., Summoned by the Hand of Death," 1. And: *West Cumberland Times* (Workington, Cumberland, England), February 6, 1886, p. 5, c. 4.

42. Kirk, Geoffrey Peter, *The Kirk Family Industrial Background*, 12. Mr. Kirk indicated he gleaned this information from the minute books of the directors' meetings for the Moss Bay Hematite Iron & Steel Company Limited which existed at the time of his writing.

43. "Moss Bay Iron Works," *Carlisle Journal* (Carlisle, Cumberland, England), March 18, 1887, p. 5, c. 4.

44. "Moss Bay Hematite Iron and Steel Company," *Carlisle Journal* (Carlisle, Cumberland, England), March 25, 1887, p. 7, c. 2.

45. "The Iron Industry," *Seattle Daily Post-Intelligencer* (Seattle, WA), April 3, 1887, p. 4, c. 1.

46. "Moss Bay Company Canadian Pacific Steel 1883," photo of rail tie, https://www.flickr.com/photos/joetourist/3855295058/in/photostream/, (accessed June 2, 2020). Sample track used to display "last spike" for CPRR at Craigellachie, British Columbia, Canada.

Chapter 6

1. Hunt, Thomas Francis, "Kirkland City's Founder," May 9, 1916.

2. Ely, *Our Foundering Fathers*, 28.

3. Jean Kellett Kaye to Arline Stokes, no date.

4. Myrtle Cecelia Robertson typescripts, #15. As told to her by Mr. J. W. Collins of Long Beach, California, a former Kirkland resident. Date unknown.

5. "New York, Passenger and Crew Lists (including Castle Garden and Ellis island), 1820-1957," digital image s.v. "Peter Kirk" Date, 1886, Aug, 23, Umbria, *Ancestry.com*. And: Jean Kellett Kaye to Arline Stokes, no date.

6. Ibid. Kellett is probably referring to Lake Sammamish when he speaks of Lake Issaquah.

7. Ibid.

8. Ibid.

9. Ibid.

10. "…Interesting Scrap of History," 5.

11. Jean Kellett Kaye to Arline Stokes, no date.

12. Sherrard, William Robert, *The Kirkland Steel Mill* (Master's thesis, University of Washington, 1958), 129. "Saturday, September 25, 1886," Sherrard referred to this in his thesis as the last entry in Kellett's journal.

13. Jean Kellett Kaye to Arline Stokes, no date.

14. Washington Governor, *Report of the Governor of Washington Territory to the Secretary of the Interior* (Washington: Government Printing Office), 1889, 12.

15. "Iron Metropolis Forbes Lake," *Kirkland News* (Kirkland, WA), September 1, 1890, George Seville Kirk Scrapbook, p. 12, Newspaper Clippings 1890's, *Kirklandheritage.org.*

16. *Weekly Puget Sound Argus* (Port Townsend, WA), December 2, 1886, p. 3, c. 4.

17. Ruffner, *Report on Washington*, 147.

18. *The Daily Morning Astorian* (Astoria, WA), August 1890, p. 3. And: *State Rights Democrat* (Albany, OR), September 16, 1881, p. 2.

19. *Corvallis Gazette* (Corvallis, OR), November 13, 1885, p. 5.

20. "Brevities," *Seattle Daily Post-Intelligencer* (Seattle, WA), January 28, 1886, p. 2, c. 3.

21. "…Interesting Scrap of History," 5.

22. *Washington Standard* (Olympia, WA), November 12, 1886, p. 2, c. 3. And: "Daily Expected," *Seattle Daily Post-Intelligencer* (Seattle, WA), May 22, 1887, p. 5, c. 5.

23. "To the Common Point," *Seattle Daily Post-Intelligencer* (Seattle, WA), October 6, 1887, p. 3, c. 3.

24. "Moss Bay (Workington) Hematite Iron and Steel Company," *Carlisle Patriot* (Carlisle, Cumberland, England), March 25, 1887, p. 7, c. 2.

25. Kirk, Geoffrey Peter, *The Kirk Family Industrial Background*, 20-21. November 24, 1886 Moss Bay board of directors meeting.

26. Ibid.

27. "Our Visitors," *Seattle Daily Post-Intelligencer* (Seattle, WA), December 22, 1886, p. 3, c. 1.

28. List of ore samples from various locations, unknown date, Accession No. 0049, Box No. 2, Folder: Financial Records, Peter Kirk Papers, University of Washington Libraries, Special Collections, Seattle, Washington. Also: Jean Kellett Kaye to Arline Stokes, no date.

29. *Weekly Puget Sound Argus* (Port Townsend, WA), December 2, 1886, p. 3, c. 4.

30. "Personal," *Seattle Daily Post-Intelligencer* (Seattle, WA), January 6, 1887, p. 3, c. 2.

31. "King County Iron Industries," *Seattle Daily Post-Intelligencer* (Seattle, WA), January 27, 1887, p. 3, c. 2.

32. "Workington," *Whitehaven News* (Whitehaven, Cumberland, England), February 17, 1887, p. 4. Also: *Carlisle Express and Examiner* (Carlisle, Cumberland, England), Feb 19, 1887; p. 6, c. 2.

33. "Cumberland Enterprise," *Carlisle Patriot* (Carlisle, Cumberland, England), July 8, 1887, p. 3, c. 5.

34. Correspondence from Charles Valentine to niece, Lily, December 5, 1896, Peter Kirk Collection, Kirkland Heritage Society, Kirkland, Washington. Lily is the daughter of Robert Valentine, Charles' brother.

35. "Washington Iron Ores," *Seattle Post-Intelligencer* (Seattle, WA), January 9, 1892, p. 8.

36. "Gun Factory Proposal," March 23, 1892, p. 4-5, Peter Kirk Collection, Kirkland Heritage Society, Kirkland, Washington. Charles Valentine's nephew, George James Valentine was Moss Bay of England's chief chemist conducting the analysis of the different ores for this report.

37. Ibid., 5-8.

38. Ruffner, *Report on Washington*, 137.

39. "Gun Factory Proposal," 2.

40. Ibid., 11.

41. Ibid. 5-6.

42. Ibid.

43. Ibid., 10-12.

44. Ibid., 11.

45. "Brevities," *Seattle Daily Post-Intelligencer* (Seattle, WA), April 6 & 7, 1887, p. 3, c. 1.

46. Ruffner, *Report on Washington*, 155.

47. "Two Items from Yakima. Purchase of Iron Claims," *Seattle Daily Post-Intelligencer* (Seattle, WA), October 8, 1887, p. 1, c. 7.

48. Ruffner, *Report on Washington*, 151.

49. "Brevities," *Seattle Daily Post-Intelligencer* (Seattle, WA), March 12, 1887, p. 3, c. 1. And March 13, 1887, p. 7, c. 1.

50. Ruffner, *Report on Washington*, 112-116.

51. "Homestead Act (1862)," www.ourdocuments.gov (accessed August 30, 2020).

52. "Alien Land Ownership," *Seattle Daily Post-Intelligencer* (Seattle, WA), January 22, 1885, p. 3, c. 4.

53. Ibid.

54. "Selected US Naturalization Records – Original Documents, 1790-1974," digital image s.v. "Peter Kirk," (filed 14 Nov. 1899), Washington, Superior Court, King County (Rolls 1-51), 1854-1928, (Roll 013) Naturalization Case Files, 1899-1901, *Ancestry.com*.

55. "Seaside Notes," *West Cumberland Times* (Workington, Cumberland, England), August 4, 1888, p. 4, c. 5.

56. Ibid.

Chapter 7

1. "Preliminary Announcement," *Whitehaven News* (Whitehaven, Cumberland, England), June 9, 1887, p. 1, c. 3.

2. Jean Kellett Kaye to Arline Stokes, no date.

3. Ibid.

4.   "New York, Passenger and Crew Lists (including Castle Garden and Ellis island), 1820-1957," digital image s.v. "Mary A. Kirk" Date, 1887, Jul, 11, Servia, *Ancestry. com.* Mary Ann and children, lines 389-97; Margaret Hughes, line 398; Wm Anderson, line 404; John G. Kellett, line 359.

5.   Ely, *Our Foundering Fathers*, 38.

6.   Jean Kellett Kaye to Arline Stokes, no date. Stories told by Mr. Anderson to Kellett children

7.   "New York, Passenger and Crew Lists (including Castle Garden and Ellis island), 1820-1957," digital image s.v. "Princess Lili'uokalani," Date, 1887, Jul, 11, Servia, lines 416-424, *Ancestry.com.*

8.   Ely, *Our Foundering Fathers*, 42.

9.   Jean Kellett Kaye to Arline Stokes, no date. Mr. Anderson's stories of the voyage with Mrs. Kirk and children told to Kellett children.

10. Correspondence from Aubrey Williams to Arline Stokes detailing history of Kirkland, October 12, 1968, Arline Stokes Andre Collection, Correspondence Folder, Kirkland Heritage Society, Kirkland, Washington.

11. The Canadian Encyclopedia, "Hotel," https://www.thecanadianencyclopedia.ca/article/hotel.

12. "Brevities," *Seattle Daily Post-Intelligencer* (Seattle, WA), July 21, 1887, p. 3, c. 1. Also: "Personals," same issue, p. 3, c. 2.

13. "Who They Are," *Seattle Post-Intelligencer* (Seattle, WA), June 1, 1888, p. 4, c. 1-2.

14. "Music was the Master When Workington Was in Unison," *Times and Star Workington,* (Workington, England), January 14, 2005. And: Aubrey Williams letter to Arline Stokes, September 25, 1968.

15. *West Cumberland Times* (Workington, Cumberland, England), March 7, 1883.

16. "Another Presentation to Mr. W. W. Williams," *West Cumberland Times* (Workington, Cumberland, England), November 26, 1887, p. 5.

Chapter 8

1.   "King County Iron Industries," *Seattle Daily Post-Intelligencer* (Seattle, WA), January 27, 1887, p. 3, c. 2.

2.   Ibid.

3.   MacIntosh, Heather M., and Crowley, Walt, "Railroad Development in the Seattle/ Puget Sound Region, 1872-1906," posted September 22, 1999, HistoryLink.org Essay 1683, https://www.historylink.org/File/1683.

4.   Ibid.

5.   "Brevities," *Seattle Daily Post-Intelligencer* (Seattle, WA), March 11, 1887, p. 3, c. 1.

6.   "The Iron Mines," *Seattle Daily Post-Intelligencer* (Seattle, WA), July 27, 1887, p. 3, c. 2.

7.   "The Iron Mines," *Seattle Daily Post-Intelligencer* (Seattle, WA), August 16, 1887, p. 2, c. 1-2.

8.   Ruffner, *Report on Washington*, 116.

9.   Ruffner, *Report on Washington*, 17.

10.   Ibid.

11.   Bulmer, *History of West Cumberland*, 304.

12.   *Locomotive Engineers Journal*, Volume 42, Brotherhood of Locomotive Engineers; Cleveland, Ohio, 1908, 428.

13.   Washington Governor, "Progress of Railroads," 24.

14.   Ruffner, *Report on Washington*, 150.

15.   "Personal," *Seattle Daily Post-Intelligencer* (Seattle, WA) January 6, 1887, p. 3, c. 2.

16.   "To the Common Point," *Seattle Daily Post-Intelligencer* (Seattle, WA), January 23, 1887, p. 7, c. 3.

17.   "Notes, Personal and Otherwise," *Seattle Daily Post-Intelligencer* (Seattle, WA), February 13, 1887, p. 8, c. 3.

18.   "A Talk with T. J. Milner," *Seattle Daily Post-Intelligencer* (Seattle, WA), March 2, 1887, p. 3, c. 3. Milner was assistant superintendent of the Columbia & Puget Sound Railroad owned by Oregon Improvement Company.

19.   "Another Road to Snoqualmie," *Seattle Daily Post-Intelligencer* (Seattle, WA), March 10, 1887, p. 3, c. 2.

20.   "Talk with Mr. McNaught," *Seattle Daily Post-Intelligencer* (Seattle, WA), April 30, 1887, p. 3, c. 2. James McNaught was the attorney for Northern Pacific Railroad. He sold his yacht *Aquilla* to Peter Kirk later.

21.   "The Iron Mines," *Seattle Daily Post-Intelligencer* (Seattle, WA), September 18, 1887, p. 4, c. 4-5.

22.   "Regarding the Denny Mines," *Seattle Daily Post-Intelligencer* (Seattle, WA), September 8, 1887, p. 3, c. 3.

23.   "The Iron Mines. An Interview with Paul Schulze Regarding Their Development," *Seattle Daily Post-Intelligencer* (Seattle, WA), September 16, 1887, p. 2, c. 3-4.

24.   Ibid.

25.   Ibid.

26.   "The Iron Mines. A.A. Denny and John Leary Discover Weak Points in Paul Schulze's Argument," *Seattle Daily Post-Intelligencer* (Seattle, WA), September 18, 1887, p. 4, c. 4-5.

27.   "Talk with Mr. Denny," *Seattle Daily Post-Intelligencer* (Seattle, WA), July 3, 1887, p. 5, c. 3. During the first 18 months that Peter Kirk was in Seattle, the newspapers spelled his name 'Kirke' much of the time. Coincidentally, when Leigh Hunt (owner of the *Seattle P-I*) entered the picture in 1888, Peter's name was spelled correctly from then on.

28. "The Iron Mines. A.A. Denny and John Leary Discover Weak Points in Paul Schulze's Argument," *Seattle Daily Post-Intelligencer* (Seattle, WA), September 18, 1887, p. 4, c. 4-5.

29. Ibid.

30. "The Other Side. Mr. Schulze Reads the Interview with A. A. Denny and John Leary," *Seattle Daily Post-Intelligencer* (Seattle, WA), September 20, 1887, p. 4, c. 2.

31. "The Iron Mines. A.A. Denny and John Leary Discover Weak Points in Paul Schulze's Argument," 4.

32. "The Other Side. Mr. Schulze Reads the Interview with A. A. Denny and John Leary," 4.

33. "The Iron Mines. A.A. Denny and John Leary Discover Weak Points in Paul Schulze's Argument," 4.

34. Ibid.

35. Ibid.

36. "The Other Side. Mr. Schulze Reads the Interview with A. A. Denny and John Leary," 4.

37. "A Talk with Mr. Jeffs," *Seattle Daily Post-Intelligencer* (Seattle, WA), March 22, 1887, p. 3, c. 2.

38. "Contract Signed," *Los Angeles Daily Herald* (Los Angeles, CA), April 30, 1888, p. 1, c. 1. And: Northern Pacific Railroad draft agreement with Peter Kirk, April 28, 1888, Peter Kirk Collection, Kirkland Heritage Society, Kirkland, Washington.

39. "Schulze's Two Big Contracts," *Seattle Post-Intelligencer* (Seattle, WA), May 20, 1888, p. 6, c. 1.

40. Northern Pacific Railroad draft agreement with Peter Kirk, 1.

41. Ibid., 3-4.

42. Ibid., 9.

43. "From Olympia.—New Corporations," *Seattle Post-Intelligencer* (Seattle, WA), May 26, 1888, p. 4, c. 2. Only lists company name. No other details listed or who officers or owners might be.

44. "Moss Bay Iron and Steel Company, Limited. Annual Report," West Cumberland Times (Workington, Cumberland, England), March 16, 1889, p. 5.

45. *The Yakima Herald* (Yakima, WA), February 20, 1890, p. 3, c. 3.

46. Kirk, Peter, King County, Washington, Coal patent No. 109; "Land Patent Search," digital images, *General Land Office Records*, US Department of the Interior, Bureau of Land Management, https://glorecords.blm.gov/details/patent/default.aspx?Accession=0447-127&docClass=CP&sid=nvjgqnhn.mb0. Registered May 3, 1888; approved April 18, 1890.

47. "Real Estate Transfers," *Seattle Post-Intelligencer* (Seattle, WA), September 9, 1888, p. 7, c. 1.

48.   "Return of Mr. James Whitfield, From Seattle," *Workington Star* (Workington, Cumberland, England), August 25, 1888, p. 3, c. 1.

49.   "Moss Bay Shareholders Meeting," *West Cumberland Times* (Workington, Cumberland, England), April 3, 1889, p. 4, c. 6.

50.   "Ellensburg's Iron Works," *Seattle Post-Intelligencer* (Seattle, WA), July 25, 1890, p. 1, c. 4.

51.   "Notice to Woodmen," *Seattle Post-intelligencer* (Seattle, WA), May 12, 1888, p. 2.

52.   "Final Arrangements for the Big Mill Completed," *Seattle Post-Intelligencer* (Seattle, Washington Territory), May 9, 1888, p. 4, c. 1.

53.   "The Proposed Navy Yard," *Seattle Post-Intelligencer* (Seattle, Washington Territory) January 12, 1889, p. 3, c. 2. And: "Moss Bay Shareholders Meeting," 4.

54.   "The Moss Bay Works.—Appointment of a Liquidator," *West Cumberland Times* (Workington, Cumberland, England), April 5, 1890, p. 8, c. 4.

55.   "Moss Bay Iron and Steel Company, Limited. Annual Report," 5.

56.   Coal Ore Analysis pages from Mr. M. Courtis, Mining Engineer at Courtis & Smith in Detroit to undisclosed recipient, n. d., p. 4, Donated by Andrew Meyers, Kirkland Heritage Society, Kirkland, Washington.

57.   Courtis coal ore analysis, 4.

58.   "Final Arrangements for the Big Mill Completed," *Seattle Post-Intelligencer* (Seattle, Washington Territory), May 9, 1888, p. 4, c. 1.

Chapter 9

1.   "Good News—Kirk's Ironworks Located at Lake Washington," *Seattle Post-Intelligencer* (Seattle, WA), June 1, 1888, p. 1.

2.   "The Claim Confirmed," *Seattle Post-Intelligencer* (Seattle, WA), June 1, 1888, p. 4, c. 1-2.

3.   "...A Talk with Mr. Kirk," *Seattle Post-Intelligencer* (Seattle, WA), June 1, 1888, p. 1, c. 4-8.

4.   Hunt, Thomas Francis, "Kirkland City's Founder," May 9, 1916.

5.   "Moss Bay Iron and Steel Company, Limited," *West Cumberland Times* (Workington, Cumberland, England), March 5, 1888, p. 5.

6.   Correspondence from J. S. Randles to W. W. Williams, March 4, 1888, Accession No. 0049, Box No. 2, Folder: Financial Records, Peter Kirk Papers, University of Washington Libraries, Special Collections, Seattle, Washington.

7.   Hunt, Thomas Francis, "Kirkland City's Founder," May 9, 1916.

8. O'Connor, T. P., October 2, 1908, Reminiscences of Leigh S. J. Hunt in article in the *T. P. Weekly*, Accession No. 4667, Leigh S. J. Hunt papers, University of Washington Libraries, Special Collections, Seattle, Washington. T. P. O'Connor was an Irish Parliament member who had met Hunt early in Hunt's life and again later.

9. US Passport Applications, 1725-1925. Passport Applications, 1795-1905, 1898-1900; Roll 537-01 Jan 1900-15 Jan 1900, p581; No. 15189.

10. O'Connor, October 2, 1908, Leigh S. J. Hunt papers.

11. Typescript of short biography of Leigh S. J. Hunt by his wife Jessie Noble Hunt, 1947, Accession No. 4667, p. 1, Leigh S. J. Hunt papers, University of Washington Libraries, Special Collections, Seattle, Washington. Several typed pages from Hunt's wife, Jessie Noble Hunt, written at age 85 and 14 years after husband's death.

12. Collins, Jim, "The Founding of Kirkland," n.d., William Robert Sherrard papers, Accession No. 0366, University of Washington Libraries, Special Collections, Seattle, Washington.

13. "Leigh S. J. Hunt (1854-1933), Adventuresome Capitalist," posted by Joel, June 5, 2004, http://faroutliers.blogspot.com/2004/06/leigh-s-j-hunt-1854-1933-adventuresome.html (accessed January 30, 2018).

14. "Political Pot-Pie," *Seattle Republic* (Seattle, WA), March 29, 1901, p. 3, c. 1-4.

15. Hunt, Jessie Noble, 3.

16. *The Indianapolis Times* (Indianapolis, IN), October 6, 1933, p. 1, c. 5.

17. Rand, Laurance B. *High Stakes: The Life and Times of Leigh S. J. Hunt* (New York: Peter Lang Publishing, 1989), 28.

18. Ibid., 40. Letter to James S. Clarkson, December 29, 1886.

19. Ibid., 36-7.

20. Ibid., 38.

21. "Political Pot-Pie," 3.

22. Rand, *High Stakes*, 33-34.

23. Hunt, Jessie Noble, 3.

24. "Furnaces and Mills," *Seattle Post-Intelligencer* (Seattle, WA), May 29, 1890, p. 5.

25. "A Talk with Mr. Kirk," *Seattle Post-Intelligencer* (Seattle, WA), June 1, 1888, p. 1, c. 4-8.

26. "Real Estate," *Seattle Daily Post-Intelligencer* (Seattle, WA), April 3, 1887, p. 5, c. 5. Bought land for $5,000 with his wife's uncle, Charles A. Cummins.

27. "An Active Market," *Seattle Post-Intelligencer* (Seattle, WA), July 15, 1888, p. 3, c. 1-3. Author added up all entries to get totals of homestead sales to Hunt and from Hunt to KL&I Co.

28. French, Harry, June 4, 1888, "French Diaries, 1880-1893," p. 36, Kirkland Heritage Society, Kirkland, Washington, http://kirklandheritage.org/wp-content/uploads/2014/06/1880-1893-Harry-D-French.pdf (accessed June 2, 2020).

29. "Real Estate Transfers," *Seattle Post-Intelligencer* (Seattle, WA), September 14, 1888, p. 3.

30. "Talk with Mr. Denny," *Seattle Daily Post-Intelligencer* (Seattle, WA), July 3, 1887, p. 5, c. 3.

31. Dailey, Tom, "Coast Salish Villages of Puget Sound," http://coastsalishmap.org/Village_Descriptions_Duwamish-Seattle.htm#14 (accessed March 28, 2019).

32. Duwamish Tribe, "Treaty of Point Elliott," https://www.duwamishtribe.org/treaty-of-point-elliott (accessed December 31, 2020).

33. Ibid., "Exile to Ballast Island."

34. Various articles on the early settlers, George Seville Kirk Scrapbook, Kirkland Heritage Society, Kirkland, Washington.

35. "Bruin Was Bold. A Bear Attacks a Fine Hog Belonging to Walter Walker," George Seville Kirk Scrapbook, 28.

36. Lindahl, Shirley. *In Christian Fellowship, Congregational Church of Kirkland 1880-1980* (Advance Printing, Kirkland Washington, 1979), 15.

Chapter 10

1. "The New City of Iron," *Seattle Post-Intelligencer* (Seattle, WA), July 27, 1890, p. 8, c. 1.

2. Sherrard, William Robert, *The Kirkland Steel Mill* (Master's thesis, University of Washington, 1958), 129.

3. "The Proposed Navy Yard," *Seattle Post-Intelligencer* (Seattle, Washington Territory), January 12, 1889, p. 3, c. 2.

4. Higson, Jacob, "Report on Mines in Washington State for the Pacific Investment Company," March 17, 1890, p. 20, Peter Kirk Collection, Kirkland Heritage Society, Kirkland, Washington.

5. "News from Kirkland," *Seattle Post-Intelligencer* (Seattle, WA), July 19, 1891, p. 8.

6. Sherrard, *Kirkland Steel Mill*, Table 6, 133.

7. Ibid., Table 5, 131.

8. Aubrey Williams to Arline Stokes, January 5, 1969. And: Sherrard, *Kirkland Steel Mill*, 22.

9. "Final Arrangements for the Big Mill Completed," *Seattle Post-Intelligencer* (Seattle, Washington Territory), May 9, 1888, p. 4, c. 1.

10. "A Talk with Mr. Kirk," *Seattle Post-Intelligencer* (Seattle, WA), July 15, 1888, p. 5, c. 1.

11. "Tacoma Has Lost A Prize," *Seattle Daily Post-Intelligencer* (Seattle, WA), March 2, 1887, p. 4, c. 2.

12. "Talk with Mr. Jeffs," 3.

13. "A Talk with Mr. Kirk," July 15, 1888, 5.

14. Ibid.

15. Ibid.

16. Ibid.

17. "Kirkland's Big Mill. One of the Pacific Coast's Big Lumber Plants," *Kirkland News* (Kirkland, WA), George Seville Kirk Scrapbook, 18.

18. "Plans of the Town," *Seattle Post-Intelligencer* (Seattle, WA), June 1, 1888, p. 4, c. 1-2.

19. Ely, *Our Foundering Fathers*, 38.

20. "Peter Kirk—Steel Mill Impossible Dream," *East Side Journal* (Kirkland, WA), July 12, 1972, p. 6, Kirkland Heritage Society, Kirkland, Washington.

21. "Plat of Kirkland," George Seville Kirk Scrapbook, 16.

22. Aubrey Williams to Arline Stokes, October 12, 1968.

23. Ibid., December 3, 1968.

24. "Lake Washington. Beautiful Little Residence Towns Spring Up," *Seattle Post-Intelligencer* (Seattle, WA), February 24, 1890, p. 8, c. 4.

25. "Notes from Kirkland," *Seattle Post-Intelligencer* (Seattle, WA), June 6, 1891.

26. "Ho! For Kirkland!" *Seattle Post-Intelligencer* (Seattle, WA), July 28, 1891.

27. "Greyhound of the Lake Damaged," *Seattle Post-Intelligencer* (Seattle, WA), June 7, 1893.

28. Ibid.

29. Aubrey Williams to Arline Stokes, September 3, 1968.

30. "A Big Contract, A Talk with Peter Kirk," *Seattle Post-Intelligencer* (Seattle, WA), August 12, 1888, p. 5, c. 3.

31. Ibid.

32. Ibid.

33. "Workington Primrose League," *West Cumberland Times* (Workington, Cumberland, England), February 5, 1890, p 4. c. 5. And: "Mr. C. J. Valentine on His American Tours," *Workington Star* (Workington, Cumberland, England), February 7, 1890, p. 3, c. 3.

34. "The Cape Verde," *Seattle Daily Post-Intelligencer* (Seattle, WA), December 14. 1887, p. 3, c. 3.

35. "Personal," *Seattle Daily Post-Intelligencer* (Seattle, WA), December 14. 1887, p. 3, c. 2. And "Brevities," *Seattle Daily Post-Intelligencer* (Seattle, WA), December 10, 1887, p. 3, c. 1.

36. "Brevities," *Seattle Daily Post-Intelligencer* (Seattle, WA), December 31, 1887, p. 3, c. 1.

37. "New York, Passenger and Crew Lists (including Castle Garden and Ellis island), 1820-1957," digital image s.v. "Peter Kirk" Date, 1890, May, 08, Majestic, *Ancestry.com.*

38. J. E. to W. W. W., March 9, 1889, Peter Kirk Papers, Seattle.

39. "Personal," *Seattle Post-Intelligencer* (Seattle, WA), December 15, 1889, p. 6, c. 3.

40.   "New York, Passenger and Crew Lists (including Castle Garden and Ellis island),
       1820-1957," digital image s.v. "Peter Kirk" Date, 1889, Jul, 20, Germanic, *Ancestry.com.*

Chapter 11

1.   Kamens, Brian, Tacoma Library, email to author referencing 1888 Sanborn Map for
       Tacoma and Tacoma City Directory, April 24-25, 2018.
2.   "Notice to Woodmen," *Seattle Post-Intelligencer* (Seattle, WA), May 12, 1888, p. 2.
3.   "Personal," *Seattle Post-Intelligencer* (Seattle, WA), June 3, 1888, p. 5, c. 4.
4.   "Stories of Old Settlers. Andrew Nelson's Early Struggles on Lake Washington,"
       Kirkland News (Kirkland, WA), n.d., George Seville Kirk Scrapbook, 25-26. And:
       Aubrey Williams to Arline Stokes, June 20, 1968.
5.   "Personal Notes," *Seattle Post-Intelligencer* (Seattle, WA), June 24, 1888, p. 8, c. 2.
6.   "A Talk with Mr. Kirk," July 15, 1888, 5.
7.   Fire insurance policy for Lots 7-10, Block 6, Kirkland for Peter Kirk, November 8,
       1889, Accession No. 0049, Box No. 2, Folder: Insurance Policies, Peter Kirk Papers,
       University of Washington Libraries, Special Collections, Seattle, Washington.
8.   Kirkland streets were originally named but changed over time. The historical society
       has since erected new street signs reflecting the old and the new.
9.   "Lake Washington. Beautiful Little Residence Towns Spring Up," *Seattle Post-
       Intelligencer* (Seattle, WA), February 24, 1890, p. 8, c. 4.
10.   Stokes, Arline, "Tour Visitor Recalls Peter Kirk and Family," *East Side Journal*
       (Kirkland, WA), September 25, 1968, p. 2, Kirkland Heritage Society, Kirkland,
       Washington.
11.   "New York, Passenger and Crew Lists (including Castle Garden and Ellis Island),
       1820-1957," digital image s.v. "Joseph Ellis" Date, 1888, Jul, 16, Umbria, *Ancestry.
       com.* And: "Moss Bay Iron and Steel Company, Limited," *West Cumberland Times*
       (Workington, England), March 5, 1888, p. 5. "Notes, Personal and Otherwise,"
       Seattle Daily Post-Intelligencer (Seattle, WA), April 10, 1887, p. 8, c. 2. Same column
       listed Peter Kirk at the Occidental Hotel and Arthur Whittle of Whitehaven,
       England had arrived same time. Alfred Whittle, son of John Whittle who was the
       Kirk Brothers distributor in Workington when the Kirks first arrived in the 1860's.
       Ellis is Moss Bay Ltd. executive.
12.   Stokes, Arline, "Tour Visitor Recalls Peter Kirk and Family," 2.
13.   Jean Kellett Kaye to Arline Stokes, no date.
14.   Stokes, Arline, "Tour Visitor Recalls Peter Kirk and Family," 2.
15.   Washington Marriage Records, 1854-2013; Marriage Return, 29 Jan 1895; Seattle,
       King, Washington for Margaret Hughes and Peter Floy. Margaret was born in 1855
       to Joe and Jean Hughes.

16. Jean Kellett Kaye to Arline Stokes, no date.

17. *Kirkland News* (Kirkland, WA), September 1, 1890, p. 1, Kirkland Heritage Society, Kirkland, Washington. Print.

18. "A Talk with Mr. Kirk," July 15, 1888, 5.

19. Margaret Hughes listed with Lot 12, Block 25 on list of lots in Kirkland plat owned by Peter Kirk on Great Western Iron and Steel Company letterhead, February 24, 1892, Accession No. 0049, Box No. 2, Folder: Miscellaneous, Peter Kirk Papers, University of Washington Libraries, Special Collections, Seattle, Washington.

20. "What Society Did, First Annual Ball," *Seattle Post-Intelligencer* (Seattle, WA), August 30, 1891, p. 12, c. 3.

21. "Personal," *Seattle Post-Intelligencer* (Seattle, WA), December 4, 1893 p. 4, c. 4.

22. Dickinson, Barbara, email to author from Lynne Carlton for Barbara Dickinson with information for "Kirk Reunion," July 3, 2005. Forwarded to Dave Cantrill at Kirkland Heritage Society, Peter Kirk Collection, Marie Kirk Bell Folder, Kirkland, Washington.

23. Music written on letterhead of Moss Bay Iron & Steel Company of America, Peter Kirk Collection, Olive Kirk D'Arcy Folder, Kirkland Heritage Society, Kirkland, Washington.

24. Typescript of conversation between Myrtle Robertson and Fanny Kirk Capron and other Kirk daughters concerning church project in Friday Harbor, Washington, n.d., Myrtle Robertson Hanging File, Kirkland Public Library, Kirkland, Washington.

25. Lindahl, *In Christian Fellowship*, 17.

26. Myrtle Cecilia Robertson photo typescripts, n.d., #26.

27. Lindahl, *In Christian Fellowship*, 23.

28. "Mrs. Olive D'Arcy Long Time Resident Called," *Friday Harbor Journal* (Friday Harbor, WA), September 16, 1944, p. 1.

29. Aubrey Williams to Arline Stokes, June 20, 1968.

30. "What Society Did, First Annual Ball," *Seattle Post-Intelligencer* (Seattle, WA), August 30, 1891, p. 12, c. 3.

31. Aubrey Williams to Arline Stokes, March 16, 1969.

Chapter 12

1. J. Ellis to W. W. Williams, November 3, 1888, Peter Kirk Papers, Seattle.

2. "Moss Bay Iron Company," *Carlisle Patriot* (Carlisle, Cumberland, England), March 22, 1889. p. 3, c. 5.

3. Washington State Legislature, "Washington State Constitution," http://leg.wa.gov/CodeReviser/Pages/WAConstitution.aspx (accessed May 31, 2020).

4. "Moss Bay Iron and Steel Company, Limited. Annual Report," 5.

5. *Workington Star* (Workington, Cumberland, England), April 11, 1890, p. 3, c. 1.

6. "Moss Bay Shareholders Meeting," 4.

7. Rand, *High Stakes*, 51.

8. Aubrey Williams to Arline Stokes, April 25, 1968.

9. Hunt, Jessie Noble, 4.

10. *Seattle Post-Intelligencer* (Seattle, Washington Territory) June 7, 1889, Kirkland Heritage Society, Kirkland, Washington.

11. "How to Benefit the City," *Seattle Post-Intelligencer* (Seattle, Washington Territory) June 9, 1889, p. 1, c. 2.

12. "New City of Seattle, Daughter of Phoenix, Born Amidst Hot Embers," George Seville Kirk Scrapbook, 50-51.

13. Ibid.

14. "Estimates of Losses," *Seattle Post-Intelligencer* (Seattle, Washington Territory) June 7, 1889, p. 2, c. 1-2.

15. "The MossBay Steel and Ironworks," *Cumberland Pacquet, and Ware's Whitehaven Advertiser* (Whitehaven, Cumberland, England), April 30, 1890, p. 5, c. 7.

16. "Moss Bay Shareholders Meeting," 4.

17. "Moss Bay Hematite Iron & Steel Co. Ltd., Workington, Directors' Minute Book," April 12, 1889, YBSC/6/2/1, Carlisle Archive Centre, Carlisle, Cumbria, England.

18. *Washington Standard* (Olympia, WA), April 26, 1889, p. 1, c. 7.

19. "Great Iron Works to be Built in Kirkland At Once," *Seattle Post-Intelligencer* (Seattle, WA), May 29, 1890, p. 5.

20. Balance sheet for Moss Bay of America, December 31, 1889, Accession No. 0049, Box No. 2, Folder: Financial Records, Misc., Peter Kirk Papers, University of Washington Libraries, Special Collections, Seattle, Washington. Henry Noble is father-in-law to Leigh Hunt. Advertisements for the bank regularly listed the directors.

21. "Great Iron Works to be Built in Kirkland At Once," 5.

22. King, Moses, *King's Handbook of the United States* (Buffalo: Moses King Corp.), 874.

23. Agreement between Peter Kirk and Great Western Iron & Steel Co., June 28, 1895, p. 1, Peter Kirk Collection, Kirkland Heritage Society, Kirkland, Washington.

24. "Great Iron Works to be Built in Kirkland At Once," 5.

25. "Indenture relating to the Workington Iron Co. Ltd," December 24, 1879, YBSC/3/1/4, Carlisle Archive Centre. Carlisle, Cumbria, England.

26. Sherrard, *Kirkland Steel Mill*, 105-108.

27. Agreement between Peter Kirk and Great Western Iron & Steel Co., 2.

28. J. E. to W. W. W., March 2, 1889, Peter Kirk Papers, Seattle.

29. "Development of Our Iron Resources," *Seattle Post-Intelligencer* (Seattle, WA), May 29, 1890, p. 4, c. 1.

Chapter 13

1. "The Kirkland Iron Works," *Seattle Post-Intelligencer* (Seattle, WA), January 1, 1891, p. 1.

2. "The Great Western Iron and Steel Company," George Seville Kirk Scrapbook.

3. Aubrey Williams to Arline Stokes, June 20, 1968.

4. "Lake Washington. Beautiful Little Residence Towns Spring Up," *Seattle Post-Intelligencer* (Seattle, WA), February 24, 1890, p. 8, c. 4.

5. Aubrey Williams to Arline Stokes, June 20, 1968.

6. "The New City of Iron," 8.

7. Aubrey Williams to Arline Stokes, October 12, 1968. And: June 20, 1968; April 25, 1968; July 17, 1968.

8. "Great Iron Works to be Built in Kirkland At Once," 5.

9. "The New City of Iron," 8.

10. "Works at Kirkland," *Seattle Post-Intelligencer* (Seattle, WA), March 8, 1891, p. 8, c. 5.

11. "The Kirkland Iron Works," *Seattle Post-Intelligencer* (Seattle, WA), January 1, 1891, p. 1.

12. "Works at Kirkland," 8.

13. "Machinery for the Iron Works," *Seattle Post-Intelligencer Seattle Post-Intelligencer* (Seattle, WA), April 4, 1891, p. 8, c. 2.

14. "All the Material Unloaded," *Seattle Post-Intelligencer* (Seattle, WA), April 1, 1891, p. 5.

15. "Kirkland Items," *Seattle Post-Intelligencer* (Seattle, WA), July 7, 1891, p. 8, c. 6.

16. "For Blast Furnaces," *Seattle Post-Intelligencer* (Seattle, WA), August 11, 1891, p. 8, c. 1.

17. "More Machinery for Kirkland, "8.

18. "For Blast Furnaces," 8.

19. "The Kirkland Iron Works," *Seattle Post-Intelligencer* (Seattle, WA), January 1, 1891, p. 1.

20. "Hail to Harrison," *Seattle Post-Intelligencer* (Seattle, WA), May 6, 1891, p. 9, c. 1.

21. Crowley, Walt, "Lake Washington Ship Canal," Posted July 1, 1999, *HistoryLink.org*, Essay 1444, (accessed February 21, 2017).

22. "Hail to Harrison," 9.

23. "Trip on the Sound. Proposal to Lunch the President on the Steamer," *Seattle Post-Intelligencer* (Seattle, WA), April 25, 1891, p. 8, c. 3.

24. "Boarding Steamer Kirkland on Lake Washington and Trip Around Lake, Accompanied by Fleet," *Seattle Post-Intelligencer* (Seattle, WA), May 6, 1891, p. 9, c. 1. Included the schedule of the President while in Seattle. Also: "The City Gaily Bedecked," same issue, p. 9, c. 3.

25. "Around Lake Washington," *Seattle Post-Intelligencer* (Seattle, WA), May 7, 1891, p. 2, c. 2. Detailed the events from the previous day in Seattle.

26. Lindahl, *In Christian Fellowship*, 18.

27. "Through the South and West with the President, April 14-May 15, 1891," p 96-99, President Benjamin Harrison Archives, Library of Congress, https://archive.org/stream/throughsouthwest00harr/throughsouthwest00harr_djvu.txt (accessed 2016).

28. Ibid.

29. "The Lake Washington Canal," *Seattle Post-Intelligencer* (Seattle, WA), February 26, 1892, p. 1.

30. "Two New Factories," *Seattle Post-Intelligencer* (Seattle, WA), July 21, 1892.

31. "Another Kirkland Industry," *Seattle Post-Intelligencer* (Seattle, WA), July 1, 1890, p. 5, c. 2.

Chapter 14

1. San Juan County Auditor's Office, "Document Search," digital images, Documents 1891-0050004-6, September 10-11, 1891, https://www.sanjuanco.com/171/Recorded-Document-Search.

2. *The Islander* (Friday Harbor, WA), August 30, 1894.

3. *The Islander* (Friday Harbor, WA), March 14, 1895.

4. Kirk, Peter, San Juan County, Washington, WASAA 096339, "Land Patent Search," digital images, *General Land Office Records*, US Department of the Interior, Bureau of Land Management, https://glorecords.blm.gov/. BLM property description for homestead: DM ID: 399277, Original Survey WA-Willamette, Twp. 036.0N, Rng. 004.0W; survey completed 10/15/1874 by Thomas M. Reed. Field notes from DM IOD: 404380, volume W0216, for WA state.

5. "The Islands as Summer Resorts," *Seattle Post-Intelligencer* (Seattle, WA), May 21, 1892, p. 1, c. 7.

6. Autograph book entry signed by Fanny V. Kirk at Mitchell's Bay, San Juan Island, August 29, 1892, Peter Kirk Collection, Fanny Kirk's Autograph Book Collection, Kirkland Heritage Society, Kirkland, Washington. Another entry from Mamma on San Juan Island, October 12, 1892, same record.

7. Greenfield, Marie Larsen Johnson, interview by Nancy R. Lindenberg, January 15, 1995, transcript, San Juan Historical Society, Washington State Historical Society oral histories collection, http://www.sjmuseum.org/community-outreach/oral-histories/. Marie Larsen Johnson Greenfield grew up at Deer Lodge after the Kirk family sold it in 1918. Transcript originally found at: http://digitum.washingtonhistory.org/cdm/singleitem/collection/oralh/id/297/rec/8 (accessed 2016).

8. "Island Landmark Destroyed by Fire," *Friday Harbor Journal (Friday Harbor, WA)*, August 18, 1949.

9. Greenfield oral history, January 15, 1995.

10. "Peter Kirk—Steel Mill Impossible Dream," 6.

11. Multiple articles from 1892-1918 in *The Islander, San Juan Islander and Friday Harbor Journal.* (Friday Harbor, WA), Chronicling America and San Juan Historical Museum Archives.

12. "Peter Kirk—Steel Mill Impossible Dream," 6.

13. Correspondence from Louis Dixon to Mary Ann Kirk concerning her inheritance annuities, December 25, 1894, Accession No. 0049, Box No. 2, Folder: Settlement of Mrs. Kirk's Estate, Peter Kirk Papers, University of Washington Libraries, Special Collections, Seattle, Washington.

Chapter 15

1. Jessie Kirk Charlton to William Sherrard, July 4, 1958, William Robert Sherrard Papers.

2. "Population of King County," *Seattle Post-Intelligencer* (Seattle, WA), June 19, 1892, p. 7, c. 7.

3. "New Home Industry: Woolen Mill in Operation, Employs 70 People," *Seattle Post-Intelligencer* (Seattle, WA), November 20, 1892, p. 8, c. 1.

4. "Two New Factories," *Seattle Post-Intelligencer* (Seattle, WA), July 21, 1892, p. 8, c. 2.

5. *Olympia Tribune* (Olympia, WA), March 7, 1892 p. 2, c. 1.

6. Lindahl, *In Christian Fellowship*, 22.

7. Typescript of Kirkland history, n.d., Myrtle Robertson, Hanging File, Kirkland Public Library, Kirkland, Washington.

8. Sherrard, William, "The History of the Kirkland Steel Mill," William Robert Sherrard Papers.

9. "How It Struck the Railroads, Panic Caused Enormous Total of Receiverships—Foreclosures Not Ripe," *Seattle Post-Intelligencer* (Seattle, WA), December 22, 1893, p. 8, c. 1.

10. Lindahl, *In Christian Fellowship*, 18-24.

11. Collins, "The Founding of Kirkland."

12. "The Mossbay Steel and Ironworks," *Cumberland Pacquet, and Ware's Whitehaven Advertiser* (Whitehaven, Cumberland, England), April 30, 1890, p. 5, c. 7.

13. Sherrard, *Kirkland Steel Mill*, 105-108.

14. Ruffner, *Report on Washington*, 112 & 137.

15. Courtis letter to McCaul, November 17, 1891, p. 2, Peter Kirk Collection, Kirkland Heritage Society, Kirkland, Washington.

16. Courtis, Coal ore analysis, p. 7.

17. "Not in It—The Ditch," *Aberdeen Herald* (Aberdeen, WA), September 1, 1892, p. 2, c. 1.

18. Correspondence from James McNaught to D. H. Gilman to support Canal Bill, February 7, 1893, Daniel H. Gilman Papers. Accession No. 2730, Box 2, File 29, University of Washington Libraries, Special Collections, Seattle, Washington.

19. Collins, "The Founding of Kirkland."

20. Sherrard, *Kirkland Steel Mill*, 105-108.

Chapter 16

1. Myrtle Cecilia Robertson photo typescripts, n.d., #15. As told to her by James Collins.

2. "Delinquent Taxpayers," *Seattle Post-Intelligencer* (Seattle, WA), May 16, 1894, p. 5, c. 1. Also, "Hotel Arrivals," *Seattle Post-Intelligencer* (Seattle, WA), May 26, 1894, p. 8, c. 5.

3. "Kirkland Plant Shipped to Ontario," *Seattle Post-Intelligencer* (Seattle, WA), August 30, 1895.

4. Agreement between Peter Kirk and Great Western Iron & Steel Co., June 28, 1895.

5. "Local Law Case—Ellis v. Kirk," *Maryport Advertiser*, March 4, 1893, p. 3, c. 5.

6. Ibid.

7. "Application by the Bank," *West Cumberland Times* (Workington, Cumberland, England), April 5, 1890, p. 8, c. 4. English debentures refer to a long-term security yielding a fixed rate of interest, issued by a company, and secured against assets.

8. "The Moss Bay Company," *Workington Star* (Workington, Cumberland, England), April 11, 1890, p. 3, c. 1. Referencing statements made by the recent issue of the *Iron Trades Journal*, the "leading journal of the steel trade."

9. "Moss Bay Co. Liquidation Meeting," *Cumberland Pacquet, and Ware's Whitehaven Advertiser* (Whitehaven, Cumberland, England), June 19, 1890, p. 8, c. 2.

10. "Steel Manufacture at Maryport," *Sheffield Daily Telegraph* (Sheffield, Yorkshire, England), p. 6, c. 2. And: "The Moss Bay Co.'s Annual Report," *Workington Star* (Workington, Cumberland, England), March 21, 1890, p. 1, c. 4.

11. "Mr. Peat of Middlesbrough, the Liquidator…," *Carlisle Patriot* (Carlisle, Cumberland, England), May 16, 1890, p. 3, c. 6.

12. "Moss Bay Iron Company," *Carlisle Patriot* (Carlisle, Cumberland, England), December 12, 1890, p. 7, c. 1.

13. "The Moss Bay Meeting," *Workington Star and Harrington Guardian* (Workington, Cumberland, England), June 20, 1890, p. 3, c. 5.

14. J. Ellis to W. W. Williams, January 21, 1891, Peter Kirk Papers, Seattle.

15.   Contract between Julian Kennedy and Peter Kirk, January 13, 1893, Accession
      No. 0049, Box No. 2, Folder: Correspondence, Peter Kirk Papers, University of
      Washington Libraries, Special Collections, Seattle, Washington. Julian Kennedy was
      one of the superintendents of the great Carnegie steel establishments at Pittsburg.

16.   Florrie and Louis Dixon to Mary Ann Kirk, December 25, 1894-January 1, 1895.

17.   Peter Gibson, death certificate, 13 Oct 1865, no. 127, General Register Office,
      Whitehaven, Cumberland, England.

18.   Hannah Quirk, death certificate, 24 Jun 1871, no. 415, General Register Office,
      Workington, Cumberland, England.

19.   "Particulars and Conditions of Sale in the matter of the estate of Hannah Quirk,"
      Cumbria Record Office, DMil/Mounsey/153/155, Carlisle, Cumbria, England.

20.   Florrie and Louis Dixon to Mary Ann Kirk, December 25, 1894-January 1, 1895.

21.   Letter from Arthur Dixon to Peter Kirk concerning Mary Ann Kirk's estate in
      England, August 28, 1909, p. 2, Peter Kirk Collection, Mary (Quirk) Kirk Estate,
      Kirkland Heritage Society, Kirkland, Washington.

22.   Receipt ledger listing many stocks and possible dividends in English pounds
      received into bank, January 1-June 20, 1907, Peter Kirk Collection, Bills and
      Receipts Folder, Kirkland Heritage Society, Kirkland, Washington.

23.   J. Ellis to W. W. Williams, March 31, 1888, Peter Kirk Papers, Seattle.

24.   "1891 England Census," digital image s.v. "Charles J. Valentine," Cumberland,
      Workington, District 12, Ancestry.com.

25.   "Cockermouth Division," Carlisle Patriot (Carlisle, Cumberland, England),
      September 18, 1891, p. 3, c. 5.

26.   "Conveyance of the Bankfield estate and mansion," August 2, 1895, YDX 473/1/3/15,
      Carlisle Archive Centre. Carlisle, Cumbria, England.

27.   Lindahl, In Christian Fellowship, 18-24.

28.   "Courts and Public Offices," Seattle Post-Intelligencer (Seattle, WA), December 28,
      1894, p. 5, c. 3.

29.   Kirk, Peter, Kirk's Centrifugal Machine for Manufacturing "Compressed Steel"
      Weldless Rings, n. d., Peter Kirk Collection, Patents and Inventions File, Kirkland
      Heritage Society, Kirkland, Washington.

30.   Ibid.

31.   "US City Directories, 1822-1995," digital image s.v. "John G. Kellett," Seattle,
      Washington, City Directory, 1893, Ancestry.com. And: Jean Kellett Kaye to Arline
      Stokes, no date.

32.   Seattle Post-Intelligencer (Seattle, WA), October 8, 1892, p. 8, c. 2.

33.   "Summons by Publication," Ellensburg Dawn (Ellensburg, WA), March 24, 1898, p.
      3, c. 6.

34. "1901 Census of Canada," digital image s.v. "William Anderson," British Columbia, Yale and Cariboo, Kootenay (West/Quest), Rossland Riding/Division Rossland), *Ancestry.com*.

35. Correspondence from I. B. Atkinson of Port Alberim, BC about ore and coal deposits to Peter Kirk, December 20, 1912, Accession No. 0049, Box No. 2, Folder: Unsorted Correspondence, Peter Kirk Papers, University of Washington Libraries, Special Collections, Seattle, Washington.

36. "City is Planning for the Ownership of Electric Plant," *The Vancouver Sun* (Vancouver, British Columbia), September 13, 1912, p. 11.

37. Aubrey Williams to Arline Stokes, September 25, 1968.

38. "1900 United States Federal Census," digital image s.v. "Walter W. Williams," Washington, King, Seattle Ward 03, District 0092, *Ancestry.com*.

39. Correspondence from Peter Kirk to Mr. Williams, December 12, 1910, Accession No. 0049, Box No. 2, Folder: General Correspondence, Peter Kirk Papers, University of Washington Libraries, Special Collections, Seattle, Washington.

40. "Washington, Petitions for Naturalization, 1860-1991," digital image s.v. "Walter Winston Williams" (February 11, 1902), Superior Court, King County, (Roll 014) Naturalization Case Files, 1901-3, *Ancestry.com*.

41. "Rousing British Meeting," *Seattle Post-Intelligencer* (Seattle, WA), February 28, 1900, p. 10, c. 1. And: "Sympathize with England," *Seattle Post-Intelligencer* (Seattle, WA), May 3, 1900, p. 7, c. 4.

42. "Political Pot-Pie," 3.

43. Hunt, Jessie Noble, 4.

44. "Leigh Hunt Gets Back to Seattle," *Seattle Star* (Seattle, WA), March 13, 1901, p. 1, c. 5.

45. "Political Pot-Pie," 3. And: "Leigh Hunt, State Man, Dies in West," *The Indianapolis Times* (Indianapolis, IN), October 6, 1933, p. 1, c. 5.

46. "Political Pot-Pie," 3.

47. "Empire Builder, Hunt Succumbs," *The Los Angeles Times* (Los Angeles, CA), October 6, 1933, p. 3, c. 1-2.

48. "Leigh Hunt…," *Washington Standard* (Olympia, WA), April 12, 1901, p. 2, c. 2.

49. "Incorporated," *Seattle Star* (Seattle, WA), March 26, 1901, p. 3, c. 1. Also: "A New Paper Is Now Assured," *Seattle Star* (Seattle, WA), March 27, 1901, p. 3, c. 1; "Leigh Hunt Gets Back to Seattle," 1.

50. "Will Sue A. P.," *Seattle Star* (Seattle, WA), April 1, 1901, p. 1, c. 3.

51. "Banquet to Leigh Hunt," *Seattle Star* (Seattle, WA), April 1, 1901, p. 4, c. 2.

52. "As was predicted…," *Seattle Republican* (Seattle, WA), July 19, 1901, p. 1, c. 5.

53. Petr Kirk vs. Leigh S. J. Hunt, 1901, King County Superior Court, case no. 32111, Washington state.

54. Correspondence from King County Superior Court to Peter Kirk, May 6, 1901, Accession No. 0049, Box No. 2, Folder: Correspondence, Peter Kirk Papers, University of Washington Libraries, Special Collections, Seattle, Washington.

Chapter 17

1. "Washington State and Territorial Censuses, 1857-1892," digital image s.v. "Peter Kirk," 1889, King, Houghton, *Ancestry.com*.
2. "Polk's Seattle Directory, 1890" digital image s.v. "James Bell," Washington State Archives- Digital Archives, https://www.digitalarchives.wa.gov/DigitalObject/View/88B288C5F8D72D5C232E88511142E2FD (accessed June 2, 2020).
3. James Bell, birth certificate, 9 Sep 1869, no. 388, General Register Office for Northern Ireland, Greyabbey, Newtownards, Ireland.
4. "Pennsylvania, Passenger and Crew Lists, 1800-1962," digital image s.v. "Mary J. Bell," T840-Philadelphia, 1883-1945, 017, *Ancestry.com*. She traveled on the *SS Hibernian*, August 8, 1892 with her children Mary A., William, Andrew, and Jennie. His father and brother had immigrated years before and were living in Pittsburgh.
5. "Selected US Naturalization Records – Original Documents, 1790-1974," digital image s.v. "James Bell," (Minor's Naturalization 28 Oct. 1892), Washington, Superior Court, King County (Rolls 1-51), 1854-1928, (Roll 005) Naturalization Case Files, 1892-1893, *Ancestry.com*.
6. "What Society Did, First Annual Ball," *Seattle Post-Intelligencer* (Seattle, WA), August 30, 1891, p. 12, c. 3.
7. "Washington, County Marriages, 1855-2008," digital image s.v. "James Bell & Mary Kirk" (marriage license 14 Nov. 1893), King county, Marriage license register 1896-1900 vol. 9, *Ancestry.com*.
8. "Washington, Marriage records, 1854-2013," digital image s.v. "James Bell" (15 Nov. 1893), Whatcom, Marriages 1898 Sep-Dec; Marriage Return #242, *Ancestry.com*.
9. Ibid.
10. "Personal," *Seattle Post-Intelligencer* (Seattle, WA), December 4, 1893, p. 4.
11. "Washington, Birth Records, 1870-1935," digital image s.v. "Vivian Bell" (birth 20 Feb 1894), no. 1773, King County, Seattle King County, Health Department Birth Records: 1891-1907, *Ancestry.com*.
12. "British Columbia, Canada, Marriage Index, 1872-1935," index s.v. Florence Kirk, Victoria, registration number 1894-09-006250, *Ancestry.com*.
13. "Personal," *Seattle Post-Intelligencer* (Seattle, WA), November 24, 1891, p. 8, c. 2.
14. "1901 England Census," digital image s.v. "Arthur L. Dixon," Cheshire, Sale, ALL, District 39. *Ancestry.com*.

15. Various correspondence from Florrie Dixon to family, various dates, Peter Kirk Collection, Florence Kirk file, Kirkland Heritage Society, Kirkland, Washington.

16. Florrie and Louis Dixon to Mary Ann Kirk, December 25, 1894-January 1, 1895.

17. Ibid.

18. "1900 United States Federal Census," digital image s.v. "Peter Floy," Washington, Kitsap, Colby, District 120, *Ancestry.com*.

19. "Launching of the Floy Burg," *The Islander* (Friday Harbor, WA), December 6, 1894.

20. *The Islander* (Friday Harbor, WA), January 31, 1895.

21. "Washington, Marriage Records, 1854-2013," digital image s.v. "Peter P. Floy & Margaret Hughes" (marriage license 29 Jan. 1895), King, Marriages 1895 Jan-Apr, *Ancestry.com*.

22. "Mitchell Bay," *San Juan Islander* (Friday Harbor, WA) August 22, 1908, p. 1, c. 5.

23. Florence Dixon to Mama (Mary Ann Kirk), October 15, 1897, Peter Kirk Collection, Kirkland.

24. Florence Dixon to Clara Kirk, January 21, 1898.

25. Florence Dixon to Fanny Kirk, April 22, 1898.

26. "Hotel Arrivals," *Seattle Post-Intelligencer* (Seattle, WA), June 19, 1898, p. 19, c. 5.

27. "Roche Harbor News Briefs," *San Juan Islander* (Friday Harbor, WA) March 30, 1899, p. 3, c. 4.

28. "U.S., Border Crossings from Canada to U.S., 1895-1860," s.v. "Florence Lucile Dixon," A3599-Blaine, Washington, July 1924-October 1956, ALL, 006. *Ancestry.com*.

29. "Bruin Was Bold. A Bear Attacks a Fine Hog Belonging to Walter Walker," George Seville Kirk Scrapbook, 28.

30. "Roche Harbor News Briefs," *San Juan Islander* (Friday Harbor, WA), June 8, 1899, p. 3, c. 4.

31. Hunt, Thomas Francis, "Kirkland City's Founder," May 9, 1916.

32. "Roche Harbor News Briefs, *San Juan Islander* (Friday Harbor, WA), September 21, 1899, p. 3, c. 3.

Chapter 18

1. "What People Say. A transient record of private opinions publicly expressed," *Yakima Herald* (Yakima, WA), November 23, 1899, p. 19, c. 1.

2. Kirk, Peter, 'Rotary Hydraulic Dredger, #632,126,' United States, 1899.

3. Florence Dixon to Fanny Kirk, April 22, '98, Peter Kirk Collection, Kirkland.

4. "Selected US Naturalization Records – Original Documents, 1790-1974," digital
    image s.v. "Peter Kirk," (filed 14 Nov. 1899), Washington, Superior Court, King
    County (Rolls 1-51), 1854-1928, (Roll 013) Naturalization Case Files, 1899-1901,
    Ancestry.com. And: "Notice for Publication," *San Juan Islander* (Friday Harbor, WA)
    November 9, 1899, p. 2, c. 7.
5. "1900 US Federal Census," digital image s.v. "Peter Kirk," Washington, King County,
    Kirkland, District 59, *Ancestry.com*.
6. Contract between Peter Kirk and A. J. Pidgeon concerning Peter Kirk's ore roaster
    invention and a new smelter operation, Accession No. 0049, Box No. 2, Folder:
    Legal Documents, Peter Kirk Papers, University of Washington Libraries, Special
    Collections, Seattle Washington.
7. Kirk, Peter, 'Combined Roaster and Smelter, patent #688,651,' United States, 1901.
8. "University on Wheels," *Arizona Republican* (Phoenix, Arizona Territory), February
    9, 1904, p. 3, c. 5.
9. Kirk, Peter, Entry in pocket notebook, circa 1900-1, Peter Kirk Collection, Kirkland
    Heritage Society, Kirkland, Washington.
10. "University on Wheels," 3.
11. "Phoenix Reduction Co.," *Arizona Republican* (Phoenix, Arizona Territory), March
    7, 1901, p. 1.
12. "Smelter at Benson," *Arizona Republican* (Phoenix, Arizona Territory), February 11,
    1902, p. 6, c. 4.
13. "Mining News," *The Oasis* (Arizola, Arizona Territory), April 5, 1902.
14. "Smelter for Benson," *Bisbee Daily Review* (Bisbee, Arizona Territory), February 19,
    1902, p. 1, c. 4.
15. "Improvements at Benson," *Bisbee Daily Review* (Bisbee, Arizona Territory), July 10,
    1902, p. 5, c. 1.
16. "Benson Smelter Now Assured," *Tombstone Epitaph* (Tombstone, Arizona Territory),
    July 6, 1902.
17. "The Benson Smelter," *Bisbee Daily Review* (Bisbee, Arizona Territory), September
    18, 1902, p. 6, c. 1.
18. "Machinery for Benson," *Bisbee Daily Review* (Bisbee, Arizona Territory),
    September 25, 1902, p. 1, c. 4.
19. "The Southern Pacific Railroad," *Arizona Silver Belt* (Globe City, Arizona Territory),
    October 2, 1902, p. 3, c. 3.
20. Summary of accounts paid by Peter Kirk, October 1901 to March 23, 1903,
    Accession No. 0049, Box No. 2, Financial Records Folder, Misc. File, Peter
    Kirk Papers, University of Washington Libraries, Special Collections, Seattle,
    Washington.

21. Canceled checks from R.A. Boggess to Peter Kirk for $500 and $2000 dated May 22 through August 1, 1903, Accession No. 0049, Box No. 2, Financial Records Folder, Peter Kirk Papers, University of Washington Libraries, Special Collections, Seattle, Washington.

22. Agreement between Peter Kirk and A. J. Pidgeon concerning Kirk's Combined Ore Roaster and Smelter patent, April 4, 1903, p. 1, Peter Kirk Collection, Kirkland Heritage Society, Kirkland, Washington.

23. "Mining News," *The Oasis* (Arizola, Arizona Territory), January 16, 1904, p. 14, c. 1.

24. "University on Wheels," 3.

25. Sale certificate indicating Peter Kirk owned 150,000 shares of common stock of Empire Smelting Co. and agreement from Boggess for the sale, September 7, 1902 & November 18, 1903, Accession No. 0049, Box No. 2, Financial Records Folder, Peter Kirk Papers, University of Washington Libraries, Special Collections, Seattle, Washington.

26. Riley Boggess promissory note for $2500 to Peter Kirk, June 25, 1904, Peter Kirk Collection, Kirkland Heritage Society, Kirkland, Washington.

27. Correspondence from R. A. Boggess to Peter Kirk at Blennerville, Victoria, BC, January 20, 1905, Peter Kirk Collection, Kirkland Heritage Society, Kirkland, Washington.

28. Ibid.

29. "Benson Touched," *Bisbee Daily Review* (Bisbee, Arizona Territory), March 10, 1906, p. 1.

30. "Riley A. Boggess Is A Bankrupt," *San Francisco Call* (San Francisco, CA), August 12, 1906, p. 47, c. 8.

31. "Creditors Claim He Has Canceled Assets," *San Francisco Call* (San Francisco, CA), August 13, 1907, p. 8, c. 5.

32. "Judgment of the Supreme Court of Arizona," *The Pacific Reporter*, March 30, 1906, vol. 85, 729.

33. "In the Courts," *Tombstone Epitaph* (Tombstone, Arizona Territory), July 7, 1907, p. 3, c. 2.

34. "Bankrupt Man Attacks Creditors," *San Francisco Call* (San Francisco, CA), January 24, 1908, p. 14, c. 2.

35. Correspondence from Dexter Horton & Co. to Peter Kirk concerning shares in Imperial Quicksilver Mining Co., August 31, 1908 & January 4, 1909, Accession No. 0049, Box No. 2, Folder: Correspondence, Peter Kirk Papers, University of Washington Libraries, Special Collections, Seattle, Washington.

36. "Pidgeon of Benson Held in Louisville," *Arizona Republican* (Phoenix, Arizona Territory), November 8, 1910, p. 3, c. 5.

37. Myrtle Cecilia Robertson photo typescripts, n.d., #15. As told to her by James Collins.

Chapter 19

1. Western Union telegram from Peter Kirk to C. S. Preston, March 27, 1901, Accession No. 3119, Box 1, Folder 9, Austin E. Griffiths papers, Correspondence, University of Washington Libraries, Special Collections, Seattle, Washington.

2. "Town and County News," *San Juan Islander* (Friday Harbor, WA) July 11, 1901, p. 3, c. 1. And: October 3, 1901.

3. Contract between timber cutter and Peter Kirk, unknown date, Accession No. 0049, Box No. 2, Folder: Assorted Correspondence, Peter Kirk Papers, University of Washington Libraries, Special Collections, Seattle, Washington.

4. Botsford, Edward W., King County, Washington, Serial Patent, Accession no. WASAA 068220, "Land Patent Search," digital images, *General Land Office Records*, US Department of the Interior, Bureau of Land Management, https://glorecords.blm.gov/details/patent/default.aspx?accession=WASAA%20%20 068220&docClass=SER&sid=25witiw5.zno#patentDetailsTabIndex=0.

5. *San Juan Islander* (Friday Harbor, WA) September 3, 1903.

6. Copy of contract between Peter Kirk and Edward W. Botsford in San Juan County, June 2, 1902, Peter Kirk Collection, Kirkland Heritage Society. Edward Botsford, a former resident of Kirkland, came to San Juan Island around the time of this contract.

7. Robert Jackson mortgage to Peter Kirk, Document number 1895-020217, January 8, 1895, San Juan County, Washington, Auditor's Office Online Document Search, https://www.sanjuanco.com/171/Recorded-Document-Search. Also: 1913-0013645; 171 acres, $1230 from sheriff's sale when Robert Jackson died in 1900.

8. "Local and Personal," *San Juan Islander* (Friday Harbor, WA), August 9, 1900, p. 3, c. 1.

9. "Sheriff's Sale of Real Estate," *San Juan Islander* (Friday Harbor, WA), January 16, 1902.

10. "Capron—Kirk," *San Juan Islander* (Friday Harbor, WA), October 10, 1901, p. 3, c. 4.

11. *Friday Harbor Journal* (Friday Harbor, WA), July 23, 1914.

12. *San Juan Islander* (Friday Harbor, WA), October 5, 1899.

13. *San Juan Islander* (Friday Harbor, WA), March 8, 1900.

14. "Capron—Kirk," 3.

15. "Smelter at Benson," *Arizona Republican* (Phoenix, Arizona Territory), February 11, 1902, p. 6, c. 4.

16. Jean Kellett Kaye to Arline Stokes, no date.

Chapter 20

1.   *Victoria Daily Colonist* (Victoria, British Columbia, Canada), November 19, 1904, p. 6, c. 4.
2.   "Blennerville contract," October 30, 1904, Peter Kirk Collection, Kirkland Heritage Society, Kirkland, Washington.
3.   "San Juan Island," *San Juan Islander* (Friday Harbor, WA), May 6, 1905, p. 1, c. 4.
4.   Correspondence to Mary Ann Kirk from her sister at 3 Prince's Road in Heaton Moor, April 24, 1905, Peter Kirk Collection, Kirkland Heritage Society, Kirkland, Washington.
5.   "U.S. City Directories, 1822-1995," digital image s.v. "Arnold Kirk," Washington, Seattle, 1901, Seattle, Washington, City Directory, 1901, *Ancestry.com*.
6.   "Notice of Election Results," *Seattle Star* (Seattle, WA), November 4, 1902, 4th Extra Edition.
7.   Lindahl, *In Christian Fellowship*, 29.
8.   Florence Dixon to Marie Bell, April 9, 1898, Peter Kirk Collection, Kirkland.
9.   Dickinson, Barbara, email to author, July 3, 2005.
10.   Bell, Mary G. and Bray, Chas., "Bonnie Scotland," 1903. Held at Peter Kirk Collection, Kirkland Heritage Society, Kirkland, Washington.
11.   Dickinson, Barbara, 2005, notes written on paper sleeve containing "Bonnie Scotland" given to Kirkland Heritage Society, Peter Kirk Collection, Kirkland, Washington.
12.   Dickinson, Barbara, email to author, July 3, 2005.
13.   Lindahl, *In Christian Fellowship*, 29.
14.   Kirk family Bible death register page, Peter Kirk Collection, Kirkland Heritage Society, Kirkland, Washington.
15.   Dickinson, Barbara, email to author, July 3, 2005.
16.   "Peter Kirk—Steel Mill Impossible Dream," 6.

Chapter 21

1.   "San Juan Island," *San Juan Islander* (Friday Harbor, WA), March 3, 1906, p. 1, c. 5.
2.   Jean Kellett Kaye to Arline Stokes, no date.
3.   *Victoria Daily Colonist* (Victoria, British Columbia, Canada), Various entries between 1909-11.
4.   *San Juan Islander* (Friday Harbor, WA), May 20, 1905, p. 8.
5.   "Republican Ticket Named," *San Juan Islander* (Friday Harbor, WA), September 15, 1906, p. 1, c. 5.
6.   Postcard to Clarence Bell from Hannah Millican, March 1905, Peter Kirk Collection, Olive Kirk Postcard Collection, Kirkland Heritage Society, Kirkland, Washington.

7. Florence Dixon to unknown recipient, no date.

8. "School Notes," *Kirkland-Redmond Sun* (Kirkland, WA), September 22, 1907, p. 6, c. 4, digital image, "Newspaper 1906-1915," Kirkland Heritage Society, Kirkland, Washington.

9. Florence Dixon to unknown recipient, no date.

10. *Aberdeen Herald* (Aberdeen, WA), March 26, 1906, p. 2. And: July 31, 1905, p. 2.

11. Kirk, Mary Ann Probate package, October 22, 1907, Superior Court of the State of Washington, San Juan County.

12. Mary A. Kirk, death certificate, 29 Sep. 1907, no. 2801, Washington State Board of Health.

13. "Death of Mrs. Peter Kirk," *Friday Harbor Journal* (Friday Harbor, WA), October 3, 1907, San Juan Museum. Print.

14. Myrtle Cecelia Robertson photo typescripts, #23.

15. Kirk, Mary Ann, probate pagers, October 22, 1907, San Juan County court, Friday Harbor, San Juan County, Washington.

16. Letter from Arthur Dixon to Peter Kirk concerning Mary Ann Kirk's estate in England, August 28, 1909, p. 2, Peter Kirk Collection, Mary (Quirk) Kirk Estate, Kirkland Heritage Society, Kirkland, Washington.

17. "San Juan Island," *San Juan Islander* (Friday Harbor, WA), January 11, 1908, p. 5.

18. "Mitchell Bay," *San Juan Islander* (Friday Harbor, WA), various articles 1908-1913.

19. Kirk, Peter, Entry in pocket notebook, January 16, 1906, Peter Kirk Collection, Kirkland Heritage Society, Kirkland, Washington. Douglas Ross married Freda Williams, W. W. Williams' daughter, in 1902. This couple sired Lannie and Winston Ross, famous for their musical talents.

20. Entry in little pocket notebook, August 22, unknown year, Accession No. 0049, Box No. 2, Folder: Notebooks, Peter Kirk Papers, University of Washington Libraries, Special Collections, Seattle, Washington.

21. Jean Kellett Kaye to Arline Stokes, no date.

22. Correspondence from D. L. Oliver to Peter Kirk concerning Fir Grove house in Kirkland, March 24, 1908, Accession No. 0049, Box No. 2, Folder: Correspondence, Peter Kirk Papers, University of Washington Libraries, Special Collections, Seattle, Washington.

23. C. L. Parrish to Peter Kirk, July 23, 1915.

24. Notes by Arline Ely about Fir Grove demise and article, "Son of Kirkland's Founder Returns to His Old Home," *Eastside Journal* (Kirkland, WA), August 14, 1919, Arline Stokes Andre Collection, Newspaper Folder, Kirkland Heritage Society, Kirkland, Washington. This only says Peter Jr. moved to Kirkland. Ely had notes about Fir Grove demise in her notes. It is unknown where she got the information.

25. "P-I 8-7-10," *The Seattle Star, Home Edition* (Seattle, WA), August 20, 1910, p. 8, c. 1.

26. Correspondence from E. Cardin of Kirkland Development Co. to Peter Kirk; June 7, 1910, June 30, 1910; and July 21, 1910, Accession No. 0049, Box No. 2, Folder: Unsorted Correspondence, Peter Kirk Papers, University of Washington Libraries, Special Collections, Seattle, Washington.

Chapter 22

1. "Mitchell Bay," *San Juan Islander* (Friday Harbor, WA), June 4, 1909, p. 8, c. 4. Also: July 30, 1909 and October 15, 1909.
2. "Mitchell Bay," *San Juan Islander* (Friday Harbor, WA), June 18, 1909, p. 8, c. 4.
3. *Friday Harbor Journal* (Friday Harbor, WA), July 15, 1909.
4. "Mitchell Bay," *San Juan Islander* (Friday Harbor, WA), April 23, 1909, p. 8, c. 4.
5. "Mitchell Bay," *San Juan Islander* (Friday Harbor, WA), August 20, 1909, p. 8, c. 4.
6. "Roche Harbor," *San Juan Islander* (Friday Harbor, WA), October 1, 1909, p. 8, c. 2.
7. "Mitchell Bay" *San Juan Islander* (Friday Harbor, WA), December 10, 1909, p. 5.
8. "Roche Harbor," *Friday Harbor Journal* (Friday Harbor, WA), December 16, 1909.
9. *San Juan Islander* (Friday Harbor, WA), December 23 & 24, 1909.
10. *Friday Harbor Journal* (Friday Harbor, WA), July 14, 1910.
11. "1910 United States Federal Census," digital image s.v. "Clarence Bell," Washington, King, Bend, District 0047, *Ancestry.com.*
12. Canceled check to James Bell for $1562.50, July 13, 1911, Accession No. 0049, Box No. 2, Folder: Financial Records, Peter Kirk Papers, University of Washington Libraries, Special Collections, Seattle, Washington.
13. Letter from Arthur Dixon to Peter Kirk concerning Mary Ann Kirk's estate in England, September 14, 1909, p. 3, Peter Kirk Collection, Mary (Quirk) Kirk Estate, Kirkland Heritage Society, Kirkland, Washington.
14. "Roche Harbor," *San Juan Islander* (Friday Harbor, WA), various dates 1909-14.
15. "Washington Marriage Records, 1854-2013," digital image s.v. "Ralph Charlton," King County, Marriages 1909 Sep-Dec, *Ancestry.com.*
16. Correspondence from Jessie Charlton to Peter Kirk, June 5, 1912, Peter Kirk Collection, Kirkland Heritage Society, Kirkland, Washington.
17. *San Juan Islander* (Friday Harbor, WA), January 28, 1910.
18. "San Juan Island," *San Juan Islander* (Friday Harbor, WA), January 21, 1910, p. 5, c. 2.
19. "Roche Harbor," *San Juan Islander* (Friday Harbor, WA), February 17, 1910. And: "San Juan Island," *San Juan Islander* (Friday Harbor, WA), March 4, 1910, p. 6, c. 4. "Mitchell Bay," *San Juan Islander* (Friday Harbor, WA), March 18, 1910, p. 8, c. 4.
20. Jean Kellett Kaye to Arline Stokes, no date.

21. Postcard from Frank D'Arcy in Anacortes to Mrs. F. A. D'Arcy in Roche Harbor, May 22, 1912, Peter Kirk Collection, Postcard Collection, p. 19, Kirkland Heritage Society, Kirkland, Washington.

22. *Whitehaven News* (Whitehaven, England), June 9, 1887, p. 1, c. 3.

23. "Friday Harbor Abolishes Saloons by Large Majority," *San Juan Islander* (Friday Harbor, WA), May 13, 1910, p. 1.

24. "School Notes," *San Juan Islander* (Friday Harbor, WA), January 21, 1910, p. 1, c. 3.

25. "Mitchell Bay," *Friday Harbor Journal* (Friday Harbor, WA), May 12, 1910.

26. *Tacoma Times* (Tacoma, WA), April 23, 1910, p. 8.

27. "Halley's Comet Speeding Away," *San Juan Islander* (Friday Harbor, WA), May 20, 1910, p. 1. Also: Edwin Emerson, "Comet Lore."

28. "Halley's Comet Speeding Away," *San Juan Islander* (Friday Harbor, WA), May 20, 1910, p. 1.

29. "San Juan Island," *San Juan Islander* (Friday Harbor, WA), May 27, 1910, p. 5, c. 2.

30. Jean Kellett Kaye to Arline Stokes, no date.

31. *San Juan Islander* (Friday Harbor, WA), August 21, 1902.

32. *Victoria Daily Colonist* (Victoria, British Columbia), July 31, 1908, p. 5, c. 7. Also: August 12, 1908, p. 5, c. 5.

33. "Washington, Marriage Records, 1854-2013," digital image s.v. Pearl C. Morrill and Clara C. Kirk (marriage 9 Feb. 1911), King County, Marriages for 1911 Jan-Apr, *Ancestry.com*.

34. Correspondence from Peter Kirk to Mr. Williams, January 1911, Accession No. 0049, Box No. 2, Folder: General Correspondence, Peter Kirk Papers, University of Washington Libraries, Special Collections, Seattle, Washington.

35. "Mitchell Bay," *San Juan Islander* (Friday Harbor, WA), February 3, 1911, p. 8, c. 2.

36. https://weather.sumofus.org/. For dates Feb 3 when brothers leave Friday Harbor and Feb 9, date of wedding.

37. Postcard sent from Seattle to Miss Olive Kirk at Roche Harbor, February 11, 1911, Peter Kirk Collection, Postcard Collection, p. 27, Kirkland Heritage Society, Kirkland, Washington.

38. *San Juan Islander* (Friday Harbor, WA), various articles in 1910 about the *Calcite*.

39. Harn, Margie and Downing, Joan, "Article Regarding Cora and Peter," June 11, 2005, Email to David Cantrill. Peter Kirk Collection, Peter Kirk Jr. Folder, Kirkland Heritage Society, Kirkland, Washington.

40. Florrie Kirk Dixon to Peter Kirk, March 31, 1914, Peter Kirk Papers, Seattle.

41. "San Juan Island," *San Juan Islander* (Friday Harbor, WA), February 20, 1914, p. 5, c. 2.

42. Correspondence from Peter Kirk Jr. to Peter Kirk Sr., August 6, 1915, Accession No. 0049, Box No. 2, Folder: General Correspondence, Peter Kirk Papers, University of Washington Libraries, Special Collections, Seattle, Washington.

43. Kirk, Peter Probate package, May 16, 1916, Superior Court of the State of Washington, San Juan County.

44. Ledger sheet indicating monies to Vic Capron from Peter Kirk referencing Cady Mountain ranch, Peter Kirk Collection, Kirkland Heritage Society, Kirkland, Washington.

45. Florence Dixon to Peter Kirk, March 31, 1915.

46. Ralph Charlton to Peter Kirk, June 8, 1914.

47. Ralph Charlton to Peter Kirk, July 5, 1914.

Chapter 23

1. "Mitchell Bay," *San Juan Islander* (Friday Harbor, WA), July 28, 1911, p. 10, c. 2. Also, April 26, 1912.

2. Postcard from Fanny to Peter Kirk, February 15, 1912, Peter Kirk Collection, Postcard Collection, p. 1, Kirkland Heritage Society, Kirkland, Washington. Florrie Kirk Dixon to Peter Kirk, March 31, 1914, Peter Kirk Papers, Seattle.

3. Cancelled checks from Peter Kirk to Mrs. Kawasaki for $7.00 and C. Kawasaki for $24.50, February 28, 1913, Accession No. 0049, Box No. 2, Folder: Cancelled Checks, Peter Kirk Papers, University of Washington Libraries, Special Collections, Seattle, Washington. Checks to this couple occur often and in regular intervals.

4. *Friday Harbor Journal* (Friday Harbor, WA), February 5, 1914.

5. "San Juan Island," *San Juan Islander* (Friday Harbor, WA), June 6, 1913, p. 5, c. 2.

6. *San Juan Islander* (Friday Harbor, WA), June 13, 1913.

7. "City Council Proceedings," *Friday Harbor Journal* (Friday Harbor, WA), August 24, 1911.

8. *Friday Harbor Journal* (Friday Harbor, WA), October 1, 1914.

9. San Juan County Assessor's Office, Document search s.v. "Peter Kirk," June 23, 1914.

10. *Friday Harbor Journal* (Friday Harbor, WA), July 2, 1914.

11. *Friday Harbor Journal* (Friday Harbor, WA), August 27, 1914.

12. Letter from Peter Jr. to Peter Kirk Sr. from Frederick Hotel in Seattle," February 1, 1915, Peter Kirk Collection, Kirkland Heritage Society, Kirkland, Washington.

13. Cancelled check from Peter Kirk to D. L. Johnson & Co. for $151.80 for graphophone, February 21, 1908, Accession No. 0049, Box No. 2, Folder: Financial Records, Cancelled Checks, Peter Kirk Papers, University of Washington Libraries, Special Collections, Seattle, Washington. And: Cancelled check to Sears & Roebuck, 1914.

14. Ibid., Cancelled checks, 1914-5.

15. *Friday Harbor Journal* (Friday Harbor, WA), October 1, 1914.

16. Correspondence from Florence Dixon to Clara Kirk Morrill, March 31, 1915, Peter Kirk Collection, Clara Kirk Morrill Folder, Kirkland Heritage Society, Kirkland, Washington.

17. *Friday Harbor Journal* (Friday Harbor, WA), January 7, 1915.

18. *Friday Harbor Journal* (Friday Harbor, WA), January 15, 1915. And March 18, 1915.

19. *Friday Harbor Journal* (Friday Harbor, WA), January 28, 1915.

20. "San Juan Island," *San Juan Islander* (Friday Harbor, WA), May 22, 1914, p. 5, c. 2.

21. Correspondence from Mr. Pontius to Peter Kirk, October 31, 1914; Peter Kirk Collection, Kirkland Heritage Society, Kirkland, Washington.

22. Ibid., December 29, 1914.

23. Ibid., October 31, 1914.

24. "Workington Coal Charity Concert," *West Cumberland Times* (Workington, Cumberland, England), December 26, 1874, p. 5, c. 4.

25. Correspondence from W. W. Williams to Peter Kirk, December 12, 1910, Accession No. 0049, Box No. 2, Folder: General Correspondence, Peter Kirk Papers, University of Washington Libraries, Special Collections, Seattle, Washington.

26. Correspondence from Robert W. Kelsey to Arline Stokes, unknown date, Arline Stokes Andre Collection, Correspondence, Kirkland Heritage Society, Kirkland, Washington.

27. "Walter Williams Dead," *Seattle Star*. (Seattle, WA), March 3, 1915.

28. Florence Dixon to Peter Kirk, March 31, 1915, Peter Kirk Collection, Kirkland.

29. Ibid.

30. Ibid.

31. "Show Changes Hands," *San Juan Islander,* September 27, 1912.

32. Family lore from Mary Jo Middleton Mazick and Gordon Middleton.

33. *Friday Harbor Journal* (Friday Harbor, WA), October 14, 1915. Weekly ads listed prices, shows, and show times.

34. Ibid.

Chapter 24

1. *Friday Harbor Journal,* (Friday Harbor, WA), January 13, 1916.

2. "Condition of Weather Month of February," *Friday Harbor Journal* (Friday Harbor, WA), March 3, 1916.

3. Bourasaw, Noel V., "1916: The Mother of All Snowstorms," *Skagit River Journal,* 2002, http://www.skagitriverjournal.com/WA/Subjects/Weather-Disaster/1916Snow1.html (accessed June 9, 2020.

4. *Friday Harbor Journal (Friday Harbor, WA),* February 1916 various dates.

5. "Fribor Theater Notice," *Friday Harbor Journal* (Friday Harbor, WA), February 4, 1916, p. 3.

6. *Friday Harbor Journal* (Friday Harbor, WA), January 13, 1916.

7. Correspondence to Mr. J. R. Pedduck from a representative of Mr. Peter Kirk, March 11, 1916, Accession No. 0049, Box No. 2, Folder: Correspondence, Peter Kirk Papers, University of Washington Libraries, Special Collections, Seattle, Washington. Also: Letter to John Bartsch, April 7, 1916, and "Peter Kirk, Sr., Summoned by The Hand of Death," 1.

8. The Mentor Magazine, "Inherited Values," http://www.inherited-values. com/2011/01/the-mentor-magazine/ (accessed June 28, 2020).

9. Correspondence from representative of Hyde Ship Brake Company to Peter Kirk, May 3, 1916, Accession No. 0049, Box No. 2, Folder: Correspondence, Peter Kirk Papers, University of Washington Libraries, Special Collections, Seattle, Washington.

10. Peter Kirk, death certificate, May 4, 1916, San Juan County, Washington Department of Health. Cause of death: mitral valve regurgitation.

11. Sum of Us Weather History, s.v. "May 4, 1916, https://weather.sumofus.org/.

12. Peter Kirk, death certificate.

13. "Peter Kirk, Sr., Summoned by The Hand of Death," 1.

14. "San Juan Island," *San Juan Islander* (Friday Harbor, WA), March 28, 1913, p. 5. E. P. Harpst was listed on Peter's death certificate as the mortician. He received a new hearse in 1913. And: Sum of Us Weather History, s.v. "May 6, 1916, https://weather. sumofus.org/.

15. Correspondence to Bert Farrar from a representative of Peter Kirk, May 16, 1916, Accession No. 0049, Box No. 2, Folder: Correspondence, Peter Kirk Papers, University of Washington Libraries, Special Collections, Seattle, Washington.

Conclusion

1. Correspondence from W. Gwilym Owen of US & Canada Steel Co., November 10, 1915, Accession No. 0049, Box No. 2, Folder: Correspondence, Peter Kirk Papers, University of Washington Libraries, Special Collections, Seattle, Washington.

2. Kirk, Peter, "Irondale Report," 2.

3. Correspondence from G. M. Sheafe to Peter Kirk, March 17, 1916, Accession No. 0049, Box No. 2, Folder: Correspondence, Peter Kirk Papers, University of Washington Libraries, Special Collections, Seattle, Washington.

4. Hunt, Thomas Francis, "Kirkland City's Founder," May 9, 1916.

5. "Cumbrian Residents at Seattle," *Carlisle Journal* (Carlisle, Cumberland, England), June 11, 1889.

6.   Florrie Kirk Dixon to Peter Kirk, March 31, 1914.

7.   Hunt, Thomas Francis, "Kirkland City's Founder," May 9, 1916.

8.   Florence Dixon to Peter Kirk, March 31, 1915, Peter Kirk Collection, Kirkland.

9.   Myrtle Cecilia Robertson photo typescripts, n.d., #15.

10.   Hunt, Thomas Francis, "Kirkland City's Founder," May 9, 1916.

Appendix B

1.   "1940 United States Federal Census," digital image s.v. "Jessie Charlton," "Fannie V. Capron," "Clara C. Morrill," and "Arnold Kirk," Washington, San Juan, Friday Harbor, district 28-6, *Ancestry.com*. And: "1940 United States Federal Census," digital image s.v. "Peter Kirk," and "Arnold Kirk," Washington, San Juan, San Juan, district 28-14, *Ancestry.com*.

2.   Florrie Kirk Dixon to Peter Kirk, March 31, 1914, Peter Kirk Papers, Seattle.

3.   Myrtle Cecilia Robertson photo typescripts, n.d., #25. Story told to Myrtle by Fanny Capron, unknown date but indicated it was during the War.

4.   England & Wales, Death Index, 1916-2007, s.v. "Arthur L. Dixon," 3rd quarter 1944, vol. 10b, p. 124, Newcastle upon Tyne, Northumberland, England. And: Kirk family Bible death register page, Peter Kirk Collection, Kirkland Heritage Society, Kirkland, Washington.

5.   Bergman, Christine, Email message of "San Juan History" to David Cantrill, June 29, 2005, Peter Kirk Collection, Kirkland Heritage Society, Kirkland, Washington.

6.   Peter Kirk Collection, Sheet Music Folder, Kirkland Heritage Society, Kirkland, Washington.

7.   "D'Arcy-Kirk Nuptials," *San Juan Islander* (Friday Harbor, WA), September 29, 1911, p. 1.

8.   "Washington, Marriage Records, 1854-2013," digital image s.v. "Francis A. D'Arcy," Whatcom, Marriages 1911 Sep-Dec, *Ancestry.com*. Frank's parents were Cyrus A. D'Arcy of Nova Scotia and Sarah Davis of England.

9.   Morrill, Dan, text message to author, November 10, 2016.

10.   "Roche Harbor," *Friday Harbor Journal* (Friday Harbor, WA), February 2, 1911.

11.   *San Juan Islander* (Friday Harbor, WA), various dates in 1910.

12.   Postcard sent from Frank D'Arcy in Anacortes to Miss Olive Kirk at Roche Harbor, February 2, 1911, Peter Kirk Collection, Postcard Collection, Kirkland Heritage Society, Kirkland, Washington.

13.   Ibid., Unsigned postcard sent from Anacortes to Miss Olive E. Kirk at Roche Harbor, April 10, 1911.

14.   Ibid., Postcard from Jessie Charlton in Seattle to Miss Olive Kirk at Deer Lodge, August 8, 1911.

15. "Washington Marriage Records, 1854-2013," digital image s.v. "Francis A. D'Arcy & Olive Kirk" (19 Sep. 1911), Whatcom County Marriages for 1911, Sep-Dec. License No. 569, *Ancestry.com.* Olive listed her age as 35 on the marriage certificate. Frank's first wife was Fannie A. Dodge.

16. "D'Arcy-Kirk Nuptials," *San Juan Islander* (Friday Harbor, WA), September 28, 1911, p. 1.

17. "Friday Harbor in a Nutshell," *Friday Harbor Journal* (Friday Harbor, WA), September 28, 1911.

18. Postcard from Florence (a friend) in Nantucket, Massachusetts to Olive, no date.

19. Correspondence from Olive at the Hotel Taylor in Anacortes to Peter Kirk in Friday Harbor, October 26, 1914, Peter Kirk Collection, Kirkland Heritage Society, Kirkland, Washington.

20. *San Juan Islander* (Friday Harbor, WA), August 9, 1912. Also: *Friday Harbor Journal* (Friday Harbor, WA), November 19, 1914. *Friday Harbor Journal* (Friday Harbor, WA), January 13, 1916.

21. Bergman, Christine, email to David Cantrill, June 29, 2005.

22. *Friday Harbor Journal* (Friday Harbor, WA), December 17, 1914.

23. *Friday Harbor Journal* (Friday Harbor, WA), December 9, 1915.

24. *Friday Harbor Journal* (Friday Harbor, WA), January 1929.

25. Dickinson, Barbara email to author, July 3, 2005.

26. "Well Known Lady Summoned by Death," *Friday Harbor Journal (Friday Harbor, WA),* September 14, 1944.

27. "Friday Harbor in a Nutshell," *Friday Harbor Journal* (Friday Harbor, WA), December 25, 1913, p. 3. And: "San Juan Island," *San Juan Islander* (Friday Harbor, WA), May 2, 1913, p. 5, c. 2. These ads went on for several weeks until June. This coincides with Capron party for the cast of the play. Both Vivian and Alfred attended.

28. Middleton, Gordon, Verbal interviews with author about family history, 2004-2010, Anacortes, Washington.

29. Smith, Greg, conversation with author at Kirk Family Reunion, 2005, Kirkland, Washington.

30. Dickinson, Barbara, email to author, July 3, 2005.

31. Mazick, MaryJo, and Middleton, Gordon, conversations with author about family lore 2004-2016.

32. Switzer, Jeff, "Case Solved in the Mystery of the Disappearing Tombstone, *East Side Journal* (Kirkland, WA), before January 15, 2005, p. A1. Copy sent to author from Dave Cantrill of Kirkland Heritage Society, Kirkland, Washington.

33. Regala, Jane, Customer Accounts for Kirkland Cemetery, email response to inquiry by author, March 13, 2020.

34. Mazick, MaryJo, and Middleton, Gordon, conversations with author about family lore 2004-2016.

35. *Kirkland-Redmond Sun* (Kirkland, WA), May 1, 1907, p. 1, c. 1, digital image, "Newspaper 1906-1915," Kirkland Heritage Society, Kirkland, Washington.

36. *East Side News and Farm Journal* (Kirkland, WA), March 26, 1909, p. 8, digital image, "Newspaper 1906-1915," Kirkland Heritage Society, Kirkland, Washington.

37. "North Bend Telephone Directory, 1910," Diorama in North Bend Museum, North Bend, Washington, as seen by author, October 2014. And: Lindahl, *In Christian Fellowship*, 29.

38. James Bell, death certificate, January 16, 1940, no. 3274, Washington State Board of Health.

39. Middleton, Gordon, Exchange of childhood stories with Kip Roberts, 2004, as told to author.

40. "1920 United States Federal Census," digital image s.v. "Victor J. Capron," Washington, San Juan, Friday Harbor, district 0077, *Ancestry.com*.

41. Florrie Dixon to unknown sister, April 24, 1905, Peter Kirk Collection, Kirkland.

42. Bergman, Christine, email to David Cantrill, June 29, 2005.

43. "In a Nutshell," *Friday Harbor Journal* (Friday Harbor, WA), April 27.

44. *Friday Harbor Journal* (Friday Harbor, WA), March 16, 1911.

45. "San Juan Island," *San Juan Islander* (Friday Harbor, WA), April 19, 1912, p. 5, c. 2.

46. Dickinson, Barbara email to author, July 3, 2005.

47. "Who's Who on the Pacific Coast, 1913" digital image s.v. "Victor James Capron," *Ancestry.com*.

48. Washington, Deaths, 1883-1960, s.v. "Victor J. Capron," November 16, 1934, *Ancestry.com*. And: Fanny Valentine Capron, death certificate, 6 Jan 1956, no. 1268, Washington State Board of Health.

49. "Washington County Marriages, 1855-2008," digital image s.v. "Victor J. Capron & August De Lion" (marriage license 15 Dec. 1898), *Ancestry.com*. Augusta De Lion was 17 when she married Victor. It is not known if she lived in Hawaii with him. They did not have any children. She soon returned to her family in Port Townsend.

50. *San Juan Islander* (Friday Harbor, WA), July 28, 1898.

51. *San Juan Islander* (Friday Harbor, WA), June 15, 1899.

52. *San Juan Islander* (Friday Harbor, WA), April 13, 1899; July 20, 1899; July 27, 1899; and September 7, 1899.

53. *San Juan Islander* (Friday Harbor, WA), April 19, 1900.

54. *San Juan Islander* (Friday Harbor, WA), June 19, 1902.

55. "Roche Harbor," *San Juan Islander* (Friday Harbor, WA), March 4, 1910, p. 9, c. 4. And: Sum of Us Weather History, s.v. "February 26, 1910, https://weather.sumofus. org/.

56. "US, WWI Draft Registration Cards, 1917-18," digital image s.v. "Peter Kirk," Washington, San Juan County, Draft Card K.

57. *San Juan Islander*, (Friday Harbor, WA). March 30, 1899, p. 3, c. 4.

58. "Roche," *The Islander* (Friday Harbor, WA), December 23, 1897.

59. Edward Scribner built Peter Kirk's first launch in 1906.

60. Harn, Margie and Downing, Joan, "Article Regarding Cora and Peter," June 11, 2005, Email to David Cantrill. Peter Kirk Collection, Peter Kirk Jr. Folder, Kirkland Heritage Society, Kirkland, Washington.

61. *San Juan Islander* (Friday Harbor, WA), January 3, 1901.

62. Harn, Margie and Downing, Joan, "Article Regarding Cora and Peter," June 11, 2005.

63. "Son of Kirkland's Founder Returns to His Old Home," *East Side Journal* (Kirkland, WA), August 14, 1919, p. 1, Kirkland Heritage Society, Kirkland, Washington.

64. "US City Directories, 1822-1995," digital image s.v. "Peter Kirk," Washington, Everett, 1926, Everett, Washington City Directory, 1926, *Ancestry.com*.

65. "1940 United States Federal Census," digital image s.v. "Peter Kirk," Washington, San Juan, San Juan, district 28-14, *Ancestry.com*.

66. Kirk, Peter Warren. *Diary of a Bataan Prisoner*. Kirkland, Washington, unpublished and held at Kirkland Heritage Society, Circa 1980's, p. 100.

67. *Friday Harbor Journal (Friday Harbor, WA)*, September 27, 1951.

68. "Washington Death Index, 1940-1996," s.v. "Cora S. Kirk," 10 Feb 1987, Snohomish, Washington, *Ancestry.com*.

69. "US, World War I Draft Registration Cards, 1917-1918," digital image s.v. "Pearl Calvin Morrill," Washington, San Juan County, Draft card M. Birth: July 17, 1887. His parents were David and Lillian (Murphey) Morrill.

70. Morrill, Dan, November 10, 2016, Facebook Messaging texts with author.

71. Baker City, Oregon, City Directory, 1908, p. 134. Digital page 70 on Ancestry. com, US City directories, 1822-1995 for Pearl C. Morrill; Baker City, Oregon, 1908. Worked for Red Boy Mines Co.

72. *Victoria Daily Colonist* (Victoria, British Columbia), July 31, 1908, p. 5, c. 7. Also: August 12, 1908, p. 5, c. 5.

73. "Roche Harbor," *Friday Harbor Journal* (Friday Harbor, WA), December 24, 1908.

74. "1910 United States Federal Census," digital image s.v. "Pearl Morrill," Michigan, Washtenaw, Ann Arbor Ward 1, District 011, *Ancestry.com*.

75. "Alberta, Canada, Homestead Records, 1870-1930," digital image s.v. "Pearl Calvin Morrill" (application #23415), *Ancestry.com*. Coordinates: SW quarter of section 34, township 35, range 12, in the 4th meridian.

76. "Washington, Marriage Records, 1854-2013," digital image s.v. Pearl C. Morrill and Clara C. Kirk (marriage 9 Feb. 1911), King County, Marriages for 1911 Jan-Apr, *Ancestry.com*.

77. "Morrill-Kirk Wedding," *San Juan Islander* (Friday Harbor, WA), February 17, 1911, p. 1.

78. Ibid. And: Wedding announcement of Clara and Pearl Morrill, 1911, Peter Kirk Collection, Receipts Folder, Kirkland Heritage Society, Kirkland, Washington.

79. Postcard sent from Fanny to Peter Kirk, Esq. at 1403 33rd Avenue in Seattle, February 15, 1912, Peter Kirk Collection, Postcard Collection, p. 1, Kirkland Heritage Society, Kirkland, Washington. Also: Postcard sent from Clara in Seattle to Mrs. F. A. D'Arcy at Roche Harbor, December 22, 1911, p. 15 of the same collection.

80. Unsourced biography for Clara Kirk Morrill written in response to 2005 Kirk Family Reunion sponsored by Kirkland Heritage Society, Peter Kirk Collection, Clara Kirk Folder, Kirkland Heritage Society, Kirkland, Washington.

81. "Mitchell Bay," *San Juan Islander* (Friday Harbor, WA), June 30, 1911, p. 8, c. 3.

82. "Alberta, Canada, Homestead Records, 1870-1930," digital image s.v. "Pearl Calvin Morrill" (application #23415), *Ancestry.com*.

83. *San Juan Islander* (Friday Harbor, WA), December 19, 1913. And: *Friday Harbor Journal* (Friday Harbor, WA), May 28, 1914.

84. Ibid. And: Pearl Morrill Alberta homestead papers.

85. *Friday Harbor Journal (Friday Harbor, WA),* March 18, 1915.

86. *Friday Harbor Journal (Friday Harbor, WA),* March 22, 1916.

87. San Juan County Assessor's Office, Document Search, Pearl Morrill, 1916-001554, September 22, 1916. And: "1920 United States Federal Census," digital image s.v. "Pearl C. Morrill," Washington, San Juan, San Juan, district 0011, *Ancestry.com*.

88. "1930 United States Federal Census," digital image s.v. "Pearl C. Morrill," Washington, San Juan, San Juan, district 0011, *Ancestry.com*.

89. *Friday Harbor Journal (Friday Harbor, WA),* September 2, 1915.

90. *Friday Harbor Journal (Friday Harbor, WA),* October 28, 1915.

91. Morrill, Dan, email to author, February 18, 2021.

92. Clara Kirk Morrill unsourced biography, Peter Kirk Collection, Kirkland.

93. Morrill, Dan, various conversations about Kirk family with author. 2014-2016, Friday Harbor, Washington.

94. "Washington, Deaths, 1883-1960," s.v. "Pearl Calvin Morrill," 3 Sep 1939, Friday Harbor, Washington, *Ancestry.com*. "1940 United States Federal Census," digital image s.v. "Clara C. Morrill," Washington, San Juan, Friday Harbor, district 28-6, *Ancestry.com*. Also, "Wallace E. Botsford," Washington, San Juan, San Juan, district 28-14, *Ancestry.com*.

95. Kirk family Bible death register page, Peter Kirk Collection.

96. "Mitchell Bay," *San Juan Islander* (Friday Harbor, WA), August 20, 1909, p. 8, c. 4.

97. Receipt from millinery, Ada Mullis Larson, November 1909, Peter Kirk Collection, Jessie Kirk Charlton Folder, Kirkland Heritage Society, Kirkland, Washington. And: "Roche Harbor," *San Juan Islander* (Friday Harbor, WA) November 19, 1909, p. 8, c. 3. And: "Washington Marriage Records, 1854-2013," digital image s.v. "Ralph Charlton," King County, Marriages 1909 Sep-Dec, *Ancestry.com*.

98. "U.S. City Directories, 1822-1995," digital image s.v. "Ralph Charlton," Washington, Seattle, 1891; Seattle, Washington, City Directory, 1891, *Ancestry.com*. Living with brother, Edward. Born to William and Minnie (Myers) in 1866 in Ontario, Canada.

99. "U.S. City Directories, 1822-1995," digital image s.v. "Ralph Charlton," Washington, Seattle, 1906; Seattle, Washington, City Directory, 1906, *Ancestry.com*.

100. "San Juan Island," *San Juan Islander*, (Friday Harbor, WA), November 26, 1909, p. 5, c. 3.

101. Letter from Jessie at Salmon Bay to Peter, June 5, 1912, Peter Kirk Collection, Jessie Kirk Folder, Kirkland Heritage Society, Kirkland, Washington. And: Correspondence from Ralph Charlton to Peter Kirk, July 5, 1914, Accession No. 0049, Box No. 2, Folder: General Correspondence, Peter Kirk Papers, University of Washington Libraries, Special Collections, Seattle, Washington.

102. Florence Dixon to Peter Kirk, March 31, 1914, Peter Kirk Papers, Seattle.

103. Ralph Charlton to Peter Kirk, July 5 & 8, 1914, Peter Kirk Papers, Seattle.

104. December 1, 1915; loan to R. Charlton and Jessie K. Charlton, for $850 due in 5 years. Estate papers of Peter Kirk. San Juan County.

105. Correspondence from Jessie Charlton to Peter Kirk, December 5, 1915, Peter Kirk Collection, Jessie Kirk Charlton Folder, Kirkland Heritage Society, Kirkland, Washington.

106. "US City Directories, 1822-1995," digital image "Ralph Charlton," Washington, Seattle, 1916, Seattle, Washington, City Directory, 1916, *Ancestry.com*.

107. "1930 United States Federal Census," digital image s.v. "Jessie C. Charlton," Washington, King, Seattle, District 0182, *Ancestry.com*.

108. "US City Directories, 1822-1995," digital image "Ralph Charlton," California, San Diego, 1921-1926, San Diego, California City Directory. *Ancestry.com*.

109. "1930 United States Federal Census," digital image s.v. "Jessie K. Charlton," California, Tuolumne, Township 5, District 0014, *Ancestry.com*.

110. "California Death Index, 1940-1997," s.v. "Ralph Charlton," 25 Jan 1940, Tulare County, California, *Ancestry.com*.

111. "1940 United States Federal Census," digital image s.v. "Jessie Charlton," Washington, San Juan, Friday Harbor, district 28-6, *Ancestry.com*.

112. Middleton, Gordon, various conversations about Kirk and Middleton family with author, 2004.

113. Morrill, Dan, various conversations about Kirk family with author. 2014-2016, Friday Harbor, Washington.

114. Jessie Kirk Charlton letter to William Sherrard, July 4, 1958, William Robert Sherrard Papers.

115. Letter from Jessie Charlton to Esther Middleton obtained at time of Esther's death, in possession of the author. Esther was wife of Gordon Middleton, grandnephew of Jessie Kirk Charlton.

116. "Last Kirk Child Dies in Calif.," *East Side Journal* (Kirkland WA), February 25, 1965.

117. "US, World War II Draft Registration Cards, 1942," digital image s.v. "Arnold Kirk," Washington, *Ancestry.com*.

118. "Mitchell Bay," *San Juan Islander* (Friday Harbor, WA), August 19, 1910.

119. "Mill on Sound Basis," *Friday Harbor Journal* (Friday Harbor, WA), April 11, 1907. Also: "The Friday Harbor Lumber Mill," August 29, 1907. And: "Additional Local News," *San Juan Islander*, April 13, 1907, p. 5, c. 2.

120. Florence Dixon to Peter Kirk, March 31, 1914.

121. "1920 United States Federal Census," digital image s.v. "Arnold Kirk," California, San Diego, San Diego, District 0323, *Ancestry.com*.

122. "1930 United States Federal Census," digital image s.v. "Arnold Kirk," Washington, Whatcom, Ferndale, District 032, *Ancestry.com*. And: "US City Directories, 1822-1995," digital image s.v. "Arnold Kirk," Washington, Bellingham, 1938, Bellingham, Washington, City Directory, 1938, *Ancestry.com*.

123. "1940 United States Federal Census," digital image s.v. "Arnold Kirk," Washington, San Juan, San Juan, 28-14, *Ancestry.com*.

124. "US, World War II Draft Registration Cards, 1942," digital image s.v. "Arnold Kirk," Washington, *Ancestry.com*.

125. "US City Directories, 1822-1995," digital image s.v. "Arnold Kirk," Washington, Seattle, 1943, Seattle, Washington, City Directory, 1943, *Ancestry.com*.

126. "US City Directories, 1822-1995," digital image s.v. "Arnold Kirk," Washington, Seattle, 1955, Seattle, Washington, City Directory, 1955, *Ancestry.com*. And: Arnold Kirk, death certificate, 12 May 1956, no. 8653, Washington State Department of Health.

Other Stories

1. Scurr, Anne, "Old Workington Facebook Group," Mar 10, 2012, https://www.facebook.com/groups/103710749754449/?post_id=132068543585336 (accessed May 31, 2020).

2.   Barnes Russell, "Old Workington Facebook Group," Feb 25, 2016, https://www.facebook.com/groups/103710749754449/?post_id=132068543585336&comment_id=834609146664602 (accessed May 31, 2020).

3.   Lihou, Amada, "Old Workington Facebook Group," June 14, 2013, https://www.facebook.com/groups/103710749754449/?post_id=353369438121911 (accessed May 31, 2020).

4.   Hargreaves, Gary, "Old Workington Facebook Group," April 3, 2015, https://www.facebook.com/groups/103710749754449/?post_id=678241122301406 (accessed May 31, 2020).

5.   Barnes, Russell, July 8, 2013, "Old Workington Facebook Page," https://www.facebook.com/groups/103710749754449.

6.   Talbot, Paul, July 7, 2013, "Old Workington Facebook Page," https://www.facebook.com/groups/103710749754449.

7.   Hucknall, Mel, "Old Workington Facebook Group," March 9, 2012, https://www.facebook.com/groups/103710749754449/?post_id=132068543585336 (accessed May 31, 2020).

8.   King, Terry, "Old Workington Facebook Group," April 1, 2015, https://www.facebook.com/groups/103710749754449/?post_id=678241122301406 (accessed May 31, 2020).

9.   Barnes, Russell W., "Bankfield Mansion, Workington, During Demolition," November 7, 2006, https://www.flickr.com/photos/russell_w_b/291401284/in/photostream/ (accessed June 3, 2020). Used with permission.

10. Sanderson, Neil, "Old Workington Facebook Group," April 2, 2015, https://www.facebook.com/groups/103710749754449/?post_id=678241122301406 (accessed May 31, 2020).

11. King, Terry, "Old Workington Facebook Group," April 2, 2015, https://www.facebook.com/groups/103710749754449/?post_id=678241122301406 (accessed May 31, 2020).

12. "The Iron and Steel Institute," *Soulby's Ulverston Advertiser and General Intelligencer* (Ulverston, Lancashire, England), September 17, 1874, p. 6, c. 6. And: *The Journal of the Iron and Steel Institute*, "Obituary. Henry Kirk," 254.

13. Ibid.

14. "Carlton Iron Works," *Daily Gazette for Middlesbrough* (Middlesbrough, Yorkshire, England), November 3, 1873, p. 3, c. 6.

15. Lancaster & Wattleworth, 134. Also: "Messrs. Kirk Brothers & Co. Ironmasters and Manufacturers New Yard and Marsh Side Iron Works Workington," *Cumberland and the Lake District, Illustrated* (Cumberland, England), circa 1895, p. 34, Arline Stokes Papers, Kirkland Heritage Society, Kirkland, Washington.

16. *The Journal of the Iron and Steel Institute*, "Obituary. Henry Kirk," 254.

17. Kirk, Geoffrey Peter, *The Kirk Family Industrial Background*, 21.

18. "The Temperance Movement," *Carlisle Express and Examiner"* (Carlisle, Cumberland, England), December 6, 1884, p. 6, c. 2.

19. "New Yard Sunday School," *West Cumberland Times"* (Workington, Cumberland, England), June 30, 1888, p. 5, c. 1.

20. "Lecture by Mr. Henry Kirk," *Maryport Advertiser* (Maryport, Cumberland, England), November 26, 1886, p. 6, c. 1.

21. "Twinkles," *Workington Star* (Workington, Cumberland, England), April 24, 1891, p. 4, c. 1.

22. "First Day," *Workington Star* (Workington, Cumberland, England), January 5, 1900, p. 8, c. 1.

23. Advertisement, *Workington Star* (Workington, Cumberland, England), October 25, 1901, p. 1, c. 4.

24. Kirk, Henry, Letter to brother Peter, July 4, 1911, Peter Kirk Collection, Kirkland Heritage Society, Kirkland, Washington.

25. Kirk, Geoffrey Peter, *The Kirk Family Industrial Background*, 18-19.

26. "Death of Mr. Thos. Kirk," *Yorkshire Post and Leeds Intelligencer* (Leeds, Yorkshire, England), July 27, 1908, p. 9, c. 3.

27. Ibid.

28. Ibid.

29. "School Board Election," *Daily Gazette for Middlesbrough* July 18, 1877, p. 2, c. 5.

30. "St. John's Ambulance Association," *Northern Echo,* July 29, 1889, p. 4, c. 2.

31. "Accidental Death at Carlton Iron Works," *Daily Gazette for Middlesbrough,* July 15, 1896, p. 2, c. 4.

32. "Conservative Working Men's Club, Workington," *West Cumberland Times* (Workington, Cumberland, England), December 16, 1893, p. 2, c. 6.

33. *Cumberland Pacquet, and Ware's Whitehaven Advertiser* (Workington, Cumberland, England), November 7, 1889.

34. "The Workington Primrose League," *Cumberland Pacquet, and Ware's Whitehaven Advertiser* (Workington, Cumberland, England), September 22, 1892, p. 8, c. 5.

35. "Lifeboat Institution's Bazaar at Workington," *West Cumberland Times* (Workington, Cumberland, England), June 11, 1887, p. 2, c. 5.

36. "St. John's Temperance Benefit Society," *Workington Star* (Workington, Cumberland, England), April 27, 1894, p. 3, c. 6.

37. "Primrose Day at Workington," *West Cumberland Times* (Workington, Cumberland, England), April 21, 1894, p. 2, c. 3. Mentions her as associated with Bankfield.

38. "Workington Primrose League," *Maryport Advertiser,* July 1, 1899, p. 5 c. 1.

39. "The Moss Bay Company," *Workington Star* (Workington, Cumberland, England), April 11, 1890, p. 3, c. 1.

40. "Preparing Speeches," *Penrith Observer* (Penrith, Cumberland, England), June 4, 1929, p. 4, c. 5.

41. "Concert," *West Cumberland Times* (Workington, Cumberland, England), November 27, 1875, p. 4. c. 5.

42. "Unveiling the Valentine Bust," *Workington Star* (Workington, Cumberland, England), October 28, 1904, p. 5, c. 1-2.

43. Ibid.

44. "The New House of Commons," *The Graphic* (London, England), February 13, 1886, p. 181.

45. "Workington Primrose League," *West Cumberland Times* (Workington, Cumberland, England), February 5, 1890, p. 4. c. 5. And: "Mr. C. J. Valentine on His American Tours," *Workington Star* (Workington, Cumberland, England), February 7, 1890, p. 3, c. 3.

46. Ann Valentine, death certificate, August 8, 1900, vol. 1b, p. 361, General Register Office, St. Giles, London, England. And: Charles James Valentine, November 5, 1900, vol. 1b, p. 358, General Register Office, St. Giles, London, England.

Glossary

Unless otherwise indicated, the definitions are from American Iron and Steel Institute website, "Steel Glossary," https://www.steel.org/steel-technology/steel-production/glossary (accessed June 29, 2020). Used with permission.

Blast Furnace—A towering cylinder lined with heat-resistant bricks, used to smelt iron from iron ore. Its name comes from the "blast" of hot air and gases forced up through the iron ore, coke and limestone that load the furnace.

Bloom—A semi-finished steel form, with a rectangular cross-section more than 8 inches. Reduction of a bloom to a smaller cross-section can improve the quality of the metal. It is smaller than an ingot.

Casting—The process of pouring molten metal into a mold so that the cooled, solid metal retains the shape of the mold.

Charge—The act of loading material into a vessel. For example, iron ore, coke, and limestone are charged into a blast furnace.

Coke—The basic fuel consumed in blast furnaces in the smelting of iron. Coke is a processed form of coal. It is made in a coke oven where coal is heated without oxygen for 18 hours to drive off gases and impurities. Unlike coal which burns sporadically and reduces into a sticky mass, processed coke burns steadily inside and out, and is not crushed by the weight of the iron ore in the blast furnace.

Flux—A mineral, such as limestone, that chemically reacts with the iron ore to form a waste product (slag) that floats to the top and can be removed, leaving a more pure liquid iron.

Forging—A metal part worked to predetermined shape by one or more processes such as hammering, pressing, or rolling.

Ingot—A form of semi-finished type of metal. Liquid metal is poured into molds, where it slowly solidifies. Once the metal is solid, the mold is stripped, and the ingots are ready for rolling or forging.

Iron ore—Mineral containing enough iron to be a commercially viable source of the element for use in steelmaking. Except for fragments of meteorites found on earth, iron is not a free element; instead, it is trapped in the earth's crust in its oxidized form.

Merchant Bar—A group of commodity steel shapes that consist of rounds, squares, flats, strips, angles, and channels, which fabricators, steel service centers, and manufacturers cut, bend, and shape into products. Merchant products require more specialized processing than reinforcing bar.

Open Hearth Furnace—A broad, shallow hearth to refine pig iron and scrap into steel. Heat is supplied from a large, luminous flame over the surface, and the refining takes seven to nine hours.

Pig Iron—The name for the melted iron produced in a blast furnace, containing a large quantity of carbon (above 1.5%) Named long ago when molten iron was poured through a trench in the ground to flow into shallow earthen holes, the arrangement looked like newborn pigs suckling.

Reducing Agent—Coal was used to remove the oxygen from iron ore in order to produce a scrap substitute. Iron ore is combined with gasified or ground coal and heated. The oxygen in the ore combines with carbon and hydrogen in the gas or coal, producing reduced, or metallic, iron.

Rolling (Cold Working)—Changes in the structure and shape of steel achieved through rolling, hammering or stretching the steel at a low temperature (often room temperature), to create a permanent increase in the hardness and strength of the steel.

Rolling Mill—Any operating unit that reduces gauge by application of loads through revolving cylindrical rolls. The operation can be hot or cold.

Slag—The impurities in a molten pool of iron. Flux such as limestone may be added to foster the congregation of undesired elements into a slag. Because slag is lighter than iron, it will float on top of the pool, where it can be skimmed.

Sleeper—A railroad tie, made of wood, iron, or concrete to form a supporting base and secure the rails.

Works Cited

Archive Collections

Carlisle Archive Centre. Carlisle, Cumbria, England.
Searched various topics concerning Peter Kirk and his industries.

Derbyshire Record Office. Matlock, Derbyshire, England.
  Kirk of Castleton/Dove Holes: Genealogical research papers
  relating to the Kirk family of Chapel-en-le-Frith. D6771.
  Kirks of Eaves Branch: Kirk Family of Glossop and
  Chapel-en-le-Frith. D513.
  Martinside branch: Kirk family of Chapel-en-le-Frith. D613.
  Needham Papers: Needham family of Peak Forest. D2575.

Gilman, Daniel H. Papers. Accession No. 2730. University of Washington
Libraries, Special Collections. Seattle, Washington.
  Early Washington publisher and promoter of railroads, mining,
  real estate, and utilities. One of the founders of the Seattle,
  Lake Shore and Eastern Railway in 1885.

Greenfield, Marie Larsen Johnson. Interview by Nancy R. Lindenberg.
January 15, 1995. Transcript. San Juan Historical Society.
Washington State Historical Society Oral Histories Collection.
http://www.sjmuseum.org/community-outreach/oral-histories/.
  Marie Larsen Johnson Greenfield grew up at Deer Lodge after
  the Kirk family sold it in 1918. Transcript originally found at:
  http://digitum.washingtonhistory.org/cdm/singleitem/collection/
  oralh/id/297/rec/8 (accessed 2016).

Harrison, Benjamin President. President Benjamin Harrison Archives.
Library of Congress. https://archive.org/stream/throughsouthwest00harr/
throughsouthwest00harr_djvu.txt (accessed 2016).

Hunt, Jessie Noble. Typescript of short biography of Leigh S. J. Hunt. 1947. Accession No. 4667. Leigh S. J. Hunt papers. University of Washington Libraries, Special Collections. Seattle, Washington.

Kirk, George Seville. George Seville Kirk Scrapbook. Newspaper Clippings 1890's. Kirkland Heritage Society. Kirkland, Washington. Online. http://kirklandheritage.org/archives/1890s-newspaper-clippings-collection#.

Kirk, Peter. Peter Kirk Collection. Kirkland Heritage Society. Kirkland, Washington.
    Legal papers, music, patents, photos, newspaper articles, and correspondence.

Kirk, Peter. Peter Kirk Papers. Accession No. 0049. University of Washington Libraries, Special Collections. Seattle, Washington.
    Financial, legal, personal correspondence, patents, receipts, bank drafts, notebooks, land, insurance, etc.

O'Connor, T. P. October 2, 1908. Reminiscences of Leigh S. J. Hunt in article in the *T. P. Weekly*. Accession No. 4667. Leigh S. J. Hunt papers. University of Washington Libraries, Special Collections. Seattle, Washington.

Robertson, Myrtle Cecelia. Typescripts of scripts for slide show presentations on the history of communities on the east side of Lake Washington. Date Unknown. Accession No. 3193. Myrtle Cecelia Robertson typescripts. University of Washington Libraries, Special Collections. Seattle, Washington.

Robertson, Myrtle Cecelia. Hanging Files. Kirkland Public Library. Kirkland, Washington.

San Juan Historical Museum. *Friday Harbor Journal* bound issues of newspaper 1906-1916. Friday Harbor, Washington.

Sherrard, William. William Robert Sherrard papers. Accession No. 0366. University of Washington Libraries, Special Collections. Seattle, Washington.

> Documents, notes, letters, and synopsis of thesis relating to Kirkland steel mill.

Stokes, Arline. Arline Stokes Andre Collection. Kirkland Heritage Society. Kirkland, Washington.

> Letters, notes, etc. Separate folders for Correspondence from Jean Kellett Kaye and Aubrey Williams.

Books and manuscripts

Bellhouse, Marguerite A. Life. *The Story of Combs, My Village.* Derbyshire: Old Brooke House, 1968.

> There is limited anecdotal material is this book, instead Bellhouse catalogued some of the ancient families and estates from old documents, court sessions and tax rolls. She includes some genealogical charts.

Bulmer, T. & Co. *History, Topography and Directory of West Cumberland.* Cumberland: T. Snape & Co., 1883.

> This business directory for West Cumberland gives details about production and earnings. It also gives available resources for the area.

Bunting, William Braylesford. *Chapel-en-le-Frith, Its History and Its People*. Manchester: Sharratt & Hughes, 1940.

> In this extensive history of Chapel-en-le-Frith, Bunting writes about the ancient families of the area. To this day, his work is the most recommended reference for anyone studying the local history. Before compiling this book, he wrote articles for the local parish newsletter about the local history. He was friends with Thornhill Kirk who encouraged him to write more.

Ely, Arline. *Our Foundering Fathers*. Kirkland, Washington: Kirkland Public Library, 1975.

> This is a history of Kirkland and some of the original families who settled there. Ely lists her sources at the end of the book but does not reference the material within the pages, making it difficult to know where information originates.

King, Moses. *King's Handbook of the United States*. Buffalo: Moses King Corp., 1891.

> A handbook containing descriptions of all fifty states (even if not yet a state), Washington D. C., and the Indian Nation.

Kirk, Geoffrey Peter. *The Kirk Family and Their Industrial Background of Iron and Steel*. Geoffrey Peter Kirk, 1973.

> A thoughtful, well-articulated, and in-depth summary of the history of the iron-producing Kirks in Chapel-en-le-Frith. He includes some genealogy of the family. Kirk writes about Peter Kirk and his brothers' enterprises in Workington. He prepared much of this information in response to inquiries from Arline Ely for her Kirkland book.

Kirk, Geoffrey Peter. *Postscript 1974*. Geoffrey Peter Kirk, 1974.

> Updated material supporting earlier Kirk family document.

Kirk, Geoffrey Peter. *Our Kirk Forefathers of Chapel-en-le-Frith, Derbyshire*. Geoffrey Peter Kirk, 1983.

Updated and expanded material supporting earlier Kirk family document.

Lancaster, J. Y. and Wattleworth, D. R. *The Iron and Steel Industry of West Cumberland, an Historical Survey.* Workington, Cumbria: CN Print Ltd., 1977.

A history of West Cumberland iron industry with discussion of the larger iron and steel works in the area. It spans over a hundred years as Britain became the world's leader producing iron, then declined and what adjustments had to be made.

Lindahl, Shirley. *In Christian Fellowship, Congregational Church of Kirkland 1880-1980.* Advance Printing, Kirkland Washington, 1979.

History of the churches and township of Kirkland from homestead days to modern times.

Sherrard, William Robert. *The Kirkland Steel Mill.* Master's thesis, University of Washington, 1958.

Discusses business aspects to Kirk's iron mill venture and possible reasons of its subsequent failure. Discusses ore samples, iron market at time, financial crash of '93, etc.

Index

About the Author

Saundra received her Bachelor of Arts in English Literature from the University of Alaska. She dabbled in journalism publishing dozens of articles in *Alaska Magazine* and *Alaska Business Monthly* and other publications.

Combining her love of writing, history, and genealogy, Saundra was recognized for her short story *Of Donkeys, Mules, & Plains Ponies* in a 2015 contest sponsored by the Kent Family History Society in England. She has produced several family history booklets for family and friends.